The Verse Miscellany of Constance Aston Fowler:

A Diplomatic Edition

Medieval and Renaissance Texts and Studies

Volume 210

Renaissance English Text Society

Seventh Series
Volume XXV (for 2000)

The Verse Miscellany of
Constance Aston Fowler:

A Diplomatic Edition

by

DEBORAH ALDRICH-WATSON

Arizona Center for Medieval and Renaissance Studies
in conjunction with
Renaissance English Text Society
Tempe, Arizona
2000

Library of Congress Cataloging-in-Publication Data

Fowler, Constance Aston, b. ca. 1621.
    A verse miscellany of Constance Aston Fowler : a diplomatic edition / by Deborah Aldrich-Watson.
        p. cm. — (Medieval & Renaissance texts & studies ; v. 210)
    Includes bibliographical references (p.) and index.
    ISBN 0-86698-252-3 (alk. paper)
        I. Aldrich-Watson, Deborah, 1954– II. Title. III. Medieval & Renaissance Texts & Studies (Series) ; v. 210
    PR3461.F667 V47 2000
    821'.4—dc21   00–058291

This book is made to last.
It is set in Caslon,
smythe-sewn and printed on acid-free paper
to library specifications.

Printed in the United States of America

In memory of my mother,
Seraphine Aldrich

Fayre Seraphina let your eyes then shine
gently upon this offering of mine
which to your outward Beauty I present,
of which your eyes are the chiefe ornament.

Table of Contents

Acknowledgments

Many scholars and friends contributed to my completion of this manuscript. I wish to thank especially the friendly and helpful personnel at the Huntington Library, the British Library, the Bodleian Library, the Stafford Record Office, and the William Salt Library for supplying me with great numbers of rare books, manuscripts, and genealogical records. In particular, Mary Robertson, Director of Manuscripts at the Huntington Library, supplied much information about HM904 and related manuscripts. Michael Webb, Assistant Librarian at the Bodleian Library, assisted with details related to Bodl. MS. Eng. poet. b. 5. Kathleen Smith of the Staffordshire Record Office, and Pauline Thomson, Assistant Librarian at the William Salt Library in Stafford, both worked patiently with me to retrieve marriage records, land negotiations, and other records of the Aston and Fowler families.

Christine Bowe, of the Stafford Landmark Trust office, graciously arranged a tour of the Tixall gatehouse for me, and Mrs. Margaret Haiggs just as graciously showed me around the now partially modernized building.

My attempts to trace what happened to the Fowler manuscript from the time it left the Fowler estate to the time Henry E. Huntington purchased it in 1925 were aided considerably by the personnel at W. Robinson, Ltd., booksellers, at Newcastle-upon-Tyne, and Jolyon Hudson of Pickering and Chatto, Ltd., Antiquarian Booksellers, of London.

Very generous in providing funding for this project were the Henry E. Huntington Library, which granted me two fellowships, the University of Missouri-St. Louis, which awarded money for several trips to England, and the University of Missouri Research Board, which provided funds for a month's stay in England. E. Terrence Jones, former dean of the College of Arts and Sciences at the University of Missouri-St. Louis, allowed me liberal time away from my duties as associate dean to pursue my research, and former associate dean Martin Sage's vast experience with parish records and Jacobean handwriting was invaluable to me during the early stages of this work.

Professor Jenijoy La Belle, who did pioneering work on Fowler's manuscript in the early 1980s, treated me to lunch, a print of Walter Aston, stories of her early days as a female faculty member at Cal. Tech., and insights into the manuscript we had both grown to love.

Elizabeth Donno, Columbia University professor emerita, now working at the Huntington Library, continues to support and encourage my work, even while she shrugs in dismay over the interest in female Renaissance writers. Professor Stanley Stewart of the University of California-Riverside helped me decipher a particularly difficult line in the manuscript when we were both working at the Huntington.

Tamara Myers, an MFA student at the University of Missouri-St. Louis, formatted the typescript and offered valuable editorial suggestions.

I am also grateful to Professor Arthur Marotti, who read through the manuscript and my typescript in detail, always offering helpful, gracious suggestions and corrections. The late Professor Josephine Roberts was very encouraging about the manuscript but died before she saw the typescript. I missed her counsel and advice while completing the project. Professor Dennis Kay gave the typescript its final letter-by-letter reading and wisely advised me (among other things) that Constance really made no distinction between her upper-case and lower-case ls.

Dr. Leslie S. B. MacCoull did a careful job of copy editing the volume, and Karen Lemiski was very helpful in seeing it to press.

Finally, I want to thank my late husband Chuck Larson, who encouraged and prodded me during much of my work on the Fowler manuscript, who traveled to Stafford and Tixall with me and took as much delight in walking along the Sow River as I did, and who died as the work was near its final stages. My colleagues in the English department at the University of Missouri-St. Louis helped me through these last difficult years and, I know, also miss Chuck, their friend, department chair, and colleague of many years.

Abbreviations and References

HM904	Manuscript version of Fowler's book
A	B.L. Add. MS. 15225
B	Bodl. MS. Eng. poet. b. 5.
HAM	Jenijoy La Belle, "The Huntington Aston Manuscript"
TL	Arthur Clifford, *Tixall Letters*
TP	Arthur Clifford, *Tixall Poetry*
DNB	*Dictionary of National Biography*
BDEC	*Bibliographical Dictionary of English Catholics*
OED	*Oxford English Dictionary*

Aston / Fowler / Thimelby / Fanshawe

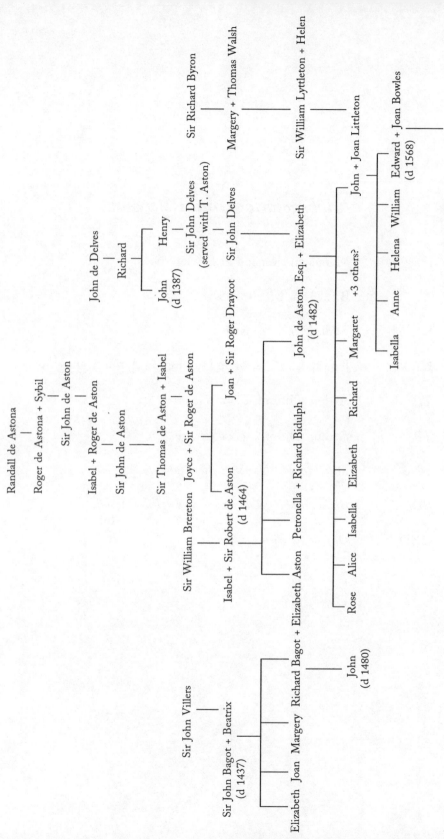

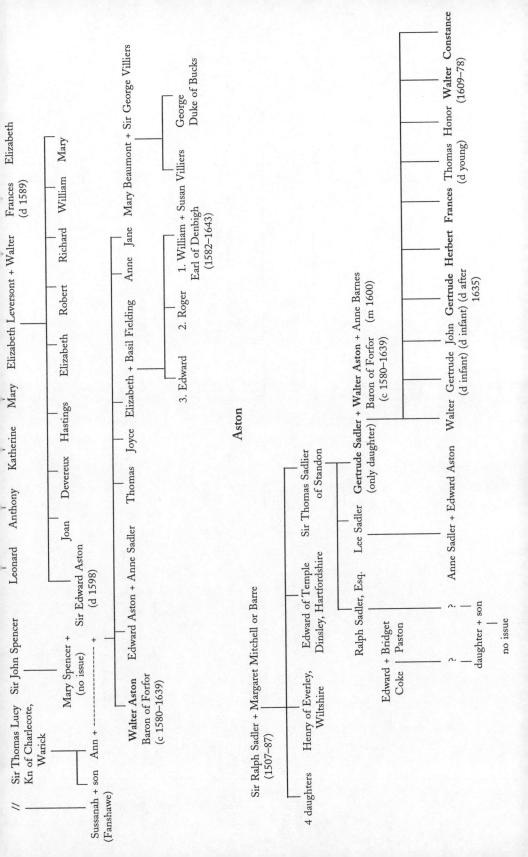

Aston

Thimelby

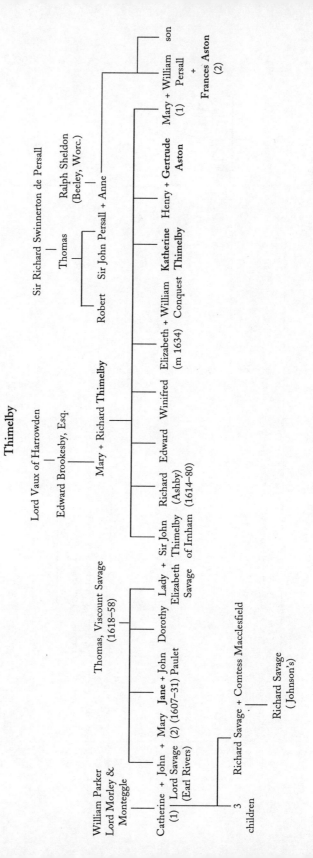

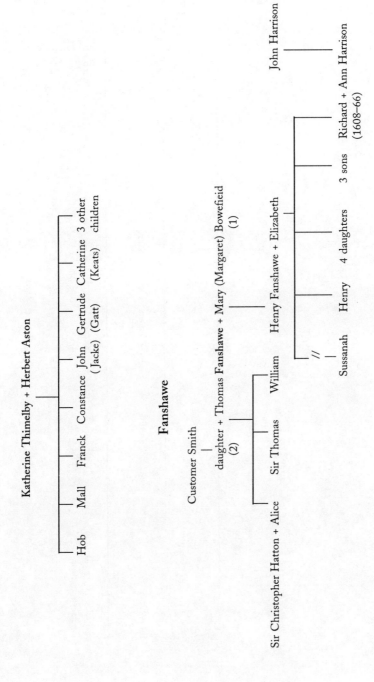

Katherine Thimelby + Herbert Aston

Hob Mall Franck Constance John Gertrude Catherine 3 other
                                (Jacke) (Gatt) (Keats) children

Fanshawe

Customer Smith

daughter + Thomas Fanshawe + Mary (Margaret) Bowefield
(2)   (1)

Sir Christopher Hatton + Alice   Sir Thomas   William   Henry Fanshawe + Elizabeth

Sussanah   Henry   4 daughters   3 sons   Richard + Ann Harrison
                                                      (1608–66)

John Harrison

Fowler

Ralph Sheldon
|
Walter Fowler of the Grange + Mary
(d 1622)

John + Anne Draycote   6 other children

Dorothy Eyre + Edward + Anne Stanningdale   Jeronima
(2)   (1)

Grace + Richard Canning   Anne + Richard Lacon   Mary (d unm)   Edward (d young)   Walter Fowler + Constance Aston
(1620–84)   (d 1664)

Frances Weston + Philip Draycote

1. Walter   2. Edward   3. William   4. Bryan   5. Thomas   6. Francis
(1645–95?)   (d young)   (d young)   (d young)

1. Constance   2. Dorothy   3. Gertrude   4. Constance   5. Mary   6. Magdalen
(d young)

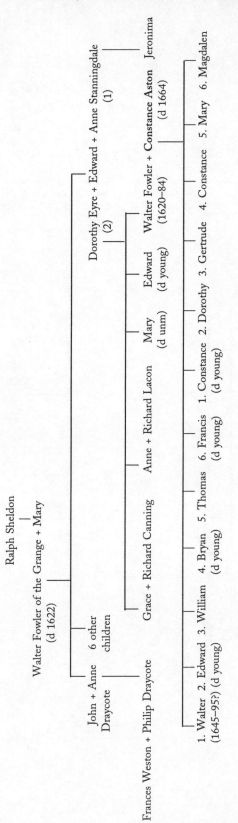

Weston

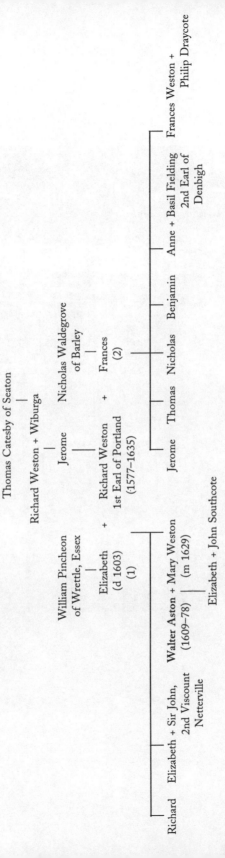

Thomas Catesby of Seaton

Richard Weston + Wiburga
|
Jerome   Nicholas Waldegrove
                          of Barley

William Pincheon   Richard Weston   Frances
of Wrettle, Essex   +   1st Earl of Portland   (2)
                          (1577–1635)
Elizabeth
(d 1603)
(1)

Jerome   Thomas   Nicholas   Benjamin   Anne + Basil Fielding   Frances Weston +
                                                  2nd Earl of   Philip Draycote
                                                  Denbigh

Walter Aston + Mary Weston
(1609–78)   (m 1629)

Elizabeth + John Southcote

Richard   Elizabeth + Sir John,
           2nd Viscount
           Netterville

The Tixall Gatehouse.
Courtesy of The Landmark Trust, Shottesbrooke, Maidenhead, Berkshire.

Introduction

In 1813, the antiquarian Arthur Clifford published a volume of poems from papers he had found in an old chest at Tixall, his ancestral home, outside Stafford, England. The chest to which Clifford was led by an elderly housekeeper contained family letters and poems written by members of the Aston family during the seventeenth century. This volume of poems and two volumes of letters (published two years later), now rare and neglected by historians and litterateurs, present by themselves a fascinating view of early modern family life and relations.

Clifford, however, did not know about another volume, a book kept between roughly 1630 and 1660, by Constance Aston Fowler, the youngest daughter in the family—a handwritten collection of poems that she copied from other sources and composed herself. This leather-bound volume, HM904 in the Huntington Library's manuscript collection, contains sixty-five poems, forty-nine of which are in Constance Fowler's hand, fifteen in her sister Gertrude's hand, and one plus a part of another in their father Walter's hand. Only four poems appear in both *Tixall Poetry* and HM904.

Thousands of commonplace books and manuscript miscellanies can be found here and abroad, ranging from John Milton's commonplace book to poetic miscellanies containing primarily one poet's work to manuscript books in which several hands have written out maxims, poems, recipes, and commentaries on current events. What makes HM904 particularly interesting, first, is Constance Fowler's gender. Arthur Marotti provides a list of diaries, commonplace books, and poetic miscellanies, including HM904, that were kept by early modern women (*English Renaissance Lyric*, 49–50), and Margaret Ezell comments that "Constance Aston Fowler was the hub of a literary group which included Lady Dorothy Shirley, Katherine Thimelby, and Gertrude Aston, in addition to Fowler's brother Herbert Aston and the Cavalier poet Richard Fanshawe" ("Canon of Women's Literature," 589). Aston's volume, then, although mainly copied rather than original work, provides the present-day reader with a document important to the study of creative thought in early modern women, as well as to the study of manuscript transmission among women and seventeenth-century literary society in general.

The poems Fowler included provide the second cause for interest in this manuscript; HM904, unlike most commonplace book-miscellanies, is not just a collection of poems that caught the writer's fancy at a certain moment, nor is it simply a collection of the writer's thoughts. Instead, HM904 combines these two elements. H. R. Woudhuysen calls the manuscript one of the important collections of verse put together by families (*Circulation of Manuscripts*, 172), and Marotti describes Fowler's book as "a good example of how a young woman assembled an anthology of poems in the context of family relations, personal devotional and literary interests, and Catholic royalist politics" (*English Renaissance Lyric*, 51). But Marotti stops short. In fact, fifty-five of the sixty-five poems in the volume relate directly to the Aston family and many are printed here for the first time. The circumstances of these poems provide us two and a half centuries later with an intimate view of a seventeenth-century woman and the relationships among her family members.

Fowler's family was a very close and loving one whose substantial literary interests and talents produced a body of work rich in the new and old poetic traditions, often innovative, and important not only to the literary scholar but to political and social historians as well. These poems provide evidence about literary influences among the seventeenth-century upper classes, about the lives of Catholics during Elizabethan, Jacobean, and Caroline times, and about family life and familial relationships.

Her own fondness for poetry along with the poetic interests of her siblings must have inclined Constance Aston Fowler to write poetry, but none of the poems in HM904 bears her initials, nor do any of the poems found among the Tixall papers. Nevertheless, I am certain that Fowler wrote poetry; at least three poems and a fragment of another, all appearing without attribution in her commonplace book, bear distinct signs of her style and what is known of her personality.

As in any collection of this sort, the quality of the poetry varies, from

Henry King's "Exequy" to the anonymous and rather tedious Catholic ballad "A certaine king married A son." However, the poetry written by members of the Aston circle is generally of high amateur quality and often rises to the level of good minor seventeenth-century verse.

This volume, along with *Tixall Poetry*, reveals a seventeenth-century family that used their own compositions and the works of others in much the same way some families today use Hallmark greetings—to celebrate births, deaths, anniversaries, and homecomings. The poems transcribed and composed by members of the Aston family possess considerable literary and historical interest. The majority of the Aston pieces have neither been printed nor, until now, made easily accessible to the students of early women's literary productions, seventeenth-century poetry, manuscript transmission, and societal and familial relationships.

HISTORICAL

Constance Aston Fowler was born about 1621, the youngest daughter of the ten children of Walter, Lord Aston, Baron of Forfor, and Gertrude Sadlier. At least five of these children survived through adulthood: Walter, second Lord Aston, Herbert, Frances, Gertrude, and Constance. A daughter, Honoria, died in Spain between 1619 and 1625, and a son, John, was still living in 1635, the date of his father's will, but probably died shortly after.

The Aston family line dates to Randal de Astona in the early thirteenth century. Ten generations later the family was prominent enough that Mary Queen of Scots was held for seventeen days under house arrest at Tixall, the family seat in Staffordshire, under the supervision of Constance's great-grandfather Walter Aston while the papers that led to Mary's execution were examined (Cutler, *County of Stafford*, 1:252). Constance's father, also named Walter, was born about 1580 to Sir Edward Aston and Ann Lucy, daughter of Sir Thomas Lucy, Knight of Charlecote. A minor when his father died in 1597 or 1598,[1] this Walter was, by Queen Elizabeth, put under the wardship of Sir Edward Coke (Clifford, *TP*, xv–xvi). Under his tutelage, Walter became an ardent Protestant, who, nevertheless, tolerated Catholics.[2]

---

[1] Arthur Clifford in *Tixall Poetry* (hereafter *TP*) dates Edward's death in 1597. Margaret Midgley (*County of Stafford*, 4:84) says that Edward Aston died in 1587; however, Clifford's careful study of the Tixall state papers and his access to manuscripts now scattered or lost suggest that his date has more authenticity.

[2] J. L. and Karl Cherry in 1908, writing without reference to Clifford, claim that Walter Aston had as

In fact, Aston may have been part of the group of nominal Anglicans who essentially retained their Catholic faith during the later years of Elizabeth's reign (Flynn, "Donne the Survivor," 18). He was almost certainly acquainted with one member of this group: the poet John Donne. In 1600, Walter Aston, still a minor, secretly married Anne Barnes, about whom little is known. R. C. Bald, Donne's 1970 biographer, uses the Aston-Barnes marriage to illustrate the danger Donne must have known he would encounter if he secretly married Anne More, as he did a year later. As Bald observes, Donne, for all the trouble his marriage caused, did not suffer the fate of Aston and Barnes (*John Donne*, 136n): all celebrants of and witnesses to the Aston-Barnes marriage were excommunicated; Anne Barnes was committed to the Fleet prison, where she remained for about a year, and Aston was absolved from his marriage. Among those sitting in judgement of Aston and Barnes was Sir Edward Coke, who would have profited considerably from his ward's marriage to a woman of higher station than Barnes's, but who recused himself from subscribing to the unanimous judgement that the marriage should be dissolved (Bald, *John Donne*, 132–33).[3]

the victim of his most virulent [anti-Catholic] animosity ... Father Sutton. In cross-examining this priest, Sir Walter put an acute accent on his questions by twice striking the prisoner with his staff, and by knocking him down. Sir Walter committed him to Stafford gaol and insisted upon giving evidence against him at the Assizes. He protested that if his evidence were not accepted he would never sit on the bench again. That was a prospect so alarming that the Court let him have his will, and shortly afterwards Father Sutton "was put off the ladder, and cut down very lively, for he stood upon his feet, and after being dismembered spoke these words, 'O, thou bloody butcher, God forgive you!' Then, calling upon Jesus and Mary, he expired." (*Historical Studies*, 73)

However, since the 1620s the whole Aston family had decidedly Catholic leanings, and in 1635, when this incident was supposed to have taken place, Walter was in Spain on his second ambassadorship. Henry Foley also recounts this story but dates it to 1588 (*English Province*, 3.233; 4.495); thus, the Sir Walter Aston named was most likely the grandfather of the Spanish ambassador.

[3] See my "John Donne and the Astons" for a fuller discussion of Walter Aston's connections with John Donne. See also Dennis Kay, who shows a further connection to Donne by attributing one poem from *Lachrimae lachrimarum* to Walter Aston ("Poems," 200–6).

Bald quotes in full a summary of this case from HL MS. Ellesmere 5920 (*John Donne*, 132).

In *Michael Drayton and His Circle*, Newdigate prints part of Sir Simon Degge's account of Aston's life and personality to Aston's grandson. In that account, a liaison or promise of marriage to a " 'yonge gentlewoman that had served his mother' " obligated him to pay £500. Of " 'this gentlewoman,' " Degge continues, " 'I can give ... noe further accompt' " (147).

Walter married Gertrude Sadlier between 1601 and 1608.[4] Gertrude was
the only daughter of Sir Thomas Sadlier of Standon, son of Ralph Sadlier,
and, as such, she brought to her marriage a good quantity of land. In 1619
Walter Aston was appointed by James I as joint ambassador to Spain with
Sir John Digby, Earl of Bristol, to negotiate the proposed marriage of Prince
Charles to the Infanta, daughter of Spain's Philip III. Through this ambassadorship, Walter developed a friendly relationship with George Villiers, the
Duke of Buckingham, favorite of James I and of Prince Charles, later
Charles I. The proposed marriage, of course, never took place, and Buckingham, Bristol, and their colleague Edward, Lord Conway faced Parliament in
1626 on charges of "High Crimes and Misdemeanors." Aston's name is
mentioned several times in the state papers concerning this parliamentary
procedure (Howell, *State Trials*, 1269 ff). However, Walter Aston, joint ambassador with Bristol, assiduously kept his hands clean during the messy
negotiations; for example, Charles I accused Bristol of "at our first coming
in Spain, taking upon you to be so wise, as to foresee our intention to
change our religion, [and] you were so far from dissuading us, that you
offered your advice and secresy [sic] to concur in it"; Bristol, Charles continued, "press[ed] to shew how convenient it was to be a Roman Catholic,
it being impossible, in your opinion, to do any great action otherwise." But
Walter Aston was not blamed because "he durst not give his consent for fear
of his head" (Howell, *State Trials*, 1277). Walter Aston was never charged
with any crime and after his six-year embassy to Spain (1619–25) returned
to Tixall. Charles, in fact, continued to place enough trust in Aston that he
returned him to Spain as ambassador from 1635 to 1638.

During either his first or second embassy, Walter converted to Catholicism; the undated letter explaining the reasons for his conversion is addressed to "My deare frend" and begins:

Where as there hath been much frendship & kindnes betwixt us for
so long a time I hope it shall not break of[f] upon this occasion of
my channging my Religion. Howsoever I am I thank God so resolved
that I had rather loose the best worldly frends that ever I had then

---

[4] The marriage was probably no later than 1608, since their oldest surviving son,
Walter, was born in 1609. He was probably Walter and Gertrude's second or third child.
Another child named Walter died as an infant, as did a daughter Gertrude, either before
or after her surviving brother. Clifford reasonably ventures 1607 as the marriage date
(*State Papers*, ii–iiin).

change againe from what I am. (Clifford, *Tixall Letters*, 1:63–64; hereafter *TL*)

Jenijoy La Belle assumes the later date for Sir Walter's conversion, while arguing that his family had converted earlier (HAM 544); however, given that Constance was married around 1635[5] to Walter Fowler, oldest son of Edward of St. Thomas Priory, a bastion of Catholicism in Stafford,[6] it seems likely that Walter Aston, if he had not already converted, continued to be very tolerant of Catholicism. In fact, in the 1620s or 1630s Tixall itself was a Roman Catholic center in Stafford (Greenslade and Johnson, *County of Stafford*, 6:250). Walter Aston died in 1639, one year after returning from Spain.

Walter, Walter and Gertrude Aston's first son to survive infancy, became upon his father's death the second Lord Aston. If the first Lord Aston was still Protestant in the late 1620s, he did not object to and indeed no doubt arranged for the marriage of his son Walter to the (probably) Catholic Mary Weston in 1629. Mary's father was Richard Weston, Earl of Portland and, since 1628, Lord High Treasurer of England. Although Richard Weston *may* never have been a Catholic himself, according to the *DNB*, he "incurred popular hatred as [a] suspected Roman catholic." There was certainly plenty of evidence to fuel such widespread popular speculation as to his religious affiliation. His wife was an acknowledged Catholic, and Weston himself seems to have raised no objection when priests were permitted to reside in his house. Several of his children were Catholic, and his oldest son married into a devout Catholic family. According to Martin Havran, Portland himself may have made a bedside conversion to Catholicism (*Catholics in Caroline England*, 135).[7]

---

[5] Clifford suggests two different dates for Constance and Walter's marriage: 1629 (*A Topographical Description*, 37–38) and 1634 or earlier (*TP*, 394). If, as I believe, theirs was a marriage arranged to consolidate land holdings, 1629, when Walter Fowler was nine and Constance Aston about twelve years old, is not an impossible date. However, 1634 or 1635 seems more likely, since Walter was then at the legal age for consent. Furthermore, the immanency of Sir Walter Aston's second ambassadorship was a likely prompt for settling financial matters.

[6] In 1602, Edward Morgan, admitted to the company of the Jesuits in 1609, lived with Walter Fowler, Esq. (the grandfather of Constance's husband), in his "mansion" near Stafford, where he attended school with two of Fowler's sons. Fowler also "enabled" the eighteen-year-old Morgan to go to Douai College (Foley, *English Province*, 4:516–17).

[7] The *DNB* continues, "Almost all the branches of the Weston family had retained a secret or open attachment to the Roman catholic religion. Sir Richard was no excep-

Herbert, the only other Aston son to survive to adulthood,[8] was the most talented and prolific poet in the family.[9] Traveling with his father to Spain on Walter's second embassy, he and Constance exchanged frequent letters. Only Constance's half of this three-year correspondence is extant (both in manuscript and as printed by Clifford), but her letters reveal a truly (and sometimes unusually) deep affection between the siblings. On 8 December ca. 1636, Constance wrote:

> Oh my dearest brother,
>
> What a grefe have you convayed in to my soule, in relating to me the danger of your last sicknesse: tounges and penes are not able to expresse it; itt being a grefe far above ther reach to utter; yet you tell me, you are perfectly recovered; but I never shall be out of fere, till I here it seconded by you in your next letter, for you say, you are yett very weake. And methinkes I would most gladly here you wer growne perfect stronge again; for I shall live in payne till then; therefore, I beg of you, if that you have not writt me word so, afore you receave this, that as sune as possible you can, that I may know it: for indeed, I shall not be confident you are so, till I here itt from your selfe; and I asure you, I shall live in much feare till then: therfore, I hope you will not be forgettfull of my misserie. I receaved with this your last letter, which is dated the 1st of Novr. another letter, which you had writt afore your being sicke, and in it you sent me a copy of your verses made to Mr Win—.[10] They are much commended by all, as they deserve; and you have ganed the English ladyes' harts extreamely by them, to see you so constant a favorite of there miritts. For my part, I must confesse, I am taken with nothinge but the praysess you give your *Seraphina*. I love her above my life, and vallew her infinitly. (*TL*, 1:96–97)

The Seraphina whom Constance adored was her friend and eventual sister-

---

tion, and with this religious belief went a political sympathy with Spain. He was favorably known to Gondomar, the Spanish ambassador, and it was through his influence that Weston was sent on a mission to the archdukes at Brussels" in 1620 and again in 1622.

[8] How old a third brother, John, was when he died sometime after 1635 is not known.

[9] Herbert Aston's commonplace book is at the Beinecke Library, Yale (Ms. Osborne B4, 1634); it shares no common poems with Fowler's collection of poems.

[10] This poem, as far as I can determine, appears in neither *Tixall Poetry* nor HM904.

in-law, Katherine Thimelby. Constance's letters to Herbert revel almost in the "conspiracy" that she (sometimes along with Katherine) had devised to link her favorite brother and her best friend in matrimony. In fact, as La Belle notes, Constance's letters to her brother resemble an eighteenth-century epistolary novel ("A True Love's Knot," 14). Constance ends the body of the previously quoted letter by enticing Herbert: "I canot tele you many thinges I else would; but I will shortly write you a longe discourse, which, I am confident, cannot be unwellcom to you; . . . . For I asure you, ther is no cause of feare, but rather of joy, if all thinges fall out acording to the wish of your most faithfull lover, and affectionat sister" (*TL*, 1:98). Her next two letters (*TL*, 1:100–6) continue the suspense as Fowler keeps promising a longer letter later. The letter that she finally writes is about 4600 words long and tells the "storye" (Fowler uses the word at least four times in the letter) of the complicated intrigue Constance and Katherine have devised for exchanging letters and of the methods Constance is using to secure the marriage (*TL*, 1:107–27). When Fowler wrote these letters to her brother, she was probably between the ages of nineteen and twenty-one, and the evidence suggests that Katherine was of approximately the same age. In 1636, Constance had been married less than a year to Walter Fowler, with whom she was not presently living. Her own arranged marriage may well have contributed to her romanticizing Herbert's and Katherine's affection. All that is known of the circumstances of Herbert's and Katherine's courtship of each other is what Fowler's letters reveal, and, from the intrigues Fowler describes, a reader would be justified in assuming objections to the match from one set of parents or the other. In fact, what seems more likely is that Fowler had a vivid, dramatic imagination and amused herself, and Herbert and Katherine too, with her tales of household spies and secretly delivered missives, indulging herself in the kind of romance that was not now conceivable in her own life. Katherine and Herbert married in 1638.

No doubt Katherine's poetic skill and love of poetry endeared her to her new family. Beyond this, several post-marriage documents attest to Katherine's acceptance into the Aston family and verify Fowler's assessment of the depth of Herbert's and Katherine's affection for each other. A 1638 letter from Herbert's father to his "Good dawter," Katherine, begins:

> Y^u have sett so great a valew of estimation upon my good affections to y^u and y^r husband: y^t I am in payn and ashamed I canot make it good wth such reall actions of advantage unto y^u as y^u deserve: (B.L. Add. MS. 36452, II fol. 36)

Herbert and Katherine seem to have been experiencing financial trouble, and

Walter, though unable to help them,[11] assures his new daughter-in-law that she is "come into a famyly ... united in trew affection one unto another" (fol. 36) and signs his letter, "Y^r Loving father I asure you" (fol. 36).

Herbert and Katherine Aston lived at Bellamour, which Herbert had constructed and named in honor of his love for his wife. Katherine, whom her husband described as being somewhat sickly throughout her life, died in 1658 after giving birth to her tenth child.

That the Astons esteemed Katherine is also clear from both the poems mourning her death and the letters to Herbert consoling him and praising her.[12] Herbert's love for his wife remained strong, as evidenced by his written description of her final days and her death (TL, 2:179–200).[13]

The Astons and the Thimelbys, who lived in Irnham, Lincolnshire, although sixty-five miles (or about a three-day carriage ride) apart, were intimately connected, both through Catholicism and through marital ties. Richard Thimelby and Mary Brookesby, granddaughter of Lord Vaux of Harrowden, had fourteen children, at least eleven of whom survived infancy. Of these, Richard Thimelby (1614–80), fifth son of Richard and Mary, joined the Jesuits when he was seventeen; he became rector of St. Omer's, in France, in 1672 (BDEC, 540),where his brother Robert died.[14] His sister Winefred was abbess at St. Monica's Convent, in Louvain, and another sister Frances took her vows on her deathbed in 1644. In addition, besides the Herbert Aston-Katherine Thimelby marriage, Frances Aston and William Pershall, whose first wife had been Mary Thimelby, married, as did Gertrude Aston and Henry Thimelby. Unlike Constance, Gertrude married

---

[11] Walter Aston and his family were always in financial straits. As ambassador, he paid most of his expenses and was not paid exorbitantly. Newdigate says of this letter that in it "he alludes to his own domestic misfortunes and to his ill-health in a touching letter addressed to Catherine Thimelby" (Michael Drayton, 155).

[12] See Tixall Letters, 1:171–77, and Tixall Poetry, "On the Death of My Dear Sister, Mrs Kath. Aston; Known by the Name of 'Good Love'" and "An Epitaph" (283–85).

[13] In "A particular accompt of ye most remarkable passages at ye happy end of Mrs Ca. Aston, and wt past 7 dayes before, wth some reflection on ye vertues and suffrings of her precedent life," Herbert says that Katherine converted to Catholicism "before she was ten yeares old" (TL 2:182) and for thirty years "there past few dayes, I believe none, wherein she suffered not some considerable sickness, or paine: few monthes that she had not a weeke at least of extremity; and twice a yeare of late, spring and fall, she had fitts that kept her for the most part of a month in bed, without ease or sleepe, for 7 or 8 days together" (2:182–83). She appears to have died of tuberculosis several days after giving birth.

[14] Several in the Aston-Thimelby circle were educated at St. Omer's, including William Habington.

relatively late in her life. As recusancy petitions from Gertrude Sadlier Aston show, her daughter Gertrude was not yet married in 1651 (*Some Account of Colton*, 135 ff). Henry Thimelby died in 1655; therefore, he and Gertrude married sometime between the latter half of 1651 and 1654, since a son of theirs died within a year of his father's death. Why Lord Aston arranged a marriage for his youngest daughter Constance when she was only fourteen instead of for her fifteen-year-old sister probably cannot now be known. Perhaps, despite Fowler's poetic enthusiasm over Gertrude's hair, the older sister was in some way physically blemished, or perhaps, given the fervor of the poems she wrote in Fowler's book, Gertrude had always intended to take religious vows. In any case (and these two possibilities are not mutually exclusive), Gertrude was in her early thirties when she married her brother-in-law. After the deaths of her husband and son, Gertrude retired to Louvain, where she took her vows in 1658 and served with her sister-in-law, Winefred. They were eventually joined by two of Katherine and Herbert's daughters.

Constance Aston Fowler's letters are interesting beyond their relevance to Herbert's marriage. Of the eight that survive, none mentions any significant events in Fowler's personal life. She comments on visits by Richard Fanshawe and the household circumstances that inspired two of his poems (59 and 61). In a letter filled with information on Katherine Thimelby and their schemes, she devotes a sentence to a visit by the king—no more. She never mentions the politics of the time nor the impending war.

Constance Aston Fowler began keeping her poetic commonplace book probably during the mid-1630s, shortly after her marriage in about 1635 to Walter Fowler, who had no doubt been a childhood playmate, given the relative closeness of the two estates. La Belle believes Fowler was about eighteen in 1635 (HAM 543), but I have not found independent verification that Fowler was born in 1617. Clifford, who is not always consistent in his dating, gives no year for Fowler's birth but never wavers in describing her as Walter and Gertrude's youngest daughter. According to the records of St. Monica's Convent, Gertrude Aston Thimelby was forty-eight when she died in 1668. If Clifford is accurate, Fowler must then have been born no earlier than 1621. Sidney Grazebrook's edition of a 1663 Staffordshire visitation indicates that Walter Fowler was born in 1620, making Constance and Walter fourteen and fifteen, respectively, when they married (*Visitations*, n.p.). Although it was somewhat unusual in the 1630s for male children outside the nobility to marry as early as fifteen, a significant land deal may have en-

couraged a precipitate marriage settlement.[15] Walter and Constance's rene-
gotiated post-nuptial marriage agreement (1649, when Walter, their first
child to survive infancy, was four years old) emphasizes the amount of land
involved.[16] Fowler bore twelve children, of whom eight survived infancy.
Beyond what her letters and her book reveal, not much more is known
about Fowler. Presumably she continued to live the life of an upper-class
matron, even through the Civil War, during which her oldest son, Walter,
fought for the King. Two daughters, Mary and Dorothy, married John
Betham and Thomas Grove, Esq., respectively. Constance Aston Fowler
died in 1664.

CRITICAL

The poems in HM904 can be divided into three categories: religious
poems, familial poems (that is, those by or about family members and
friends within the Aston-Fowler-Thimelby circle), and miscellaneous poems
fitting neither of the first two categories.

Sixteen of the poems in HM904 are overtly Catholic (2, 3, 4, 7/8, 9, 10,

---

[15] Lawrence Stone in *The Family, Sex and Marriage* argues that arranged marriages
between young men and women not yet physically or emotionally mature enough to
consummate their relationship, especially when significant amounts of land were involved,
continued into the early 1700s. Catholic families were more prone than Protestants to
assert their parental rights in arranging their sons' and daughters' marriages (129–35).

[16] "This indenture ... made the [left blank in doc.] Day of May Anno Dom one
thousand six hundred forty and nine between Walter Fowler of St Thomas in the countie
of Stafford, ... in consideration of a marriage formerly had and solemnized betweene the
said Walter Fowler and Constance his now wife the daughter of Walter Lord Aston
deceased and for the settling a suffient [sic] and competent joynture for the livelihood
and subsistance of the said Constance in case she shall outlive the said Walter as also for
establishing and settinge of the state of the said Walter Fowler and his name and blood
the said Walter by indenturebearing date the thirtieth day of April and anno thousand six
hundred forty nine enrolled in the high court of chancery hath for the consideration
therin expressed granted bargained and sold alyen and confirmed unto the said Arthur
Shirland and Robert Chilmand her ... assigned will that the scite of the dissolved
monastry of St Thomas the Martyr nere Stafford called the Mannor upon Sowe wth the
rights members and appurtancies therof in the said county of Stafford and all those the
severall mannors of Colton [+ 5 others] wth their and every of their rights memberd and
appurtenences and all those fifty messuages ... and fourefront cottages five hundred acres
of arrable land on [several words unreadable because of the MS. fold] of meadows or
thereabouts six hundred acres of pasture ... twenty acre of wood or thereabouts and two
hundred acres of ... heath or thereabout. ...." (William Salt Library, Stafford, England.
Bundle 20, doc. 20)

11, 12, and 26 through 33).[17] There are no religious poems after fol. 46. Four of the Catholic poems are by Robert Southwell, the Jesuit priest, who was jailed in the Tower of London in 1586 for his Jesuit proselytizing and executed for treason in 1595. The first printed editions of Southwell's poems appeared almost immediately after his execution. In addition, at least five manuscript versions of his poems circulated during the mid-seventeenth century (Southwell, *Poems*, ed. McDonald and Brown, xxxv). Thus, the four Southwell poems in HM904 ("The prodigall childs soule wracke" [11], "Man to the wound In christs syde" [12], "A Child my Choyce" [26], and "Lifes Death, lous life" [27]) were a standard part of the poetic canon for seventeenth-century English recusants and readily available to Fowler, probably in manuscript (see below, p. lxxix). At the same time, these particular four suit Fowler's personality as it is displayed in the other poems in her book and in her extant letters.

First, faith, while an integral part of her life, was neither complex nor all-consuming. Constance had certainly read widely in sixteenth- and seventeenth-century poetry, and some of the poems she allowed in her book echo Donne's poetry, including his religious poems.[18] However, she includes not one of Donne's Holy Sonnets or Hymns (with their hard and intricate arguments) or even the more Catholic "La Corona." The religious poems she copies convey an uncomplicated, direct Christian message—"Let folly praise y^t fancy loues / I praise And loue that child," for example, rather than Donne's "Wilt thou love God, as he thee! then digest, / My Soule, this wholesome meditation" (1–2) or even Southwell's "Burning Babe." She anguishes over Christ's physical passion but allows the poems in her book to reflect no doubt about what that passion means.

Thus, her letter to Herbert seeking to comfort him on the death of his (and her) beloved Katherine in 1658 (probably twenty years after she regularly worked on her book) is above all practical. She does not offer the standard Christian consolation that Katherine is happy now in heaven; they both

---

[17] La Belle indicates that the poem beginning "O lord direct my hart" (7/8) is in Fowler's hand. However, the handwriting through line 21 is the same hand as that in Poem 1: that of Fowler's father. At line 22, the hand is Fowler's. Given the change in handwriting, the interruption in chronology (with line 22 backtracking through some of the events already described in the preceding lines), and the torn-out pages before these lines, the poem may be considered two separate compositions following the same plot and theme.

[18] See, for example, Poem 7/8, ll. 84–88.

know she is. Her concern is for his life now, on this earth. To that end she writes that their older brother Walter has asked that "if I had any powre with you, I would trye if I could obtaine of you to come abroade amongest your frindes" (*TL*, 1:171). Later she admonishes, "Deare brother, consider this oft, and let it move you to seeke more to preserve your selfe, and give me the comfort to here you are at Tixall some times, and I will be as sat-isfy'd as if I had seene you" (*TL*, 1:171). Her only explicit reference to her faith, "My humble duety to my lady, and servis to the rest, desireing of there good prayers, having a most weeke hart. God helpe me, and remember you will doe nothing to comfort it" (*TL*, 1:172), reflects an awareness of God's love, and at the same time acknowledges the necessity of men's and women's immediate actions. For Constance, the four Southwell poems may have been appealing because they reflect the first part of this dichotomy without inter-fering with the second. God is mighty and powerful; his redemptive power calms "the boysterous seas" (11.13) of life; with his love she "cannot liue Amisse" (26.8). The straightforward doctrine of these poems may well have appealed to Fowler's practicality, evident in her knowlege twenty years after Gertrude copied the poems that God will ease her brother's grief but will have a much easier time doing so if Herbert returns to the human society at Tixall.

Second, those Southwell poems Fowler included in her book display, more than many of his other poems, an ingenuous fondness for words and word sounds, abounding in alliteration, balanced lines and half-lines, and word repetition. For example, in "Lifes Death, lous life," a variation of the verb "to live" appears twenty-four times and "to love" (or a form of it) twenty-one times within the poem's thirty-two lines. The repetition of these two words, which are often juxtaposed, turns the poem into something of a religious conundrum.

Constance herself was fond of riddles and wordplay, as her letters demon-strate. Certainly her letters to Herbert dramatically promising to tell him of Katherine's fondness for him in the next letter—and then putting him off until the next—demonstrate a cleverness, a love of games and words, that is also evident in all four Southwell poems. La Belle notes Fowler's fondness for puns, especially those involving her own name: a short letter (*TL*, 1:96–99) "includes *conveyed, seconded, confident* (twice), *constant* (twice), *confess, conceal, contended,* and *conjure*" ("A True Love's Knot," 14–15).[19] Another

---

[19] La Belle continues that Constance "plays upon her name to suggest the kind of

letter ends "Tis con and none but con that is, / Your ever most afectionat / sister, ..." written in an arc over her initials (*TL*, 1:135).[20]

That these poems are in Gertrude Aston Thimelby's hand does not necessarily contradict the theory that Fowler herself preferred to dictate what poems would be included in her book. The blank book was most probably given to Fowler by her father, since Walter Aston copied or wrote the first dedicatory poem in it to Constance, perhaps shortly before his second embassy to Spain and shortly after his daughter's marriage to the fifteen-year-old Walter Fowler. (In the poem, Fowler is still, like Mary, "a uirgin wife" [1.6].) La Belle says that this poem is "in Constance's hand, but hastily written" (HAM 554). However, the hand of Poem 1 matches that in the commonplace book that Walter Aston kept during his travels to Spain.[21] What would become Fowler's beloved book of poems and her family record was, then, begun with a very hastily scrawled, messy, but earnest verse and given to her on the occasion of her marriage by her father, who would soon leave the family again.

Aside from this and a very few others, all the poems in HM904 are neatly copied and decorated, indicating that Fowler cared very much just what works covered its pages. After fol. 46, only one poem, the last, is not in her own hand. It seems probable, then, that Constance and Gertrude (the sister to whom she appears to have been closest) cooperated in choosing and in copying the first poems in Fowler's book. Perhaps Gertrude had borrowed or been given a printed or manuscript edition of Southwell's poems and copied those that appealed most to her sister or that Fowler chose. That thirty-one Southwell poems appear, in Gertrude's hand, in a manuscript at the Bodleian Library (11, 12, and 27 from HM904)[22] also testifies to Gertrude's affinity for Southwell and Fowler's more limited taste for his poetry: if Fowler had allowed her sister to copy whatever Southwell poems Gertrude wanted to copy, HM904 would no doubt contain more than a mere four.[23]

---

constancy which she hopes will exist between her, her brother, and finally Katherine" ("A True Love's Knot," 15).

[20] See also La Belle, "A True Love's Knot," 14.

[21] Walter Aston's commonplace book is at the County Record Office in Stafford.

[22] B; see Textual Introduction, pp. lxxvii–lxxx for the editorial importance of this manuscript.

[23] No printed edition of Southwell's poetry appears in the 1899 Sotheby, Wilkinson and Hodge sale catalogue of "Valuable Books & Manuscripts" from the Tixall Library,

In fact, Gertrude copied fourteen of the sixteen religious poems into her sister's book; all but three of these also appear in her handwriting in the Bodleian manuscript.[24] Poems 28 through 33 are all rather uninteresting examples of Catholic ballads or poetic renderings of parables; one might believe that Fowler lost control of her book for a period, and Gertrude included poems to suit her own taste, which seems to have tended toward verses like the following from a poetic rendition of the biblical tale of Abraham and Isaac:

> The Angels Asked Abraham
> where sarah Did Abyde
> who Answered And sayde
> In the tent A little beside
> then spake these heauenly Angels
> within the time of life
> A child shall be conceiued
> by sarah thy owne wife. (30.33–40)

Similarly, poems 9 and 10 are Catholic ballads that appear in other Catholic song or commonplace books. Both can be found, for example, in the Bodleian manuscript (in Gertrude's hand) and in a British Library manuscript of Catholic ballads. Fowler may have been attracted by the drama of these poems, or, during the early months of keeping her book, she may simply have been inconsistent in what she allowed to be copied. Poem 2, "O Iesu, thou my glory Art," in Gertrude's hand, is similar to 9 and 10.

"Off the Blessed name, of Iesus," Poem 3, also in Gertrude's hand but unique (as far as I can tell) to HM904, differs little in sentiment from the other unattributed religious poems in this volume; certainly it is far removed from the dense and anguished arguments of the metaphysicals. However, aside from being an acrostic, the poem shows more wit and more affinity with some metaphysical religious poems than others copied into the volume do:

> Iust as the sunn beames — In the midst of Dai
> Expell the worlds — Eclipsing shads frō uewe

---

but many reasons for this absence are possible, including that Gertrude carried it with her when she joined her sister-in-law Winefred Thimelby at Louvain.

[24] Poems 4 and 7/8 are in Fowler's hand; of the fourteen additional religious poems in Gertrude's hand, only Poems 2, 3, and 26 do not appear in B.

soe is renew'd by Ie — sus glorious — rayes
uile Ignorance Dull — uailes while he ye tru
sunn of sweete Iustice — sence to reason swaies

When sunbeams are "in the midst of Dai," no shadows, no eclipses, are cast. As Donne writes in a love lyric about sun and shadows: "But, now the Sunne is just above our head / We doe those shadowes tread; / And to brave clearnesse all things are reduc'd" ("Lecture upon the Shadow," 6–8). The sunbeams at noon rid the corrupt world of shadows and reveal only the pure light of truth. In the same manner, the beams of the "sunn of sweete Iustice" remove the veil cast by ignorance and the deep shadows of natural valleys that block man from God, both by being dark and by being low. Ignorance is renewed, reborn as truth because of the Son's "glorious rayes." Once this happens, one can see clearly that the things of this earth all keep man in an eclipse until the Son sways sense (or sensation) to reason and God's love. Clearly, this poem exists on a higher intellectual plane than the previously discussed unattributed poems.

The poem is also, of course, a series of acrostics: reading down the first letters of the poem, the first letters of the words after the caesura, and the last letters of each line produce JESUS. The first version of the poem, written above the second, corrected, version, shows Gertrude or Constance and Gertrude jointly playing with the vagaries of seventeenth-century spelling to puzzle out the end acrostic.

Only one and a half religious poems are in Fowler's hand, Poems 4 and 7/8, and both are quite different from the poems in Gertrude's hand in their dramatic intensity. That Fowler had a penchant for the dramatic is obvious to anyone reading her sometimes unusual letters to Herbert. For example, in one already cited letter, she describes to her brother how she and Katherine Thimelby work to keep their affection secret and of how her proxy courtship of Katherine is progressing. These involve transmitting secret letters between her dear friend and her:

> For about three weekes after we partted at Tixall, she [Katherine] sent me a letter by a messeinger knowne onely to her selfe and me, for we had sent him often betwixt us, he being of great trust, foir no body could gett any thinge out of him tha[n] he list him selfe, nether here nor none with her. (*TL*, 1:112)

Her tale of intrigue continues with disguised handwriting and secretive maids (113). In another letter, she is quite aware that she is stringing her brother along to create tension and suspense:

> I write now in very great hast, therfore I canot tele you many thinges
> I else would; but I will shortly write you a longe discourse, which, I
> am confident, cannot be unwellcom to you; but till then, I beg you
> will not emagin, nor be fearfull to know what it may be. For I assure
> you, ther is no cauwse of feare, but rather of joy, if all thinges fall out
> according to the wish of your most faithfull lover, and affectionat
> sister. (*TL*, 1:98)

Constance is consciously heightening the theatricality of the situation for the
pleasure of her audience, which consists not only of Herbert but of Katherine as well.

    This same sense of the dramatic in "On the Passion of our Lord and sa-
uiour Iesus" (4), an unattributed poem in Fowler's book, suggests Fowler as
the composer. Following Christ from the Garden of Gethsemane through
the Crucifixion, the speaker shows a personal involvement in Christ's
passion:

> O say (deere Iesus) was it for my sake
> For me vile sinner thou didst undertake
> such pains, such cruell torments, what am I
> That thou for me shouldst suffer misery
> But O my soule I feele my conscience say
> I was an Actor in this bloody play
> gaue thee some wounds, my guilty soule descries
> Too where they were, t'was neere those sacred Eyes
> O tell me where I hitt, and frome this Day
> These constant uows religiously I'le pay
> Once euery day to fix a sorrowed Looke
> vpon the place, and say o there I strooke:
> His sacred flesh thus all to peices torne. (159–71)

Christianity teaches that each person through sin is responsible for wound-
ing Christ, and Fowler uses this doctrine to involve herself in a very personal
way in the drama of the Crucifixion. Her use of "actor" and "play" illustrates
her awareness that she is now creating a play, a scene (albeit a very serious
one), just as she does in her letters to Herbert, which stress the drama of
her, his, and Katherine's relationship. Fowler's dramatization of the life of
Christ is firmly rooted in the Catholic tradition; the Catholic mass, after all,
is the priest's reenactment of the Last Supper. Furthermore, Fowler's poem

fits perfectly into the Catholic meditative tradition. According to Ignatius Loyola, a crucial phase of the exercise is to imagine oneself on the scene during the Crucifixion or some other stage of Christ's life and to imagine with such detail that the supplicant does actually believe she is really there. A number of other unattributed religious poems in the commonplace book loosely follow the meditative tradition, but none achieves the dramatic, visual detail of this poem. In fact, the poem gets so caught up in Christ's final days and hours that the narrative overwhelms most of the remaining meditative exercise. Her promise that

> ... frome this Day
> These constant uows religiously I'le pay
> Once euery day to fix a sorrowed Looke
> vpon the place, and say o there I strooke: (4.167–70)

conforms to the Ignatian injunction that one should each day fixate upon one aspect of Christ's passion, but the dramatic intensity Fowler creates prohibits her from progressing further in her meditation. As in her letters, Fowler in this passage makes a very serious pun on her own first name when she writes about these "constant uows." This reading does not make the poem less serious; far from it. As with Donne's puns on his name in "A Hymne to God the Father," Fowler's dramatic sense and the punning inclusion of her personally at the scene bring her and her audience closer to the pain and passion of the Crucifixion.

In addition, after describing herself as an "Actor in this bloody play," the narrator wounds Christ "neere those sacred Eyes" (4.166). Except for one reference to Christ's being blindfolded and struck before being crucified (Luke 22:64), the New Testament makes no mention of wounds to Christ's eyes. Fowler, then, must be referring to the crown of thorns, which wounded his head near his eyes. In her second, explicit, reference to the crown of thorns in the following lines, she comes back to this idea of his head wounds:

> Now I behold, and see my selfe most Cleere
> Agent in all that happened to him heere
> My costly clothinge made him naked goe
> My easy Lodginge forst his scourginge soe
> My curious Diett Hungar to him brought
> My foolish Ioyes presented him sad thoughts
> My pleasurs in vaine glory breed his scorns
> My often curlinge weau'd his crown of Thorns: (4.179–86)

Her confession now that "My often curlinge weau'd his crown of Thorns" represents where, many lines earlier, she struck him and refers to the artificial curling of hair, common for seventeenth-century women.[25] This, along with the general tenor of the passage, identifies the writer of the poem as female, and combined with the sense of drama and personal involvement, strongly suggests Fowler herself as the poet.

Poem 7/8, "O lord direct my hart," appears at first to be two poems: lines 1–21 are in Walter Aston's hand; Fowler's hand begins at line 22 and continues to the end. The poem, in fact, seems primarily Constance Fowler's creation, exhibiting above all, Fowler's characteristic sense of drama:

> Come now wee'le here the judgment; nothinge proud
> pilate was mou'd
> To pitty; yet the vulgar uoyce preuayl'd
> A rogue let free, Iesus to the crosse nayl'd
> I: heare them crye
> giue us this Iesus, weele him crucifye:
> Now see him stript; now crown'd with thornes, while they,
> Mock't him, smoate him, jeard him, soe led our christ away.
> (73–80)

Like Poem 4, "O lord direct my hart" concentrates on the physical presence of the speaker at the crucifixion, placing her at the scene in the Catholic meditative tradition:

> I trauell'd up the mount; where Iesus wept
> All others slept,
> His weepinge not as ours, t'was a huge flood,
> And all his pord's were eyes, where gusht out blood.
>
> lord can I write
> And shed no teare, uiewing this gastly sight?
> And can my soule be light, and thine heauye
> Euen unto death, and all cause I might not dye. (25–32)

Constance has ended the poem with the initials M. W. S., presumably indicating Mr. William Stafford, the second husband of Lady Dorothy Shirley, Fowler's good friend. Significantly, this is the first poem in her book to be associated with any specific person and the only poem for which attribu-

---

[25] Gertrude, it should be noted, had naturally curly hair; see Poem 61, Fanshawe's "Celia hath for a brothers absence sworne."

tion to Stafford is even a possibility: no other poem bears his initials in the normal place of attribution. The only other poem directly associated with William Stafford is Randolph's "The Constant Louers" (65), a pastoral rendering of the familial opposition on both sides when the Protestant Stafford married the Catholic Dorothy Shirley. That Stafford himself would have composed a poem as Roman Catholic in its sentiment as Poem 7/8 seems unlikely. Far more likely is that Fowler composed the poem herself and, as a novice compiler, used the initials of her friend's husband, as a tribute to the triumph of their love over religious differences. In this case, the initials—the first appearance of initials in the book—function not so much as an attribution as a dedication. The initials appear after a series of final flourishing loops, unlike the other initials in the volume, which immediately follow the poems' final words. The physical characteristics of the poem—begun by her father, with pages torn out in the middle—indicate that Fowler was still experimenting with what she wanted her book to be. Her inclusion of Stafford's initials following a poem she wrote would welcome him into the Tixall circle of poets and of Catholics.

The second group of poems—secular pieces by and about Fowler's friends and family members—forms the largest and most interesting section of the manuscript. In this group can be found, among others, a poem celebrating Walter Aston's return from Spain, love poems from Herbert to Katherine, and poems describing chance events in the Aston-Thimelby household. In La Belle's words: "In some ways the anthology becomes like a personal journal—implicitly revealing Fowler's attitudes towards the authors or their subjects" (HAM 545). Without a doubt, given the contents of her book, Fowler was fond of her family and friends and cognizant of her family's most extended relationships. What seems unusual at first glance, then, is that having created this family-oriented miscellany, Fowler does not in her surviving letters once mention her husband, childbirth, child deaths, or living children, although letters among other family members regularly discuss their own familial matters of this sort. She refers to Gertrude, her brother Walter, and her father in her letters to Herbert; and upon Katherine's death, writes the above-cited letter of consolation. Although her failure to mention her husband and children may be interpreted as unhappiness with her married life, in fact, Fowler between 1635 and 1638 was not living with her husband nor had they yet conceived children: Fowler wrote in her letters about what she knew—life at Tixall and the family and visitors there.

Besides the sixteen religious poems, thirty-six poems in HM904 are certainly or almost certainly by or about family members and friends (two are

only loosely linked); three others, in addition to the two religious poems discussed above, may have been composed by Fowler; and ten (to be discussed
as the third category) are seemingly not connected in any obvious way with
Fowler.

Typically, several of the familial poems in Fowler's book mourn a death.
Curiously, none of these is an elegy on a close relative. *Tixall Poetry* provides
several examples of elegies on Fowler's nieces, nephews, and sister-in-
law from which she could have chosen. However, even though she made
changes in her book as late as 1656, it is not certain that she added any
actual poems after the Civil War, or, for that matter, after 1638. Thus, that
Fowler copied no elegies on her immediate family in HM904 may simply
mean that no such deaths occurred during the years that she actively kept
her book.

Two elegies do celebrate the deaths of two distant relatives. The first, "An
Elegy on the death of The Lady Frances Draicott" (18), was probably writ-
ten by William Pershall, about Fowler's cousin by marriage. Lady Frances
Draycott (or Drascot or Draycote) had several close connections with the
Aston family. She was the daughter of Richard Weston by his second wife
Frances Waldegrove. Lady Frances Draycott's half-sister Mary, Richard
Weston's daughter by his first wife, married the second Walter Aston, Fow-
ler's brother. Frances's husband Philip Draycott and Constance's husband
Walter Fowler also had the same grandfather, Walter Fowler of the Grange
(d. 1622), and like the Fowlers, the Draycotts were prominent Staffordshire
Catholics (Foley, *English Province*, 5:429–31). When Lady Draycott died is
uncertain.

Fowler also copied Ben Jonson's "An Elegie on the Lady Iane Paulet
marchionesse of winchester" (1607–31) (42). As Jane Savage, she married,
in 1622, John Paulet, the fifth marquis of Winchester. The marriage of her
sister, Lady Elizabeth Savage, to Sir John Thimelby of Irnham made Jane
the sister-in-law of Katherine Thimelby Aston. Probably neither Constance
nor Katherine was old enough to remember Lady Jane, but Fowler's loyalty
to and love of her friend were such that this poem became a part of her
family volume.[26] That Jonson wrote this poem about Lady Jane was probably the reason Fowler included Poem 58, an anonymous elegy on Jonson's
death, and Poem 24. Initialed B I, this poem, titled elsewhere "My Mid-

---

[26] Fowler might well have copied this poem from a manuscript rather than a printed
version, given the interesting textual variations (see Appendix).

night Meditation," was written by Henry King.[27] (The same kind of mistaken attribution undoubtedly caused Fowler to include a poem dubiously attributed to Suckling—Poem 46—which she clearly believed was written by "M. H. T.," her brother-in-law Mr. Henry Thimelby.)

A third elegy of a sort (38) is rather unusual and is the only overtly political poem in Fowler's book. It is one of the few poems written on the death of George Villiers, Duke of Buckingham, that mourns his death and praises his actions on behalf of his country, and it is the only one of its kind that I have found that is not apologetic in tone.

The poem is followed by the initials "Mr. A. T.," and La Belle suggests Aurelian Townshend as the poet (HAM 553), but Cedric Brown does not include this poem in his edition of Townshend. As La Belle notes, Fowler no doubt included this commendatory poem on George Villiers, Duke of Buckingham, in her book because of the Duke's high regard for her father Walter Aston, as the following letter makes clear:

> My Lord; for all businesses I must refer you to ye dispatches wch Mr Secrie Calvert sends by this bearer (Mr Digbie,) and by those lres, you wyll understand how well his matie is satisfied wth ye proceedings of my lo. of Bristol, and yorselfe, in ye business of ye marryage, wch we hope wyll now grow to a happie conclusion.
>
> For yor own ptcular, I must entreat you to believe that I have the same care as if it concerned myselfe, and that ther needeth no other solicitation wth me then yor own merritt in his maties service; unto whome I have soe lyvely represented the inconveniences you suffer for want of yor paymt, as he hath been pleased to give order and comaundmt unto my lo. treasurer that yor debt be discharged in ye receyt, and you shall find me soe good a solicitor for ye future as I hope you shall have no more need to press yor friends in this kind hereafter, butt yt you may cherefully go on in his maties service. Soe with my best wyshes, I rest
>
> Your faithful friend
and servant,
G. BUCKINGHAM

Whitehall, the 7th
of Ja. 1622. (*TL*, 1:46–47)

---

[27] See Crum, *The Poems of Henry King*, 157–58.

Aston and Buckingham were also distantly related: Walter Aston's sister Elizabeth married Basil Fielding (or Feilding), and one of their children, William, first Earl of Denbigh, figured prominently in the negotiations to arrange a marriage between Prince Charles and the Spanish Infanta; he married Susan Villiers, Buckingham's sister. Thus, Buckingham was the brother of Walter Aston's niece-in-law.[28]

Extant poems commending Buckingham are rare: David Underdown, who has studied printed and manuscript seventeenth-century poems on the Duke written before and after his death, has indicated that the incidence of complimentary poems was slight ("Kings, Courtiers, and Countrymen"); Frederick W. Fairholt, in the introduction to the Percy Society collection of poems on Buckingham, also found few commendatory poems.[29] Buckingham's Catholic sympathies also would have made him a sympathetic figure in the Aston household. According to Lockyer, the Duke, although "he never abandoned the protestant faith in which he had been brought up" (*Buckingham*, 9), remained tolerant of different religious views (58). In August 1619, Buckingham was negotiating with Katherine Manners's father, the Earl of Rutland, for his Catholic daughter's hand in marriage. At about the same time, Buckingham's mother was on the verge of her own conversion to Catholicism (Lockyer, *Buckingham*, 58–59). If it had not been for James I (who, indeed, involved Buckingham from 1618 on in the marriage negotiations between his son Charles and the Infanta of Spain), Buckingham would not have objected to marrying Katherine; however, James insisted that Katherine convert to the Church of England, and so, at least nominally, she did.

---

[28] Roger Lockyer, Buckingham's most recent biographer, shows the relationship to be much closer: his genealogical table of the Feilding family shows Elizabeth Aston to be Walter's daughter; William Denbigh would then be Walter's grandson and Buckingham the brother of Walter Aston's granddaughter-in-law (*Buckingham*, 72). In fact, Walter and Gertrude Aston had no child named Elizabeth.

[29] Fairholt comments: "The collection of Poems, &c., which have formed the present volume, will sufficiently show how strongly and bitterly popular feeling went against the duke, even amongst educated men, and how slight was the contrary spirit. The few apologetic or defensive rhymes in the following pages, is the result simply of the non-existence of more. . . . His secure dependance on royal favour, and proud contempt for the people, engendered and fostered the deep seated aversion of the large majority of Englishmen, until his foul murder was hailed as a national deliverance; and the condemnatory poems which followed the duke to the grave, could only be exceeded by the laudations which were showered on Felton" (*Poems and Songs*, xxx–xxxi).

I suspect that given the fairly close business and personal relationships that existed between George Villiers and Walter Aston, someone in the Aston family (probably Walter himself) commissioned this poem upon Buckingham's assassination and that the poem (which perhaps *was* written by Townshend) did not circulate outside the family and, for this reason, is not found in other manuscript copies of Townshend's poems.

Poems 5 ("Dote not on that") and 6 ("goe hence a way") have a more tenuous political connection to the Aston family. Although they are not initialed in HM904, La Belle believes them to have been written by Robert Herrick. Poem 5, La Belle notes, appears ascribed to Herrick in a Folger Library manuscript (HAM 554). J. Max Patrick includes 5 as a poem ascribed to but not verified to be by Herrick and does not mention 6 at all (Herrick, *Complete Poetry*, ed. J. Max Patrick, 552). More important, however, is whether Fowler believed the poems to be Herrick's. If she did, perhaps she included the poems in her mainly-family volume because Herrick was chaplain to Buckingham on his expedition to the Isle of Ré in 1627; Walter Aston may have known him.[30] "When by sad fate" (63) was probably included for a similar reason: its poet, Owen Felltham, besides being one of the group of seventeenth-century Catholic-leaning poets, including William Habington, Richard Fanshawe, and Thomas Randolph, associated with the Astons, also wrote "*On the Duke of Buckingham slain by Felton, the 23. Aug. 1628.*", which is another rare compliment to the dead duke.

In fact, Fowler's father was acquainted with a number of contemporary poets. Besides John Donne (discussed above), he was Michael Drayton's patron, and Drayton dedicated several of his works to Aston, including the Epistles of Edward the Black Prince and Alice Countess of Salisbury (1602), the *Barron's Wars* (1603), and *Poemes Lyric and Pastorall* (1606) (Newdigate, *Michael Drayton*, 148–53).[31]

The poet Thomas Randolph (1605–35) was connected with the Astons through the marriage of Fowler's close friend Lady Dorothy Shirley to William Stafford, whom Randolph knew from his association with William's

---

[30] John Donne's second son George accompanied Buckingham on this mission (Lockyer, *Buckingham*, 374).

[31] Newdigate indicates that "There is no evidence that Drayton resumed his intimacy with Aston and his family when the ambassador was recalled ... in 1625" (*Michael Drayton*, 155).

uncle Anthony Stafford of Blatherwycke Northamptonshire (Smith, *Thomas Randolph*, 29).[32]

William, who had succeeded as a child to the family estate at Blather-wycke, had from his first marriage three sons (Smith, *Thomas Randolph*, 30), one of whom Randolph tutored (Aubrey, "*Brief Lives*," 196). When Ran-dolph contracted smallpox in 1634, he lived first with his father and then with his friend William Stafford and his new wife Lady Dorothy Shirley, daughter of the second Earl of Essex and Philip Sidney's widow, Frances Walsingham Sidney. When Stafford and Shirley married, she was the wid-ow of Sir Henry Shirley, second Baronet of Staunton Harold and Ragdale Halls, both in the county of Leicester, who died in 1632 in the "Lappe of his Holy Mother the Catholike Apostolike Roman Church" (Harl. 4928, fol. 110v).

The courtship between Shirley and Stafford had "weathered a period of storm," as Newdigate puts it (Newdigate, "Constant Lovers," 1:204), because the Catholic Shirleys, and probably the Astons also, opposed Lady Doro-thy's marriage to the Protestant Stafford ("The Constant Lovers," 2:216). As Newdigate quite appropriately points out, the initials MWS and LDS at the beginning of Randolph's pastoral "The Constant Louers" (65) indicate that the subject was the courtship of William Stafford and Lady Dorothy Shirley ("The Constant Lovers," 1:204).

G. C. Moore Smith believed that Randolph's poem on the marriage of Richard Love, dated January 1634, was probably his last (*Thomas Randolph*, 30–31); in fact, however, the HM904 poem on the courtship of William and Dorothy, married sometime after January 1634, succeeds it. When Ran-dolph died in 1635, he was buried in the Stafford family graveyard.

"A Pastorall Egloune on the death of Lawra" (66), by William Pershall, mourns the death of Dorothy in 1636 or 1637.

Lady Dorothy herself composed at least two poems (40 and 55) included in her friend's book. In the former, a female lover complains that the man she thought loved her has turned away:

---

[32] When Randolph's *The Jealous Lovers* was published in 1632, it included verses to, among others, Anthony Stafford. Probably in 1634, Randolph, in John Aubrey's words:

> rencountred captain [William] Stafford (an ingeniose gent. and the chief of his family, and out of which the great duke of Bucks brancht) on the roade . . . [sic] He gave him a pension of I thinke C¹ per annum, and he [Randolph] was tutor to his son and heir. ("*Brief Lives*," 196)

> Why did you fayne both sight's and teares to gayne
> My hart frome mee and afteward disdayne
> To thinke upon those oth's you did protest
> As if men soules were to be pauned in Iest. (40.1–4)

Her complaint is answered in Poem 41, "If you would know," in which her former friend protests that when he swore his oaths of love to her, he thought he and she were one; when he saw her laughing with others, however, he realized that they were not united in love. A variation of Poem 41 appears also in BL MS. Eg. 2725, fol. 92v, and its appearance there raises some interesting questions: did Lady Dorothy Shirley write 41 also and the copier of Eg. 2725 change her version? Did this person and Lady Dorothy copy the same poem from different sources? Did Lady Dorothy write her questions in Poem 40 as a prelude to 41? Or did a male member of the Aston-Thimelby-Fowler circle of family and friends write the response, which was then copied into at least one other poetic manuscript miscellany? Indeed, perhaps Lady Dorothy did not write either poem herself, but merely gave her copies of both poems to her friend Constance, who copied them into her own book, assuming that Lady Dorothy had written the female-voiced poem. However, Fowler may have found the poem not inconsistent with what she knew of her friend and her friend's social life.

Two other poems in HM904 provide a statement and response. In "upon the L D saying K T could be sad in her company" (54) and "The L. D. ansure" (55), Lady Dorothy and Katherine Thimelby write to each other in verse about a fairly unremarkable occurrence. Both poems are in Constance Fowler's hand and copied before 1638 when Katherine married. Katherine was visiting Lady Dorothy at her home, either at Staunton Harold Hall or Ragdale (Newdigate, "The Constant Lovers," 2:216), both close to Tixall. Lady Dorothy remarked upon Katherine's apparent moodiness, and Katherine responded with a gracefully complimentary verse to her friend:

> why I am sad oh worde of most hiegh powre
> To torne me misserable with in the howre
> For I am griued that my exteriour show
> shuld contradick the joy I haue From you. (54.11–14)

Lady Dorothy apologizes, graciously complimenting Katherine and belittling herself:

> I feare'd you sad because that smileing grace
> which oft hath Ioye'd me was not in your face

> Ioy me it did, because it made me see
> you please'd to tollerate this place and mee. (55.7–10)

These represent coterie poetry in its most intimate and most casual form.

Besides the two poems by William Pershall already mentioned, three others bear his initials. One of these, Poem 45 ("on Lovers Teares"), is a slight poem elaborating on Petrarchan love paradoxes. Poem 23, "A congratalation For the happy Retorne of ᵀL: A: From spaine," reflects much more the familial nature of Fowler's book. In it, Sir William Pershall welcomes his (or his prospective) father-in-law, Walter Lord Aston, home in 1638 from his second stay in Spain. The poem reflects what was important to the Aston household—Walter's literary skill—rather than what might be expected in a poem to either an important diplomat or a father-in-law: Pershall compares his own verses to the songs of birds: full of a desire to be beautiful but lacking in art and skill. Pershall implores Aston, "who weare[s] Apolloes lawrell in our hemisphære" (19–20), to condescend to accept the neophyte Pershall's oration to him.

In fact, Aston did write poems himself. Mostly, according to Clifford, they were translations, now lost (*TP*, xix) but much admired in their day. In a 1636 letter to Herbert, Fowler writes:

> Sence I received this letter from you, which I have now writ you of,
> I have receaved another from you, some five dayes agoe, which you
> writ to my sister, and mee together; and in it sent us most admirable
> verses of my lord's translateing, which are justly admired by all here.
> (*TL*, 1:89)

"A stranslation" (62) in HM904 compares, with some poetic skill, the speaker's lover to a mountain whose surface changes with the seasons but remains essentially a mountain. The closing initials indicate that it was written or, more likely, translated by Lord Walter Aston; it, a poem in *Lachrimae lachrimarum*,[33] and Poem 1 are as yet the only extant poems by the man Clifford calls "the head of the authors, and collectors" of the poetry produced at Tixall (*TP*, xix).

Finally, William Pershall's poem "The first Alter" (15) begins with a line very similar to William Habington's Elegie 5, one of eight elegies written on

---

[33] Discussed by Kay ("Poems," 198–206).

the death of Habington's good friend George Talbot. Habington initially
compares his friend's words to a nun's vow:

> Chast as the Nuns first vow, as fairely bright
> As when by death her Soule shines in full light
> Freed from th' eclipse of Earth, each word that came
> From thee (deare *Talbot*) did beget a flame
> T' enkindle vertue ... (*Poems*, ed. Allott, 105–6.1–5)

The remainder of the poem is a tribute to Talbot's guidance in worldly
temptations and his adherence to the values of Renaissance male friendship.
Heterosexual love (typically) suffers by comparison:

> .... To every Sirens breath
> We listen and even court the face of death,
> If painted ore by pleasure: Every wave
> Ift hath delight w' embrace though 't prove a grave. (25–28)

"The first Alter" begins

> Chast Flames of sacred virgins purely bright
> Like hallowed Tapers on the Alter; Light
>   My zelous loue: while heere confin'd
>   In this darke closett of my Minde
>   Obscur'd: my early uows I pay
>   And make a thought of her my day:
>   Of her (faire Cælestina) shee
>   whose euery thought's a Deity
>   sprunge from the uertues of her soule. (1–9)

The first two lines of these poems are similar enough (although obviously
not exact) to indicate that Pershall had read Habington's verse and, imitat-
ing the first two lines, turns the poem, with some talent, from a grieving
celebration of chaste male friendship to one of passionate love.

William Pershall, Constance Fowler, Katherine Thimelby, and probably
many other of the Tixall poets knew Habington's poetry. In fact, until Newdigate examined HM904 in the early 1940s, the manuscript was believed to
be William Habington's commonplace book.[34] Besides Pershall's imitation,

---

[34] In his introduction to his edition of Habington, Allott says:

In the Huntington Library, California, there is a manuscript wrongly described as

HM904 contains two poems associated with Habington: Crum, but not Al-lott, attributes to Habington "The Complemement" (35), which, while slight, is among the better seventeenth-century lyrics of this sort; the other, "To the honourable G T" (51), is an authentic Habington poem. This latter poem attempts to console George Talbot for the unfaithfulness of his mistress, disguised under the name Astrodora, by assuring him that there are available to him in the sky "Ten thousand other fires, some bright as she" (13).

Katherine Thimelby, in Poem 52, wittily answers Habington. Her under-standing, she says, is that virtuous love does not depend on the changeable-ness of the lover, but rather once a person truly loves, that love remains no matter how fickle the beloved. She concludes:

> For if I lou'd who now am free
> shuld he retorne no loue to me
> I must loue ther eternally. (41–43)

Her response to Habington is witty, easy, and intimate, indicating a close relationship between Habington (also a Catholic) and the Tixall circle.

A third poem by Katherine Thimelby (21) is a complaint to dreams, which can make sad sleepers happy until they awake to reality. The persona concludes that she would rather always be awake or always asleep, and thus not suffer from the extremes of joy and sadness. A skillful poem, it hints at a poetic ability that manifests itself more when Katherine deals with a less conventional topic than dreams.

Katherine's husband, Herbert Aston, was, outside the "professionals," the most prolific poet in the Aston-Thimelby-Fowler circle. He is also the poet whose poems Fowler copied into her book most frequently: eight poems, compared to five of William Pershall's. Jenijoy La Belle in "A True Love's Knot" explicates five of these poems: "The perfect Louer" (13), "whilest I here absente" (14), "whilest here eclipsed" (34), "I striue to loue" (36), and "A true loues knott" (60). By juxtaposing the wittiness and the puns in Fowler's

---

a commonplace book of William Habington. . . . It contains one poem certainly by Habington and three other poems of some interest: two addresses to Castara and a reply to the authentic Habington by a lady, Mrs. K. T. . . . Mr. Norman Ault printed one of the addresses to Castara in *A Treasury of Unfamiliar Lyrics* (1938) and commented in a note, 'The appearance of Castara in a few of the poems sug-gests that they at least are correctly ascribed.' This is to assume too much. The genuine Habington poem, '*To the Honourable*, G. T. . . . ,' is signed W. H. while the two addresses to Castara are signed with a cipher of crossed lines. (*Poems*, lxi)

letters to Herbert against the wit of Herbert's poetry about his love for Katherine Thimelby, La Belle illustrates "some interesting facets of seventeenth-century poetic sensibility" ("A True Love's Knot," 22), including metaphysical elements, in Herbert's poetry. "The perfect Louer," La Belle says, is in the "tradition of love definition[s]," adding that the "self-conscious rhetoric and love of intellectual games" evinced in Fowler's letters influence the "artificiality" of Herbert's definition ("A True Love's Knot," 24–25). "whilest I here absente," "whilst here eclipsed," and "I striue to loue," according to La Belle, all center on Petrarchan themes of the lover's faithfulness when absent from his mistress and of the pain and pleasure of love ("A True Love's Knot," 22–24). "A true loues knott," also a definition of love, has as its conceit that love, as a knot, fails if it is tied too tightly or too loosely ("A True Love's Knot," 26). Each of these poems ends with a visual device that Fowler used to designate her brother's poems. As described by La Belle:

> the key to its [the cipher's] meaning was not to be found in the major outlines, but in the interstices between the intersections, where Constance has intricately woven together the initials H. A. of her brother's name and the word gOD, written twice to form a cross of five letters. The lower-case 'g' and upper-case 'D' are so constructed that they can be read interchangeably depending upon which way the cipher is turned, and thus the word gOD can be found four times in this cipher of five letters. ("A True Love's Knot," 19)

A sixth poem, "To his Mrs on her outward Beauty" (25), explores the poet's love for his "Seraphina." The last page of the poem is torn out; thus the poem is incomplete and has no identifying device or initials. However, Seraphina was Herbert's poetic name for Katherine, and so the poem is undoubtedly his.[35] The controlling simile is of the poet as a humble priest, who, doubting his own piety and overzealously performing his duties, appears to the gods more devout than the artful but less devout priest who performs the sacrifice flawlessly. Herbert himself doubts his own writing skill when he calls on his Seraphina:

> Each word I write, sometimes I doe blott out
> what I before did Interline, and then

---

[35] Fowler writes her brother: "For my part, I must confesse, I am taken with nothinge but the praysess you give your *Seraphina*" (*TL*, 1:97). See also La Belle (HAM, 558).

what I new blotted out strate like agen,
sometimes I thinke this uerse it doth not flow,
This word too common, this expression low
Feare which with true deuotion you'le find
Always united so orerules my mind. (25.28–34)

He asks that his "offering" to her be accepted as his devotion to her war-
rants, and the fragment ends with an insistence that unlike other lovers'
mistresses, "Instead of cupids in your heauenly eyes, / A legion of Angells
houering flyes" (76–77).

The other two poems by Herbert that Fowler copies are written to family
members. An epideictic piece addressed to their sister-in-law Mary Weston
Aston is rather conventional:

How blest is then your family in you
How happy are those eyes that daily view
Those two life giuing lights, and heare your voyce
By which man knowes how Angells doe reioyce. (50.93–96)

The Westons, "your family," have daily seen her "life giuing" eyes and heard
her angelic voice; now, with her marriage to Herbert's brother Walter, the
Aston-Thimelby-Fowler family can have the same pleasure. If she does not
write poetry, as most of the others in her family do, her beauty and her soul
connect her with Daniel's Delia, Greville's Caelica, Drayton's ideal woman,
and most especially Sidney's Stella, whose star prefigures Mary's sun (50.33–
54).

Herbert wrote another poem (53) to his sister Gertrude Aston Thimelby,
who, according to Clifford, "appears to have employed herself occasionally
in writing verses, not with a view of being thought a poetess, but merely
from a strong desire to pour forth her feelings on such subjects as excited
her sensibility" (TP, xxiv). Herbert does not have such a partial view of his
sister's poetry:

... though I know
loue is a tribute; which all men doe owe
To Beauty, to your uertue then far more;
This they affect, the other they adore;
....
Yet nether Beauty, uertue; nor the name
of brother; doth so much my mind inflame
To honour you; as doth that witt, and skill

By which you guide your high poetique quills
I loue you for the rest, this I admire;
in nothinge more then this doe I desire
To imitate you in; by this you tye
Etternall luster to our familye:
How short's Ioue borne minerua of your will,
How short are all of us in honoring it;
How blest were one to dye if on his herse,
As others dropp a teare, you sticke a uerse:
For nothinge you can write, But will suruiue
when the world's ashes, it will be aliue. (87–90, 95–108)

The poem is, in fact, a pastiche of a number of Donne poems,[36] including, for example, an allusion to Donne's "Valediction: forbidding mourning" (53.60–62) and "Elegie: Death" ("Language thou art too narrow") (53.48–50). These and a reference to Donne's strong-lined "Anatomy" and "Progress" (53.5–6) enhance Gertrude's status as a poet, as well as reinforce the importance of the poetic endeavors of their circle of family and friends.

One of those friends, the poet Richard Fanshawe, was also a family member and professional acquaintance of Walter Aston. He visited the Astons at least once at Colton, an Aston family property about six miles from Tixall, probably in autumn 1636 (*Shorter Poems and Translations*, ed. Bawcutt, 104). According to Lady Ann Fanshawe, her husband "was about the year 163[5] made Secrettary of the Ambassy when my Lord aston went ambassador" (*Memoirs*, ed. Loftis, 113). In addition, Lord Aston's wife, Gertrude Sadlier Aston, had years earlier stood as godmother to Ann Harrison, the future Ann Fanshawe (*Memoirs*, ed. Loftis, 108), and, in fact, Richard Fanshawe and Lord Aston were related. Richard Fanshawe's sister Sussanah married the son of Sir Thomas Lucy, Knight of Charlecote, Warwick. This son's sister Ann was the wife of Sir Edward Aston and mother of Walter Aston, first Baron of Forfor. Thus, Walter Aston was Richard Fanshawe's nephew-in-law.

Constance copied three of Fanshawe's poems into her commonplace book. "The nightingall" (64), the third in order of appearance in Fowler's book (and probably the last of the three that she copied), is a somewhat loose translation of Luis de Góngora's sonnet "Con differencia tal, con

---

[36] I am grateful to Dennis Kay for pointing out the prevalence of Donne allusions in this poem, especially those to Donne's "Language thou art too narrow."

gracia tanta" (*Obras poéticas*, 1:55). The subject of both sonnets is Philomela's rape by her brother-in-law Tereus and her subsequent transformation
into a nightingale. While it is an interesting and a lovely poem, Fowler
probably included it because of Fanshawe's first two poems, which were
written for and about Fowler and Gertrude. Fowler is so pleased with these
two poems that she writes a charming letter to Herbert about them:

> Dear Brother,
> That you may see how Mr Fanshaw has spent his time here, I have
> sent you these verses, which are of his making, sence his coming
> hither, and he presented them to my sister and mee. The first were
> made upon this occasion: Wee wer all walking in the owld halle, and
> looking upon Trent, and I was speaking how you used to course your
> boy Dick about that medow, and talking of many things. But the
> next morning he came out with these verses, which I doe not think
> but you will like very well, for methinks they are very prity ones, if
> they had bin made of better subjectes. Wee made him beleeve that
> you should fight with him when he came into Spaine againe, for
> abusing your sisters so, in flattering of them so infinightly as he has
> don in these verses. But now to come to speeke of these other verses
> of his, which are made in particular to my sister Gatt [Gertrude
> Aston Thimelby]. The occasion of making of them was this: We had
> bin one eavening at bowles, and when we caime in, my sister was
> opening her hayre with her fingers, and bid him tell you that she
> would not curle her hayer no otherwaies than it curled itselfe till she
> saw you againe. Uppon which theame he made these other verses,
> which are much admired by all here, and by the Thimelbyes. (*TP*,
> 215)

The first poem to which Fowler refers, "I saw two swans come proudly
downe the streame" (59), is a graceful compliment to Constance and Gertrude, who as proud swans exceed even Venus's beauty. They are allied to
Phaëthon and implored to become salamanders, since so many men are on
fire for love of them. Another manuscript version of this poem is titled "Of
two most beautifull Sisters rowed on the Trent; under the allegorie of
swans" (HM116).

A second Fanshawe poem (61) was, as Fowler indicates, written for Gertrude, who refused to curl her blonde hair (which cannot take on the black
of mourning) until her brother Herbert returned from Spain. The hairs,
however, have other ideas and curl themselves—proving that no matter how

Gertrude neglects her personal appearance she cannot disguise her beauty.

Constance may have included another poem in her book because of its association with Fanshawe. Poem 43, "Tell me (Lucinda)," is probably by Thomas Carey, younger son of the first Earl of Monmouth. There may be a familial reason for including a poem by Carey, since his grandfather, Henry Carey, first Baron Hunsdon, had been involved in the plot to remove Mary Queen of Scots to Tixall; however, a clearer reason for its inclusion is that this poem appeared in Fanshawe's 1648 printed edition of *Il Pastor Fido, The faithful Shepherd, with an addition of divers other poems.* There it is attributed to " 'Mr. T. C. of his Majesties Bed-Chamber,' " and Fanshawe "has rendered it into Latin" (Dighton, ed., *The Poems of Sidney Godolphin*, xxxv–xxxvi).[37] Fowler knows the poem is not one of Fanshawe's but copies it anyway because of its associations with the poet who acted as courier between Herbert and her when her brother was in Spain and with whom she had such a delightful time when he visited.

Three unattributed poems pursue the theme of sisterly closeness captured in the Fanshawe poems: "On Celestinæs goinge a Iorney in wett-weather," "on castaraes sittinge on Primrose banks," and "upon casteries and her sitters goinge A foote in the snow." Although Fanshawe's poem on Gertrude's hair uses Celia as the poetic addressee, it seems very probable that in these three closely grouped poems (16, 17, 19) Castara is Gertrude and Celestina is Constance; indeed, Walter's presentation poem to his daughter Constance (Poem 1) is addressed to Celestina.

"On Celestinæs goinge a Iorney," written by Gertrude for her sister and copied perhaps several years later by Fowler into her book, reveals the same enjoyment with word play and word sounds that attracted Gertrude and Constance to some of Robert Southwell's more ingenious poems at the beginning of the book. For example, lines 13–16 show Gertrude's playfulness as well as her awareness of Fowler's frequent puns on her own name:

---

[37] George Saintsbury prints this poem in volume 2 of *Minor Poets of the Caroline Period* (260–61) from B.L. MS. Harl. 6917, where it is titled "A Dialogue betweene a Lover and his Mistress" and ends with Godolphin's name (Dighton, ed., *The Poems of Sidney Godolphin*, xxxv). Saintsbury says of the poem: "But the Pindaric dialogue . . . has attractions of various kinds, including a certain shy rather than sly humour, not absolutely unrelated to Suckling's robuster and more boisterous variety" (234).

See also La Belle (HAM, 562). *Tixall Poetry* contains a verified Godolphin poem beginning "Unhappy East! not, in that awe / You pay your lords, whose will is law;" (216–18). This poem is printed in Dighton (*The Poems of Sidney Godolphin*, 21) and Saintsbury (*Minor Poets*, 244).

But Th'Relicks of her presence made
Faire weather; and the Tempest stayde:
As pleas'd to shew the Raynbows Fame
In the first letter of her Name: (13–16)

That is, a *C* turned forty-five degrees creates a rainbow.
Later, Gertrude puns again:

Blest Mayde retorn: (or if that Mayde)
To nature bee prophanely sayde
Take any Ayde that bears the sence
Of saints or naturs Excellence
looke back but with one gratious eye,
Els wee, the springe, and all must Dye: (41–46)

The same spelling for *Mayde* and *Ayde* is too close for the poet not to be punning deliberately: if the designation *mayde* is too irreverent for mother earth (here identified with Celestina) then Celestina should, the poet continues, take any *Ayde* or assistance that will bring her back to the poet; that is, she should take any help and she should take any designation ending in *ayde* that emphasizes her saintliness and her excellent qualities.

"On castaraes sitting on Primrose banks" continues the image begun in the previous poem of the young woman competing with or affecting the fragrance of primroses and violets. Castara is like the moon whom the stars fear will be wakened by their flickering lights and thus waken a fitfully sleeping lover. As the moon is to the stars, so is Castara to the flowers: sitting amid the evening primroses, she causes them to pull their fragrance back into their own ranks (with a pun on how these primroses smell compared to Castara). Castara herself is the violet, the most treasured of wildflowers, and even though lily-white shepherdesses might think she is the lowly gillyflower, she is instead a plant meant for princes.

In the third poem in this group, "upon castaries and her sitters goinge A foote in the snow," Castara/Gertrude and her sister Celestina/Constance arise one morning to a foot of snow through which they need to walk—an occasion that Castara's sister turns into a teasing joke: Castara has so often expressed boredom at the same walk every day that the heavens have forced the earth to do penance for its sin in a robe of snow. This presents Castara with two options: Castara's eyes can behave as they did after the last snow—enameling it with their diamonds and making a bright path for her eyes and a slippery one for her feet—or, like the sun, they can melt the snow creating a muddy walk for the two young women. In either case the tedium vanishes.

These three poems are prototypes of the extraordinary instances of female friendships that a number of the poems in Fowler's book illustrate, most notably Fanshawe's poems 59 and 61 and Katherine Thimelby's and Lady Dorothy Shirley's poems to each other (54 and 55). The coterie formed at Tixall among both the women and the men, related through blood, marriage, or love of verse, produced comradeship, intense friendship, and joy in one another's company that led to the verses in Constance Aston Fowler's family book.

The third group of poems in HM904 contains ten poems not associated in any discernible way with Constance Fowler or her circle. Poems 20 ("An Eglogne betweene Melibeus and Amyntas") and 22 ("Loue's Meritt"), one a pastoral addressed to Celestina, the other a forty-nine-line poem about the noble effects love of Celestina has upon the poet, could compete in terms of quality (especially the latter) with any by Felltham or Habington. Celestina's appearance in the poems may indicate that they were addressed specifically to Constance Fowler, and thus found a place in her book. The remaining eight appear in the last half of the manuscript, after fol. 38v.

Three of these, "To weepe were poore" (39), Henry King's "The Exequy" (49, "D K on the Death of his Wife"), and Philip King's "An elegie on his Mrs death" (56),[38] mourn the death of a lover. Despite sections of blank and torn-out pages, there is little reason to believe that Constance Fowler copied her poems in any order but that in which they appear in the manuscript; therefore, tempting as it is, I cannot associate these poems with the death of Katherine Thimelby in 1658. Although Fowler was making changes in her book as late as 1656 (see below, p. lxxxi), it seems unlikely that she would have returned to middle sections of her book in 1658 to copy elegies on others' deaths in honor of her sister-in-law and friend. As previously noted, however, enough deaths occurred in Fowler's circle and in society in general to justify inclusion of elegies commemorating deaths of those she did not know simply because they were good poems.

"Mistres godmorow" (47) and "A louer if beloue'd" (48) are both four-line poems, probably by the same unknown poet; "Eyes gaze no more" (37) and "on the Departure of two Louers in Teares" (44) are mediocre love poems, the former tending toward Petrarchism, the latter initialed "Mr G. B." Poem

---

[38] La Belle attributes the poem to Philip King on the basis of the attributions in B.L. Harl. 6917 and B.L. Add. MS. 25707 (HAM, 567).

57, "O loue whoes powre and might," is a piece of delightful foolishness (found in several extant miscellanies) in Fowler's hand but very different from any other poem in the volume.

It was quite natural for Constance Aston Fowler to include poetry of various kinds and levels of competency in her beloved book. She grew up in an atmosphere of bucolic natural beauty and consistent exposure to poetry, both contemporary and a generation old. The Astons were, and continued after the seventeenth century to be, avid readers; the 1899 sale catalogue of the Tixall Library contains 739 items: more than one-fourth are pre-1660 texts, and one can assume that a large number of additional manuscripts and printed editions that Fowler's father collected or inherited were distributed to family members as they left the estate and that the library was also parceled out during its post-1660 history. The 1899 sale catalogue contains such items as a first edition (1633) of Donne's poems and editions of some of his miscellaneous pieces, the Countess of Pembroke's translation of the Psalms, Sidney's *Arcadia*, Shakespeare's Second Folio, an edition of Spenser's works, and a work by Aphra Behn. These works may have come onto the Tixall estate years after Fowler's death; however, it is, I believe, safe to assume that the Tixall library during Fowler's life was filled with manuscripts and printed editions of her contemporaries' and their predecessors' works.[39]

The Tixall mansion was built near the confluence of the Sow and Trent rivers. Clifford in 1813 described the parish of Tixall as a "Peninsula, formed by the rivers Sow, and Trent; the former of which, though the larger stream, loses its name, as it falls into the Trent, at the village of Great Haywood" (*A Topographical and Historical Description*, 11). The mansion, when it stood, was clearly magnificent. After Clifford visited his ancestral home, he described the ruins in great and loving detail (*A Topographical and Historical Description*, 91–95). All that remains now, however, is the gatehouse, clearly built to impress neighbors with the ambassador's and his ancestors' wealth, and it continues to impress today, with its four turrets around the entryway and the spacious rooms and halls above it.

---

[39] No edition of Southwell is listed in the Sotheby catalogue, but a 1671 signed presentation copy of Izaak Walton's *Lives* of Donne, Wotton, Herbert, and Hooker, and a first edition(1670) of this same work are. The inscription on the presentation copy reads "FFOR MY LORD ASTON, IZ: WA:" below which, as the catalogue notes, is written, "Izake Walton gift to mee June ye 14, 1671, wh. I ffor his memory off mee acknowledge a great kindnesse, Walter." Izaak Walton often fished from the Sow River in Stafford, his home town, close to Tixall.

When Constance looked left through the south windows of the gatehouse or manor, she would have seen Great Haywood, the canal formed by the rivers, and the groves of nearby Shugborough. Looking straight before her, she would see then as now (as Clifford romantically but truthfully describes)

> the whole of the smiling landskape below, ... charmingly contrasted, and terminated both beyound, and above the wood, by the brown heathy distances of Cannock Chace, whose elevated ridges, surmounted by irregular clumps of firs, high-waving in the blast, mingle the wild horizon with the sky. (*A Topographical and Historical Description*, 96–97)

Within this rich, beautiful manor and estate, Fowler was nurtured by her family's love of reading and composing poetry. Fowler's book is her more-or-less private contribution to the coterie poetry of her family and friends, but Clifford's edition of *Tixall Poetry* provides a fuller vision of the family's poetic activities. There one can find many occasional poems on friends but many more on family members and the milestones in their lives: "Mrs Thimelby, on the Death of Her Only Child" (85–86), "To Her Husband, On New-Years-Day, 1651" (86), "Upon a Command to Write on My Father" (92–93), "To My Brother and Sister Aston, On Ther Wedding-Day, Being Absent" (94), "Upon the Lady Persalls Parting with Her Daughter without Teares" (97), "To Sir William and my Lady Persall, Upon the Death of their Little Franke" (99–100), "To Sir William and My Lady Persall, Upon the Death of theire and our Deare Mall" (103–4), "To the Lady Elizabeth Thimelby, On New-Yeares-Day, 1655, Looking Dayly for her Sonne from Travaile" (104–5), "On the Death of My Dear Sister, Mrs Kath. Aston; Known by the Name of 'Good Love.'" (283–84),[40] and "The Poore New Yeare's Gift of Wishes Cobled Together" (292–93).[41] These

---

[40] Clifford cites a folio MS. of the pedigrees of all the families in the Pyrehill Hundred (the parish in which Tixall is located): Herbert Aston named his home "Bellamour" because " 'it was finished by ye benevolence and affection of his friends'" (*TP*, 396). The house either gave its name to its mistress, or Herbert gave his mistress's name to the house.

[41] The last lines of this poem have a column of initials along the right margin. Clifford says:

> These lines, dictated by affection, and good sense, appear to have been written by, or in the name of, several individuals of the Aston family, probably collected at Tixall, or Bellamore, and were addressed perhaps to the Thimelbyes of Irnham. But I am puzzled to make out some of the Christian names. They may, however, be

are only some of such poems that illustrate that this particular circle wrote
poems at any excuse, for any occasion. In Fowler's family, poetry was the
preferred means of communication. Therefore, it should not be surprising
that among the poems Clifford found in his family's chest was one addressed to Constance, one that she chose not to include in her book:
To Mrs Constance Aston[42]

> As in the summer a soft falling shower
> Tempereth Sol's beams, and cooles the parched earth,
> Refresheth every field, to every flower
> More sweetness yields, and gives to new ones birth;
>
> So in this cloud of griefe your beauty weares,
> Your eyes but warme whom they were wont to burne,
> Your lovely face thus gently dew'd with teares,
> For every drop doth a fresh charme returne.
>
> And as this sorrow doth your beauty raise,
> By it of future joyes yourselfe assure;
> It is their dawne; those are the fairest days,
> Whose morning light mists for a while obscure.

TEXTUAL

The Huntington Library's HM904 contains 200 leaves (or 400 pages), of
which 140 pages are blank. The quarto is 7 3/4" long, 5 3/4" wide, and 1
1/2" thick, including the covers. The leaves were bound and sold as a blank-

---

read, John, Constantia, Katherine, Gertrude, R—? Walter, Frances, and Mary, a
daughter of the second Lord Aston.
  I am surprised that H. for Herbert, is not among them; but as the A. is quite in
his hand, I suspect he held the pen, on this occasion; and the lines being sent perhaps from Bellamore, his signature was therefore considered unnecessary. (*TP*, 394)
  [42] Clifford says of this poem:

I found these beautiful lines, on a scrap of paper, which belonged to a letter, part
of the direction on the back of it, being still legible as follows: "These for Mrs
Constance Aston, at the Lady Marchiones of Clanricard's, dowager, Red Lion
Square—." This must have been written at least as early as 1634, for about that
time, or sooner, Constance Aston changed her name, and became Mrs Fowler.
(*TP*, 394)

paged book, to be used as a diary or a commonplace book. It is in its original speckled calf binding, from England in the first quarter of the seventeenth century, with sixteenth-century vellum under the end-cover pages. The front and back covers have identical gold and blind tooling—a 7 x 5 1/4" double-lined rectangle enclosing a 5 3/8 x 3 3/8" double-lined rectangle. Between each set of blind-tooled lines shaping the rectangles is a line of gold dots. The smaller rectangle, decorated at each outside corner with a petal-and-leaf flower, encloses a gilt crest, an English imitation from a French model. The long outer edges of the front and back covers have two small holes each, about 1 3/4" from the top and bottom edges and 1/2" from the outer side edge. These holes plus the paper tears on the inside cover pages indicate that the volume was at some point tied with ribbon. The six-hole spine binding is decorated with nine sets of double-dotted lines in gold at right angles to the rectangle on the front and back covers. The gilt-edged pages are worn. The binding indicates that the volume was of higher than ordinary seventeenth-century quality, as one would expect the family of an ambassador to purchase. Watermarks are posts and pillars, resembling four others from the mid-1630s but identical to none (Heawood). In the lower right-hand corner of the inside back cover, in Fowler's hand, is written "C T," indicating either "Catherine Thimelby," whose poems in HM904 are consistently marked "K T," or, more probably, "Constance Fowler," her "T" differing from her "F" only in the absence of a cross-bar. The ends of poems are usually indicated with drawn, abstract borders, often elaborate, in Constant Fowler's hand. Below is an example of one of her more elaborate ones (fol. 15v). Others include elaborate diamonds formed by connected small circles with dots within each diamond (fol. 26v), diagonal dotted lines alternating with rows of dots within circles (fol. 27v), and the pattern on page lix (fol. 28v). Fowler follows thirty-four poems with borders. Three additional borders are intertwined around the poet's initials. Of the thirty-four borders, she repeats one pattern six additional times; two patterns are each used one additional time.

//o\\o//o\\o

Constance concludes several poems by Herbert Aston with the cipher previously described. Those poems not in Fowler's hand bear a tag word at the end of the page. About a dozen pages in the volume have been torn out.

In 1656, Constance Fowler amended her book for, as far as is evident, the last time. As La Belle notes, Fowler returned to her book to scratch through at the end of five poems the initials of her brother-in-law William Pershall, who disgraced himself financially and in 1656 brought a land suit against Fowler's brother, the second Lord Aston (HAM 551).

It is unlikely that after Constance Fowler's death in 1664 her book was returned to Tixall. Neither the Sotheby, Wilkinson, and Hodge sale catalogue of the Tixall library (London, 1899) nor the Evans and Evans catalogue (Bank House, Stafford, 1913) lists any manuscript volumes resembling HM904.

The book appears next in 1925, in the sale catalogue (as Item 472) of William H. Robinson, an English bookseller, from whom the Huntington Library purchased it. No earlier provenance is given in the catalogue or in the Huntington's records. Mr. William Cornish, the current owner of W. Robinson, Ltd., in Newcastle, indicated that the firm had turned over its records of early holdings to Pickering and Chatto Antiquarian Booksellers, in Pall Mall. Pickering and Chatto has a multitude of records and sale catalogues of items from the sixteenth and seventeenth centuries, and notice of the sale of what would become HM904 is probably among these. Unfortunately, the records are unavailable while the bookseller negotiates with the Victoria and Albert Museum to catalogue them.

Most likely, the Fowler manuscript was left at St. Thomas Hall, the residence of Constance's husband and his family until 1733 when, after several disputes over the will left by William Fowler, the estate was judged to be the property of William Fowler's two sisters. William, a grandson of Constance and Walter, bequeathed the estate to his nephew, who was married to Katherine Cassey, granddaughter of Constance and Walter. Lord Fauconberg, husband of Katherine Cassey, was forced to relinquish most of the estate. He was, however, able to keep the manor house, which he sold to the Duchess of Marlborough, and after her death, the Spencer family put it up for lease. In January, 1914, when the Fowler estate was sold by public auction for tithe rent charges,[43] Fowler's book was probably part of one of the lots sold to William Robinson, the Newcastle bookseller, who eleven years later sold it to the Huntington Library.

Constance Fowler's book, however, apparently found itself in other hands some time prior to this 1914 sale. Not unexpectedly, some of the religious poems in HM904 (Southwell's, for example) are also found in other contemporary and older manuscripts.[44] Poems 9, 10, and 29 from HM904 are also in A, compiled in 1616 by an "ardent Catholic" (*Old English Ballads*, ed. Rollins xxviii–xxix), with the expected number of textual variations.

More interestingly, these three plus eight other poems (11, 12, 27, 28, 30, 31, 32 [twice], 33) are found in Bodl. MS. Eng. poet. b. 5 (B), which F. M. McKay describes as a recusant manuscript probably compiled by Thomas Fairfax, a Warwickshire yeoman, who, in 1656, refused the Oath of Abjuration renouncing Catholicism ("A Seventeenth-Century Collection," 189). Indeed, in the manuscript, the following passage appears:

> Anno dom
> 1654 August the 18th, betweene nine and tenne of the clock att night was John Fairfax the sonne of Thomas & Isbell Fairfax borne, & the 20th day of the same moneth was the sayd John Baptized & ye 26 day of ye same moneth, he changed this life. (B, fol. 87)

Thirty-six pages earlier is written "finis, thus ends y[e]. /. of Anna Alcoxs Songes sent frõ Alveston[45] at Christmas last 1651 written by herselfe" (fol. 51). McKay believes "the six-year-old Anna" sent Fairfax the poems (191). Although a precocious child could conceivably have copied and sent these

---

[43] The information for the above paragraph appears in an article, dated 17 January 1914, which was clipped from a Stafford newspaper and placed in a book on Staffordshire history (Cherry, *Historical Studies Relating Chiefly to Staffordshire*, 1908) at the British Library. The article is titled "Tithe Rent Charge Sale at Stafford. A Romance of St. Thomas's Priory Recalled." The information also appears in *A Topographical and Historical Description of the Parish of Tixall* (Clifford, 37–40).

[44] F. M. McKay notes the remarkable textual similarities between Eng. poet. b. 5 and the contemporary manuscripts (as opposed to the printed editions) of Southwell's poetry. He adds, "Could more instances such as that provided by Eng. poet. b. 5 be found, one might be able to establish that although by 1650 there had been twenty editions of Southwell's poetry it was still circulating in manuscript" ("A Seventeenth-Century Collection," 187). HM904 is an important such instance.

[45] Alveston is in Warwickshire, about four miles north of Stratford-upon-Avon.

poems, it seems unlikely. What McKay did not know was that the twelve poems (including the duplicate) before B fol. 52 that appear also in HM904 are written in the same hand as the second hand (Gertrude's) in Fowler's book. In addition, there is every reason to believe that these twelve poems were copied from HM904. The three Southwell poems (11, 26, 27) that appear in both manuscripts are very close, not only in phrasing but in punctuation and orthography as well. For example, the text of Poem 11, "The Prodigall childs soule wracke," in HM904 differs from A more than twice as many times as it does from B (sixteen obvious differences to seven). Significantly, B is described by McDonald and Brown, Southwell's editors, as the only commonplace book they examined "to draw directly upon manuscript sources" (*Poems*, li). Therefore, when Gertrude copied the Southwell poems into her sister's book, she must have been working from one or more of the five manuscript copies made from Southwell's own collection of his short lyrics (*Poems*, ed. McDonald and Brown, xxxv–xxxvi). Three of the Southwell poems were then copied along with others into B.

The textual differences between all twelve duplicate poems in these two manuscripts are insignificant (see Appendix), and, in fact, in two instances the copier of B copies mistakes from HM904. For example, in poem 28 from HM904, line 26 is written "In Egypt seauen yeares I we stayd"; in B, the line is written exactly as it appears in HM904; the phrase "I we" was then crossed out and replaced with "we." In the same poem, the B hand copies exactly the variant and rare spelling of "eisell," or vinegar (l. 47), as "Isall." These along with the remarkable similarities in spelling and punctuation lead to the conclusion that Gertrude either spent some time in Warwickshire or that Alcoxs had access to HM904, possibly when she was visiting the Fowler family at St. Thomas Priory. I have, unfortunately, been unable to find further information on Anna Alcoxs. A John Alcock (1651–1704), who took the alias Gage (probably his mother's maiden name) was a student at St. Omer's and had two brothers and two sisters (Foley, *English Province*, 5:949n), one of whom might have been Anna. The third Walter Aston married Catherine Gage, and so there may be some familial connection among the Astons, Gages, and Alcocks. Certainly, knowing more about Anna would provide more information on Constance Aston Fowler and the circulation of her book.

In this diplomatic edition of HM904, I have distinguished *i*s and *j*s, although both Constance Aston Fowler and Gertrude Aston Thimelby most often use what looks like a modern *i* for lower-case *i* and *j*. Occasionally, Fowler uses a modern *j*, extending the tail below the line and looping it upward. In both hands, the upper-case *J* is indistinguishable from upper-case *I*. Gertrude Thimelby only rarely uses what looks like a modern *v*; I have therefore transcribed all her letters resembling a modern *u* as *u*, even when conventional spelling calls for a *v*. Constance Fowler uses a letter resembling a modern *v* more often than her sister does, but she most often renders her *v* as a modern *u*. I have used modern typographical practice to reproduce these letters in Fowler's hand.

Fowler's upper- and lower-case *l*s are often difficult to distinguish; she seems, in fact, to have been quite unconcerned about any consistency in forming the letter. Although Fowler appears to intend an *l* with an open upper loop and a base stroke that dips noticeably below the written line to be upper case in such words as *Lawra* (poem 65) and *Lucinda* (poem 43) and often in the initials for *Lord* and *Lady* (poems 23 and 65, for example), she is not consistent in this practice. While an intention to capitalize these *l*s seems approriate to modern readers, Fowler was apparently more interested in the flourish of the letter than in the appropriateness of using an upper or lower case. Thus, for example, in "Tell me (Lucinda)" Fowler forms almost all the poem's *l*s with a flourish we usually associate with capitals, even those occurring within words. Fowler is particularly apt in all her poems to use an elaborate *l* in -*ly* endings and in double *l* combinations. To complicate the matter further, Fowler's *l*s do not always have the same flourishes, floating indeterminately between what we would consider upper and lower cases. For these reasons, I have adopted modern convention in transcribing Fowler's *l*s.

I have reproduced letters that are crossed over (d͟o͟n͟e͟) when I have been able to recognize them; when I have not, I have used a series of crossed out *x*s (**xxx**), each *x* representing a letter.

I have not attempted to recreate the borders or visual devices Fowler uses at the end of some poems.

Portrait of Walter, First Lord Aston.
From an engraving by H. Robinson.
Courtesy of Jenijoy La Belle.

But vertue soone all clowdy fires had calm'd
And her bright soule with holy Acts imbalm'd
At Last was grown to Angells thoughts. so nigh
Except shee had made Earth Heauen, shee needs must dye

upon castaxies and her sisters goinge
Afoote in the snow

The Heauens knowinge that the tedious way
Did rauish ease from fayre castara; Lay
Their sentence on the Earth, and thinke it meete
It should doe pennance in a snow-white sheete
As it hath done this morninge: for the Last
Enameld at your sights did sparkles cast
Like hardest diamonds and were proud to bee
This is my feare least like faire Phæbus Rays to see
Your eyes might melt the snow, and make wett ways.

An Eglogue betweene
Melibeus and Amyntas:

Melibeus: Tell me Amyntas why you Looke
So sadly on this murmuringe brooke,
As though you had some Distemper tooke:

Hope well; the fates may bee Inclinde
propitious to your troobled minde,
And Cælestina will be kinde.

Amyntas: O Melibeus   True I Loue
Faire Cælestina farr aboue
The thoughts, that common Louers mine:

The Verses

[1]¹

verses presented with
a beautious picture to
celestinae

          image shee

[fol. 6r] Except² earth's saint this beautious
whose glorious eyes Angells reIoyce to se
to you belonges the honore of her sight
for you deserue to be her fauerite
nor ist a derogacion to her life   5
To say you'ar yet³ as she a uirgin wife⁴

---

¹ The hand in this poem matches that of Walter Aston in his commonplace book found at the county record office in Stafford. Walter's daughter Constance was married while she kept her book, and it is probable that Walter presented this book to his youngest daughter as a gift with this poem of praise to her written in his hand. The somewhat convoluted poem may in fact have been composed by Walter himself. (Poem 62, in Constance's hand, is one of his translations.)

The "beautious image" would seem to be a picture of the Virgin Mary.

² Context indicates this should be "accept."

³ Ever, always, or still.

⁴ Constance married Walter Fowler when she was about fourteen and he fifteen; the marriage probably had not yet been consummated.

fayre as the soule of beauty can deuise
to dresse her selfe to tempe a hermits eyes
and yet soe good as if that she did giue
                              saue
uertue enoefe[5] to *tempe* all soules as liue   10
o then admired goodnes since you are
                                        far
soe neare in grace to her and I soe
                                        that she
with follded[6] armes sometimes imploere
may for you and you to her for me[7]

[fol. 6v] Blank

---

[5] Enough.

[6] The initial letter looks more like an *s* than an *f*, but *folded* makes more sense as a gesture characteristic of melancholy.

[7] The syntax of these last four lines is garbled. I believe they should read as follows: Since Celestinae ("admired goodnes") is so near to the Virgin Mary and the poet claims to be so far from Mary in grace, he asks Celestinae to intercede for him with Mary as Mary intercedes for Celestinae with Christ.

Walter Aston, according to most sources, converted to Catholicism during his second embassy to Spain (1635–38). Other members of his household, including Constance whose husband was Catholic, converted before him. This poem, in which Walter seems to indicate that his daughter has preceded him in the Catholic faith, dates the commonplace book between 1635 and 1638.

[2]¹

[fol. 7r] O Iesu, thou my glory Art
          in thee will I reioyce
          And not Good Iesu in my selfe
          nor yet in that mans uoice

          That worldly honour may me giue   5
          to set me up on high
          to rule Among the sonnes of men
          And sit in Dignitie

          These Are but shadowes to compare
          to glory thats with thee   10
          sweete Iesu, for thy gloryes sake
          haue mercy now on mee

          O Iesu meeke, O Iesu sweete
          O Iesu sauiour mine
          most gracious Iesu to my Call   15
          thy gratious eares Incline

          Now I good Iesus yet Doe Call
          thou knowest what I would haue
          Iesu I know thy grace it is
          that bids me mercy craue   20

          O Iesu Deare, whose precious bloud
          was shed on crosse of tree
          sweete Iesu for thy passion sake
          haue mercy now on mee,
                         O Iesu²

[fol. 7v] O Iesu meeke grant that I may   25
          repose my trust In thee

---

¹ In Gertrude Aston Thimelby's hand.
² Only the poems in Gertrude Aston Thimelby's hand are marked with tag words.

for thou sweete Iesu Art the peace
And true tranquillitie.

Thou Iesu Art the uery peace
And quietnesse of mind   30
the onely rest unto the soule
that seeke thy fauour finde

Therefore sweete Iesu Doe uouchsafe
my soule this peace may see
And for thy painfull passion sake   35
haue mercy now on mee,
    Amen,

[3][1]

Off the Blessed name, of Iesus,

[fol. 7v] Iust as the sunn beames, — In midst of day i
Expell the worlds — Eclipsing frō uewe
rayes
soe is renew'd, by Ie — sus glorious ~~name~~
uile Ignorance Dull — uailes while he ye tr^{u}
sunn of swete Iustice — sence to reason swais

Iust as the sunn beames — In the midst of Dai
Expell the worlds — Eclipsing shads frō uewe
soe is renew'd by Ie — sus glorious — rayes
uile Ignorance Dull — uailes while he ye tru
sunn of sweete Iustice — sence to reason swaies

[1] Both versions of this poem are probably in Gertrude Aston Thimelby's hand. The spelling differences between the two versions and the omission of words in the first clearly indicate that the second is a revision of the first.

The poem is an acrostic, the first letters in the left-hand margin, the near right-hand margin, and the far right-hand margin spelling "Jesus." In the first draft, the poet is working with the flexibility of seventeenth-century spelling to get the far right-hand "Jesus" to work out. The center of the poem, the middle of the third line, pivots on "Jesus."

[4]¹

On the Passion of our
Lord and sauiour
Iesus:

[fol. 8r]   When that æternall word, with sacred loue
In nature's robes came clothed from a boue
suited unto our shape, and halfe an Age
Had suffered heere a painfull pilgrimage
Now ready to Imbarke, and bidd farewell   5
To all the world till hee had conquered Hell
Retiringe to the gardeine which hee us'd
Deuoutlly to frequent, and there refus'd
Th'Attendance of his chosen, only three
Hee tooke as witnes of his Agony: 10
where hee th'æternall preist that hell controuls
said vespers for Th'uniuersall states of soules
His zeale was to redeeme the world, the booke
Hee pray'd in was, the flesh of us hee tooke
The rumours of the Iews the Eueninge bell   15
His closett was a solitary cell
The Earth his cushen, and his Taper Light
was the pale Moone that trembled at his sight
This was the Eue of sadnes, and the day
succeedinge, was saluations Holly-day: 20

---

¹ In Constance Fowler's hand and probably composed by her. See Introduction, p. xxxiv.

Although this poem does not follow the meditative *Exercises* of St. Ignatius Loyola, as described by Louis Martz in *The Poetry of Meditation*, it clearly contains some meditative elements, primarily using "the image-forming faculty to provide a concrete and vivid setting for a meditation on invisible things" (Martz, 28). In fact, the majority of the poem consists of the speaker's imagining that she is in the Garden of Gethsemane, at Jesus's trial, and finally at the Crucifixion. According to Martz, "to imagine oneself present in the very spot where the event occurred" is one of the three ways to compose oneself for meditation (*Poetry of Meditation*, 30).

The visualization of Christ's last days leads the poet, as it should (*Poetry of Meditation*, 33), to reflect upon her own sins and trespasses and to recognize God's mercy.

But o where are my sences! what strange sight
my soule beholds; that bright æternall Light
The hope of nations, hee whose glorious name
gilded the penns of prophets to proclaime
saluation to the Earth; at whose aspect   25
Angells doe quake like little children checkt
Behold him kneelinge from his sacred Eyes
Like the red sea oceans of teares Arise
[fol. 8v] And how could lesse suffice; when heere hee ment
To weepe the tears of euery penitent: 30

O strange Affliction: heere behold a loue
Rarely Deuine and true; so farr a boue
our Aery lou's that in Disorders range
At euery heate, and thawe at euery change
whose pale Effects produce a watry flood   35
But his pure flames dide² all his tears in blood
Nor were they only Tricklinge Dropps let fall
From his bright Eyes alone, for ouer-all
His sacred flesh a scarlet Robe appears
As though hee had putt on a coate of tears: 40

Then with a sorrowed sigh, enough to winne
Mercy for more then Hell could know to sinne
Prostrate hee falls sealinge the Earths release
And sweetly Kist the grounde in signe of peace
The sunne made hast to bedd, loath to giue light   45
To the conception of this fatall Night
The clowds Assembled, and the Horisons bounde
Did skreene the light in the æthereall rounde
All was a sable Canopy, and stood
Expectinge of a new destroyinge flood;   50

Heere in the center of all sadnes hee
Laments our state, deplores our misery
The noise and rumors of our cryinge synns

---

² Dyed.

As loud as thunder, in his Eare beginns
To enter, And he knew Th'æternall laws   55
Decreed him to pale Deathes Insatiate Iaws'
His poore Afflicted Mother hee had left
Widow'd of all her comforts, and bereft
[fol. 9r] Of her deere sonne; O see her sadly weepe
prepard with teares his funerall to keepe   60
Hee saw Th'Inraged Iews Like sauage Doggs
plottinge his ruine in their synagougs
The scribes (their own deuourers) stood in strife
To bloott their names out of the booke of life
All these lapt in a labourynth of fears   65
His greiued soule, and caus'd a sea of tears:

Thus comfortlesse, hee riseth vp from prayer
willinge to trye his Deere Disciples care
But they regardles of their masters right
were close a sleepe, as lapt in shades of night   70
greiu'd at the sight hee approachћeth neere and sayth
Arise from sleepe (o peter) whers thy Fayth
A regiment from Hell is up in Arms
Against thy Lord threatninge with lowd Alarm's
A torteringe conquest, o remember how   75
Thou promist mee; nor violate thy vow
But nothinge moou'd, they still supinely lye
As if they Intended not to sleepe but Dye:

Now was the time when Armed troops Arriu'd
To Arrest deere Iesus, and their plotts contriu'd   80
with the Infernall traytor, that a kysse
should bee the Signe: good oft is turnd a misse:
The sawcy Iews like seriants[3] sent from Hell
seinge their prey so neere with Horror swell
And with confused noise lay violent hands   85
On the worlds sauiour, and with Iron bands

---

[3] Sergents.

[fol. 9v] Like a notorious traytor, binde him fast
And to the Earth his sacred body cast

Bold plebeians say! who seald your writts
To Arrest Th Almighty Emperor that sitts   90
On his Imperiall throne, when you know this
your master belzebub his Iaylor is,
Hell and the Th'Inferior o'rbs his prisons are
who must commit him then, who canne, who dare
Restraine that hand, that might haue done but Iust   95
To graspe the Earth, and crumble it to dust:
Away they Hurle him, all his freinds forsake
him in Distresse, for they too late did wake
Their pantinge hearts, perswads them all to flye
Liue with their Lord they wisht but loath to Dye   100
They looke behinde, but hee (Alas) is gone
Lockt in the center of the furious thronge
No hand, no weopen there, but had a part
To wound my sauiour and Increase his smart:

Midd-night it was, when they in triumph bringe   105
To syon's citty Earth and Heauens kinge
Tumultuous throngs affrighted rise to see
As if Arriued were some prodigy
To Annas[4] first in strange Derision borne
Then tost to caiphas with hatefull scorne   110
where legions of Accusers doe Attende
little regardinge oaths to gaine their Ende
No forme obseru'd of conscience nor of laws
[fol. 10r] Nor Aduocate allow'd to plead his cause
The Infernall plaintife on his side did winne   115
False witnesses, and brib'd the Iudge with synne
while Th'Innocent Lambe accus'd, made no replies
But mildly heard them speake, with downe cast eyes
His answeare was in silence; his Defence
was patience; and his guilt was Innocence: 120

---

[4] Father-in-law of the high priest Caiaphas; see John 18:13.

Behold the damn'd proceedings of his foes
Instead of Euidence they giue him blows
That sacred Face which Angells Ioy to see
prophan'd with poisenous spittings, was not free
But euery base, Mechanick was Allow'd   125
To Abuse and presse him in the Hellish crowde:

peter was in the thronge, who sore afraide
Of questions askt him by a silly Maide
Deuoutly vow'd, hee neuer saw the manne
whom they Accus'd: when straight the cock began   130
To rowze his guilty dreams, and to Impart
Not breake of day to him, but breake of heart:
For O when hee beheld that Heauenly looke
Of his deere Lord upon him, how it strooke
Contrition to his soule, remembringe how   135
Hee told this token of his breach of uow:
To pilate next, our Deere redeemers sent
To be condemn'd in his high parliament
[fol. 10v]   They thought defect of proofe would bee supplide
By policy:⁵ but hee not satisfyde   140
Endeauour'd to release him; when the Iews
Threatned to cæsar they would him Accuse
That word affrighted Iustice and deprest
            his
All fauour for priuate Interest:

Behold what heere succeeded, neuer Eye   145
saw such an obiect, hee who cloth'd the skye
with spangled lights, whose tender care prouids
garments to keepe us warme and food besids
Is now Disrob'd: fast to a pillar tide,
And scourg'd as would haue tyrants terrifide   150
Let phebus witnes that so bright appears
If in his trauells many thousand years
About the world, hee euer yeat could tell

---

⁵ That is, by conniving or politics.

A tragedy that this could paralell
To see his flesh plow'd up and where hee stood   155
The ground all paued with his pretious blood
No gall of Asps or vipers could expresse
such cruelty or sauage wickednes:

O say (deere Iesus) was it for my sake
For me vile sinner thou didst undertake   160
such pains, such cruell torments, what am I
That thou for me shouldst suffer misery
[fol. 11r]   But O my soule I feele my conscience say
I was an Actor in this bloody play[6]
gaue thee some wounds, my guilty soule descries   165
Too} where they were, t'was neere those sacred Eyes[7]
O tell me where I hitt, and frome this Day
These constant uows religiously I'le pay
Once euery day to fix a sorrowed looke
vpon the place, and say o there I strooke: 170
His sacred flesh thus all to peices torne
They wound his head with cruell wreaths of Thorne
Framinge a crowne and beatinge it with clubbs
They pierce him to the braine with sharpned stubbs
And in Derision for a scepters grace   175
A waueringe reede in to his hand they place
O Monarks boast not of your glisteringe gemms
When christ Aſk is crownd with Thorny Diadems:

Now I behold, and see my selfe most cleere
Agent in all that happened to him heere   180
My costly clothinge made him naked goe
My easy lodginge forst his scourginge soe
My curious Diett Hungar to him brought
My foolish Ioyes presented him sad thoughts

---

[6] Throughout this poem, Constance Fowler displays a sense of drama that is also characteristic of her letters. Constance might have seen plays by traveling troupes of actors in the market square in Stafford.

[7] Luke 22:64 is the only gospel that mentions Jesus being struck specifically on the face.

My pleasurs in vaine glory breed his scorns   185
My often curlinge⁸ weau'd his crown of Thorns:
[fol. 11v]   Heere ended not their fury, sentence past
vpon him, to mount caluery they hast
Iustice allows to euery commen slaue
A means to bringe him to his Death and graue   190
But they Allow him none the waigty loade
Of his own crosse hee carries all the roade
Forcinge his cruell wounds to bleede anew
And from his face Distills a Holy Dew
Passinge the Dolorous way where euery doore   195
Laments his state thus comfortles and poore
The tender hearted weomen did relent
And for his sake their bitter teares present
These did Inioy when coward mann did faile
courage to follow; Pitty to bewaile: 200
Happy then are your sex for you had grace
To Follow Iesus to his Dyinge place:⁹
where now arriu'd his foes triumphinge waite
with all their Magazine of Engins fraight
To torture him: heere on the tree hee's cast   205
And through his hands and feete is nayled fast
O thinke but of the paine, for custome takes
Away the sence of sorrow, and it makes
Only Impression in ungratefull hearts
To speake the words, but not to Iudge his smarts: 210

Behold our sauiour's now exalted high
Vpon the crosse, and Iust prepard to dye
The feild is fought, and hee uictorious stands
Now ready to dissolue Hells murderinge bands
[fol. 12r]   And purchase us æternall life, for bye   215
His death upon the Crosse, Hee made death dye:

---

⁸ The vanity of artificially curling one's hair was more common to women than to men in the mid-seventeenth century.

⁹ These lines seem to present a female perspective. For a similar treatment, see Aemilia Lanyer's *Salve Deus Rex Judaeorum*.

His Holy heart Inflam'd with sacred loue
Implor'd his Heauenly father)to remooue
His Iudgments from his foes, let's learne by these
Truely to pardon all our Enimies: 220
see how the soldiers gratefully replide[10]
they giue him gaull and scoffs thus to deride
                              loue
His patience meeke and ʌ in death—[11]
                              his
They force a spere in to tender side[12]
woundinge him unto death: Then mildly hee   225
Commends his spiritt to the æternity
Of his deere father; when these words were saide
It brought the news to euery creature made
                                    r
For first the temples ueile in sunder ẃent
                            w
And rocky buildings all to peices ŕent   230
The sunne Amaz'd him-selfe in mourninge kept
Cloath'd in Cymærean[13] darknes sadly slept
A sable garment round the Earth is spred
Like a dark region peopled by the dead:
Confusion raign'd, all order layd Aside,   235
As if the Uniuerse had lost her guide:
Nature beganne to grope, and quakinge felt,
whether shee had not lost the zodiaks Belt:
The Tropicks trembled, and distracted guesse
They now should loose their fixt Antipodes: 240
Death was Inraged, and sends out her spies
To learne the truth, by dead Anotomies

---

[10] Probable place for the following two lines, which are scribbled in the right margin at right angles to the text.

[11] Following the dash are the only totally illegible words in the entire manuscript. The words look to be written over. "They chide" makes metrical and contextual sense, but this is only a guess.

[12] John 19:34.

[13] Cimmerians, mythical people described by Homer, inhabited a region of perpetual darkness and mist.

[fol. 12v]   They walke like ghosts, all who that noise did keepe
             In naturs name that dead menn could not sleepe
             yeat all these strange portents did not Infuse   245
             one Atome of beleife to th'raginge Iews:
             O madnes farr more poisenous then if Hell
             Had lodged in your brains a charmed spell.
             Did not the Heauens speake him to bee right
             And true messias by that heauenly light   250
             That did report his comminge to bee true
             And were three kings slight messengers with you
             Did not the sea and waters closely meete
             And make a marble pauement for his feete
             saw yee not xxx how the Earth when that he Dide   255
             with tremblinge palsies syon terrifide:
             The stupide stones and walls his power speake
             when like sad mourners they in peeces breake
             yeat your dull souls deceiu'd with senceles toyes
             Nothinge beleeue but what (true Faith) destroyes: 260

             But O my Heart! Behold deere Iesus dead
             His soule departs, nature decline's his head:
             His Arme extended on the cruell tree
             yeat seeme to Imbrace the Earth in charity
                                  to
             Thus humbly kneele I that sacred signe,   265
             My will and understandinge I resigne
             vnto the crosse: and to his crowne of Thorns
             And peirced head bequeath all that Adorns
             My useles haire: to both those wounded hands
             And feete I giue all Ioyes the Earth commands   270
             Into his side whence loue and mercy flow'd
             I place all Follies that my youth hath sowd
             And For his loue contrition shall force roome
             within my soule, and make my heart his tombe.

[5]¹

[fol. 13r] Dote not on that which may but cause thy woe
            Curbe thy desires let not afection growe
            Beyound due limitts, though the thinge be such
            as thou mayst loue, yet loue it not too much
            let reason still possesse thy better part   5
            elce with thy loue thou wilt ingage thy hart
            which ought to be preserued pure and free
            onely for him who gaue his first to thee
            loue god alone and doe such riches chuse
            as by no time or fortune thou canst loose   10
            giue him thy hart and with a soule resign'd
            Beare all unequalls with an equall mind.

---

¹ In Fowler's hand. La Belle speculates that the poem may be by Robert Herrick:
"Compare similar use of the polyptoton in the last line ... with last line of Herrick's
'Loading and Unloading' from *Noble Numbers*. ... Further compare meaning of this last
line of MS. poem with Herrick's 'An equall mind is the best sauce for griefe' (from
'Sauce for sorrowes')" (HAM 554).

$$[6]^1$$

[fol. 13r]   goe hence a way and at thy perting know
             T'was not my uoyce but Heauins that bids thee goe[2]
             For uoyce of xxx fame and uoyce of Heauin haue thundred[3]
             we both are lost if both of us not sunderd
             Fould then thine armes and in thy last looke rear   5
             One sigh of loue then coole it with a teare
             since pert we must let's kisse that done retire[4]
             with as much frost as erst we met with fire
             And such white uows as time canot deseuer
             With Fath knit fast and so farwell for euer   10

---

[1] In Fowler's hand. Also found in B.L. MS. Harl. 6917; ascribed to "Ro Herrick" in MS. Folger 1669.2, fol. 270v.

J. Max Patrick (*Complete Poetry*, 552) prints this poem in "A Supplement of Poems Not Included in the 1648 Edition," that is, poems not in *Hesperides* or *Noble Numbers* but attributed to Herrick by seventeenth-century sources: "[L. C.] Martin [1956] prints 25 other poems in his edition because internal evidence or proximity to works known to be Herrick's or attribution to 'R. H.' suggests his authorship. But without stronger evidence, such attributions are little more than guesses. Manuscript collections of seventeenth-century writings contain hundreds of anonymous poems which could, with more or less plausibility, be attributed to Herrick" (*Complete Poetry*, 536). Variations from Patrick are given in the Appendix.

If Constance Fowler believed this and the preceding poems to be Herrick's, she may have copied them because he was chaplain to Buckingham on his expedition to the Isle of Ré in 1627. According to Martin, Herrick wrote poetry between around 1610 and around 1647 (*Poetical Works*, xxxvii–xxxviii).

[2] Followed in Patrick by: "Spring hence thy fate nor think it ill desert / I find in thee that makes me thus to part."

[3] Probably; the letters are very compressed to make them fit on the manuscript page.

[4] Compare Drayton, "Since there's no help, come let us kiss and part."

[7/8]¹

[7/8][1]

[fol. 13v] O Lord direct my hart, direct my soule
                    O Lor'd controle
          my weaker fancy, let thy spirit rayse
          my calloe muse to a hight that so thy prayse
                    poore I may sing   5

          In allelueses[2] grant this heuenly King
          and grant deare sauioure thats first of all
                                        funeral
          I proue cloase morner at this thy gran[3]
                              but I
          my thoughts haue aim'd at something good
                    could not discry   10

---

[1] Beginning at line 22, the handwriting becomes considerably neater. It is at this line also that the poem back-tracks: Judas twice delivers his kiss, at lines 21 and 41. Between fol. 13v and fol. 14, several leaves have been clumsily removed. These facts probably indicate that the poem was drafted hastily; the poem was then revised and rewritten on the pages following, and the draft torn out (except for fol. 13v, the recto of which contains two poems). In doing so, however, Constance removed the verso side of the revised poem and the last recto page of the draft.

The poem is initialed M. W. S. Jenijoy La Belle attributes it on this basis to Mr. William Stafford, husband of Constance Fowler's close friend Lady Dorothy Shirley (HAM 38) and identifies the hand throughout as Constance's. The poem is, nonetheless, in two hands: Fowler's starting at line 22, and another, the same hand as the first poem in the volume, that of Constance's father Walter Aston. It seems that Fowler either revised or recopied the poem after tearing out her father's draft, Fowler herself having composed the lines in her hand. The first twenty-one lines differ in style and substance from the remaining lines. The lines in Fowler's hand have a much keener sense of drama than do the opening lines, a sense of drama that Fowler's letters also exhibit.

The presence of two hands in one poem, with leaves torn out for revision, illustrates the casual intimacy with which Fowler's book was treated in the family and perhaps an evolution in Constance's ideas about it. The forty poems before the first group of blank leaves are in three different hands, Fowler's predominating; after this break, all the poems save the very last are in Fowler's hand. It seems likely that when Fowler first began her book, she allowed others close to her to contribute to the collection. Later, she seems to have made a conscious decision to keep the book to herself. Alternatively, she moved to her husband's estate where her family had less easy access to it.

The last line indicates that this poem was written on Easter day.

[2] *Hallelujahs.*

[3] *Grand.*

my selfe compainion in thy lesse[4] paine
and yet dare I presume to expect the gaine
                t'wer impudence
wants all inunewety[5] wants all sence
to imagin that we can be freed from sin   15
                                    ing
and nere desire to pertake in his sofer
I traueld with those tw that did prepare
                with humble care
                                    Lords
thy last prouision where the Lord of
                c   words
there feete with water wash the soule with   20
                I saw the kess[6]

[seven pages torn out]

[fol. 14r]   Thy blessed actions, each thy act was best.
              I saw the caytiffe take that soppe, wherein
              The Diuell was inclos'd, with all his monstrous sinn.

              I trauell'd up the mount; where Iesus wept   25
                        All others slept,
              His weepinge not as ours, t'was a huge flood,
              And all his pord's[7] were eyes, where gusht out blood.
                        Lord can I write

----

[4] An odd use of "less" to mean "more." According to the OED, the word was "used peculiarly by Shakespeare with words expressing or implying a negative, where the sense requires 'more.'"

[5] "Ingenuity" in the senses of high birth or stature and intellectual capacity. According to the OED, "ingenuity," as it was used in the seventeenth century, combined the meanings of "ingenious" and "ingenuous." Walter Aston seems to have gotten the rhythm and meaning of "ingenuity" but was uncertain about the exact pronunciation of this relatively new seventeenth-century word. The OED dates its first use in these senses to 1598–99.

[6] The OED lists "kesse" as a variant spelling of "kiss."

[7] Pores (OED); i.e., blood gushed as if from every pore. See Luke 22:44: "and his sweat became as drops of blood running down upon the ground."

And shed no teare, uiewing this gastly sight?   30
And can my soule be light, and thine heauye
Euen unto death, and all cause I might not dye.

----

                              a
Here uiew our sauiour, in bloody trance
                    castinge a glance
Oth'⁸ cursed traytor; se him rise, and walke   35
with all-commandinge courage; here him talke
                    mildly; my Friend
why coms't thou thus to me? why thus unkind
why thus as to a theife, with club, and bill⁹
I dayly preach'd ith'temple, neuer did you ill.   40

Fe'w see the the Diuell Iudas, marke his kisse
                    Beware thy blisse
[fol. 14v] Be not soe lost as his; a smoother sinn,
Often makes way for greater to come in;
                    And know each thought   45
If ill, crucyfies him againe, who bought
with pretious blood thy soule. Lord clense my hart
And grant that I may feele of thine a little smart

----

see it more wonder; see th'Allmightys hand
                    which often spand   50
the polds; bound in cords; the feet that of't bestryd
The glorious Heauens, see manacled and ty'd;
                    see how the lambe
Of god most innocent, of him selfe came
To this their Hellish slaughter, see him come   55
That's Iudge of all, to suffer their false Iudges doome.

----

⁸ Presumably, *on the*; *O the*, while possible, makes less syntactical sense.
⁹ A weapon of war consisting of a blade and a wooden handle.

see how the multitude of diuells runn
To see it done
scorninge their Iesus; and which greiues him most
All his desciplas, all his freinds are lost.   60
see'em spit in's face,
see 'em buffet, smite with rods; ther's not one place
I'th'Allmighty's fleshly robe but seem'd all torne
As an offreikninge[10] suite, in a long leaguer[11] worne.
[fol. 15r] Come trauell with him, to the Iudgment Hall   65
wher peeple all
view him as if a monster; see his looke
And reade it, nere was printed better booke:
there are uertues
Humility, patience, in their perfect hues: 70
sweete Iesus giue me grace to follow thee
In this example of thy greatest uictorye

Come now wee'le here the judgment; nothinge proud
pilate was mou'd
To pitty; yet the vulgar ẙ uoyce preuayl'd   75
A rogue let free, Iesus to the crosse nayl'd
I: heare them crye
giue us this Iesus, weele him crucifye:
Now see him stript; now crown'd with thornes, while they,
Mock't him, smoate him, jeard him, soe led our christ away.80

But now me-thinks, I feele my memory
ore-pres't my eye
Fearefull, and dull, back to its caue doth sinke;
How can it lesse, this made the sunn to winke:

---

[10] Presumably, "offreckoning," which the *OED* defines as "A deduction; formerly, in the British army, the name of a special account between the government and the commanding officers of regiments in reference to the clothing, etc. of the men." An offreckoning suit would then be a government-issued, probably cheap uniform. This use of "offreckoning" predates the *OED*'s 1687 citation.
[11] Siege.

                              It might not uiew   85
[fol. 15v]   The sunn of god Eclips'd, by this dire crewe
             Of Iews, Athiests: thy footstoole; lord, did cracke,
             graues opend, nature shrunk, viewing this Heauye wracke.[12]

             Yet though I cannot looke on's crosse; Ile thinke
                              of gall, his drinke   90
             I'le thinke of's blood, that flow'd as if a tyde
             From's head, from's hands, from's feet, from's hart, and side
                              Enough t'haue bin
             A ransome for ten-thousand worlds of sinn.
             O Blessed sauiour, hanging on thy tree   95
             pardon my sinns, nayle 'em to it, me to thee.

             And if this day, which to thy passions memoryc
                              Is dedicated, I
             which am but mud wal'd-earth, doe passe a way
             In thoughts not worthy it; pardon I pray   100
                              And let it be
                thy[13]
             For this bitter death sufferd for me
             And grant Deare sauiour, I neuer may
             Forgett thy mercy, in sufferinge this happy day.

                              M. W. S.

---

[12] The preceding lines (along with lines 49–51) echo Donne:

> It made his footstoole crack, and the Sunne wink.
> Could I behold those hands which span the Poles,
> And turn all spheres at once peirc'd with those holes?
> "Goodfriday, 1613. Riding Westward." (lines 19–23)

[13] "Thy" was added after the line was written to regularize and complete the metrical pattern, the irregularity probably occurring because "sufferd" is spelled to be sounded as two rather than three syllables. "Thy" should precede "bitter."

[9]¹

the soulse meditation
of heauenly thinges

[fol. 16r] Amount my soule from earth Awhile
swoure² up with wings of loue
to see where saints And Angells Dwell
with christ In Blisse Aboue

I silly wretch In earth Alone³   5
Amongst professed foes
the world, the flesh, the diuell And none
but such As seeke my woes

Remember thou A stranger Art
A wandring pilgrime heare   10
A pilgrime till that thou Depart
to saints thy fellowes there⁴

---

¹ In Gertrude Thimelby's hand. This poem also appears in A (pp. 6–12) and B (pp.
18–21). In commenting on A, the B.L. manuscript, Hyder Rollins says of the poem:

> This unique ballad is a remarkable one. No man knows the glory of the New
> Jerusalem save he who actually experiences it, says our ardent Catholic poet; yet
> he manages to give a concrete and detailed account of its unparalleled joys. Into
> these joys, however, only true Catholics can hope to enter: there is no place for
> heretics or for those potentates who use Tyburn and the rack in an attempt to
> root out the true faith. The other ballads in this volume [A] describing Heaven
> are only slightly Catholic in tone, and were, with slight and judicious excisions,
> acceptable to Protestants. The present ballad would mortally have offended. (*Old
> English Ballads*, 152)

Variations in HM904, A, and B of one line or less are given in the Appendix.

² I.e., soar.

³ In B, this stanza and every second stanza after it are indented; in A, this stanza is
omitted.

⁴ In A, this stanza follows:

> An exile poore in earth alone
> Amonge professed foes
> The world the devill the flesh and non
> But such as seeke thy wooes.

O spouse of christ why Dost thou stay
to build thy house upon the sand
the bridgroome comes the minstrills play   15
thy wedinge Is At hand

ffor here A weding thou must haue
I meane a uertuous life
for other garmēt Are not uane
for such A princes wife   20

Therfore renounce all worldly pelfe
A heauenly race to runne
forsake this world And frame thy selfe
to liue As saints haue Done,⁵
                                        A Cittie

[fol. 16v] A Cittie there renowned is   25
of statly statures rare
A princly place Adorn'd with blisse
of building passinge faire

Ierusalem this place is call'd
most sumtuous to be hold   30
the gates with precious pearles Are fram'd
the streets Are pau'd with gold

The walls wᵗh precious stones Are made
And Rubies Doe Abound
the precious pearles that can be nam'd⁶   35
therin Are plenty found

---

⁵ A follows with:

Passe over ayre aizar skye
and thinges that mortall bee
Above the spheare of heaven to flye
if thou those joyes would see

⁶ According to Rollins, "namde" in A is a substitute for "made" (*Old English Ballads*, 154).

Thorowe the streets the floud of life
with siluer streames Doth flow
hard by whose banks there thou shalt find
the tree of life Doth grow[7]   40

This tree Doth Euermore beare fruit
And Euermore Doth springe
there Euermore the Angels sitt
And Euermore Doe singe[8]

This cittie shines with endlesse blisse   45
In glory passinge bright
there god himselfe the lanthorne is
And lampe which giueth light.
                                                    The

[fol. 17r] The bodies there of Euerione
            Are like to Cristall fine   50
            showinge more brighter then the sunn
            when it most Cleerly shines[9]

            There shalt thou see the Cherubins
            In glorious state excell
            the Angells And the saraphins   55
            where soules of saints Doe Dwell

            There noah And all the Iust remaine
            there Doth the prophets stands
            the patriarks old Doe there remaine
            with sᶜepters In their hands   60

---

[7] Upon whose banks the tree of life / in statelie sort doth growe, in A.

[8] In A, this stanza is replaced by:

> Whose pleasant fruite of everie kind
> Delighting mortall eies
> Hard by whose roote there you shall finde
> where heavenlie manna lyes

[9] And showes as bright as doth the sunne / when it most cleare doth shine, in A.

There prophets And Apostles liue[10]
there sacred uirgins stay
there they doe liue, there they doe giue
Attendance Euery way

Our lady there most heauenly sings   65
with sweete melodious uoyce
the saints And all Celestiall thinges
for Ioy of her Reioyce

Good magdalen hath left her mone
Her siths And sobbs Do cease   70
And sith her plaints And teares be gone
she liu^es In endlesse Blisse
                                        Where

[fol. 17v] Where thousands thousands Angels dwell
And soules in glory braue
And Euery one reioyce to see   75
the Ioy his fellowes haue

The precious pearle the marchant sought
with longe And endlesse toyle
Is now to uew[11] the ground he bought
with his most happie soyle   80

Ten thousand tongues cannot expresse
nor Angels skill Indite
the perfect pleasures there Remaine
And Ioyes with their Delights

There do thy faithfull friends Remaine   85
there do thy parents Dwell
And thou in blisse shalt meete Againe

---

[10] In B, *stay* is crossed out, and *live* is written in.
[11] I.e., view.

with them thou loudst[12] soe well

O blissefull Ioy to meete our friends
And louinge kinsfolke there   90
And liue in blisse that neuer ends
with them thou lou'dst soe Deare

There doth thy good progenetors
both wish And waite for thee
And thousands of thy Auncestours   95
which thou didst neuer see
                                        Noe

[fol. 18r]   Noe blisse no pleasure there doth want
             which man Doth wish to haue
             no braue nor fine delight is scant
             Thou canst request or craue   100

             Yf wealth or honour thou Desire
             or Ioyfull D̶a̶y̶e̶s̶ Dayes to see
             there nothinge wants thou canst desire
             for thou A kinge shalt bee

             Thy Clothinge shall be All of blisse   105
             And thou A scepter beare
             of Diadeame that beaten is
             that earthly princes weare

             In Aged yeares yf thou request
             to liue with faithfull friends   110
             with saints And Angels thou shalt dwell
             In blisse that neuer ends

             yf thou Desirest Daintie Chere
             or rich or costly meate

---

[12] I.e., lovedst. In A, the next stanza is omitted.

the bread And drinke of life is there   115
And foode which Angels eate[13]

or yf thou wouldst by good Aduice
the will of god goe Doe
there is the priest And sacrifice
the church And Alter too   120
                                    There

[fol. 18v]   There god himselfe doth here o[r] plaints
And pitties christians case
his louinge friends and holy saints
behold him face to face

There Euery word And godly thought   125
each greefe And great Annoy
And Euery worke in uertue wrought
Rewarded is with Ioy

The widdowes mite hath there reward
cold water wants no meede   130
for god respects And hath regard
to each good worke And Deede[14]

The glorious Ioyes which thou shalt see
were not with siluer bought

---

[13] In A, this and the previous stanza are reversed and followed by:

If learning skill or wit thou would
in booke of life that's there
most plainlie there thou shall behould
the thinges thou knowest not heere

[14] In A, the following is included:

No eye hath seene, nor eare hath hearde
no creatur ever found
nothing on earth may be compard
to joyes that there abound

for gold or pearle or siluer sold   135
Are things which nature wrought

Noe ualue worthy was to buye
these Ioyes thou hast to see
till christ the sonne of god Did Dye
to purchase them for thee   140

O then what Ioyes may these be esteem'd
how sweete how uery good
that with no prise could be redeem'd
but with o^r sweete sauiours blood[15]
                                              Saint

[fol. 19r]   Saint paul wch did these secrets see   145
could not those pleasures name
the glory no man knowes but hee
which Doth enioy the same[16]

Noe eye hath seene no eare hath hard
noe liuinge creture found   150
the perfect pleasures there remaine
And Ioyes that there Abound

There thou shalt rest out of the reach
And wayes of wicked men

---

[15] After this stanza A adds:

> O blisfull joyes nothinge there was
> in heaven or earth below
> But Christ alone to bring to pass
> that men such joyes should know

[16] A replaces the following stanza with:

> No neede is there noe want of wealthe
> no death nor deadlie paine
> where Christ the cause of all our health
> and heavenlie life doth raigne

blaspheamous tongues And filthy speach   155
shall not Annoy thee then

Noe threatninge words to prison uile
shall not torment thy mind
but Angels sweete And saints most mild
shall welcome thee most kind   160

ffor no blaspheamers there remaine
none that in bloud Delight
noe uile Adulterors there do liue
noe lewde nor wicked weight[17]

Nor persecutinge potentate   165
Doth rule or gouerne there
no temperrisinge schismatike
hath office there to beare
                                            There

[fol. 19v]   There tyborne nothing hath to doe
             No rope nor rack is knowne   170
             tormentors All And sathan too
             Are wholy Ouerthrowne[18]

---

[17] In A, this stanza is followed by:

> Noe rude nor raillinge heretikes
>   that new religions make,
> Noe temperisinge scismatickes
>   that Christ and Church for-sake;
> Noe persecutinge potentate
>   doth rule and gouerne there;
> Noe workmaister or pursivant
>   hath office there to beare.

A then omits lines 165–68 in HM904.

[18] In A these lines are followed by:

> There triumph over sinne is wonne
> the Devill and death devided
> the kingdome of the just begunne
> and they in glorie placed

Concupiscence is rooted out
temptations All Doe cease
no motion of the flesh Doth rest   175
In that triumphant place[19]

ffor it was made for purged soules
before the world was made
where they receiue both crownes & stoles
of Ioy that neuer fades   180

Then o my soule, take up the wings
of faith of hope of loue
And sore Aloft to uew the thinges
prepar'd for thee Aboue

O happie time when thou shalt leaue   185
this flesh those Ioyes to see
no hart can thinke or once conceiue
the Ioyes prepard for thee

Almighty god grant my request
And boone which I Doe craue   190
O lord my soule in heauen to rest
And there my Dwellinge haue
                              amen,

---

[19] In A, these lines are followed by:

Nothinge that lastes of wickednesse
nothing defield with sinne
Doth harbour there or hath accesse
that place to enter in

[10]¹

[fol. 20r]   O God of thy great might
              strengthen our frailty soe
              stoutly to stand in feight
              Against our Infernall foe²

              Sathan sustaines the foyle   5
              christ gaines the uictory
              the world may well requoile³
              the flesh is fraile wee see⁴

              Let us march on Amaine
              christs Crosse be oʳ good speede   10
              full resolu'd to sustaine
              what Iesus hath Decreede

              In measure of oʳ faith
              rewards Doth bear Away
              then let us stand upright   15
              In midst of our Aray

              And neuer be Dismayd
              At Any D⁵ Aduersitie

---

¹ In Gertrude Aston Thimelby's hand. Printed in *Old English Ballads*, ed. Rollins (1920), 71–74. In A (fols. 31–33), written in four-line iambic hexameter stanzas. Titled in A, "A songe of four priests that sufred death at Lancaster to the tune of Daintie com thou to me."

On pages 96–97 in B. Variations among the texts are given in the Appendix.

² This stanza is followed in A by:

      The Campe in Order standes,
      where many a Champion bould
      In their victorious handes
      eternall Tryumph hould

³ *Recoil.*

⁴ This and every second stanza is indented in B.

⁵ This stray letter appears in the manuscript as an upper case *D* without the back stroke. Apparently, the writer began a word and changed her mind without crossing out the letter.

saith christ o^r lord hath sayd
take thy crosse follow mee   20

Our lord is gone before
with his crosse rufully
layd on his shoulders sore
towards mount caluery

                                   Our

[fol. 20v] Our Blessed Lady sweete   25
            when she this sight Did see
            when she her sonne did meete
            Loaded Soe heauily

            The sword of sorrow then
            pierced her louinge hart   30
            Amongst All Blessed men
            christ doth his crosse Impart

            ffrom Abell to Zachery
            The scripture showeth plaine
            with grieuous cruelltie   35
            many sweete saints were slaine

            Oh the seauen maccabees
            with their sweete mother deare
            those grieuous Cruelties
            these Blessed martyres bare   40

            would uerily pierce I thinke
            the hardest hart to thaw
            yet would they neuer shrinke
            From gods most sacred law

            Each prophet And each saint   45
            of the old testament
            In hart did neuer faint
            But with his crosse was content

                                   walkinge

[fol. 21r] walkinge on willingly
saint paul doth plainly say 50
because to them theire might bee
more Ioy Another Day

saint Iohn that prophet Iust
whome christ Did soe Commend
reprouing herods lust 55
whome lew^dly Did offend

A wench herods fancy fed
what with her Dancing skill
that saint Iohn lost his head
at A lewd womans will 60

All the Apostles Deare
whose happie lots were such
their painfull Crosses bore
for god Did loue them much

Saint peter principall 65
upon A crosse was killd
his louing Duties All
to god was soe fulfild

Saint paul that Blessed weight
gods elect uessell Deere 70
in trauaile day And night
his painfull crosse did beare

And

[fol. 21v] And As the story saith
with sword he lost his head
in defence of his Church 75
he lost his Dearest blood

Saint Andrew by gods Ayde
when he his crosse Did see
O good crosse then quoth hee

welcome thou Art to mee   80

Receiue me with Ioyfull cheere
which long haue wished thee
to see my master Deare
which hath redeemed mee[6]

Likewise saint Iames the Iust   85
for his fedilitie
downe from A tower was thrust
brained most Cruelly

Saint barnabee likewise[7]
for his feruent Desire   90
in defence of gods church
his body was burn'd with fire

Saint Bartholomew likewise
Aliue he lost his skin
flayed from top to to   95
whereby gods grace to winne[8]

                                          Saint

[fol. 22r]   Saint laurance eke God wott
              long time did broyle And fry
              upon A gridiron hot
              for Iesus sake Did Dye   100

---

[6] In A:

Take me with gladsome cheere,
who long have wished for thee
For soe my Savior Deare
thus hath redemed mee

[7] This stanza is omitted in A.
[8] Thereby gods blisse to winne, in A, followed by:

St. Stephen, stoned to death
by the Jewes feirce and fell
Through bloodie tormentes past
in endlesse joyes to dwell

And saint sabestine quick
unto A stake was bound
shot thorrow wth Arrowes thick
with many A greiuous wound[9]

Oh who can write with penne   105
or wth tongue who can show
what loue these Blessed men
to christ our lord Did owe

Infinite martyres more
whome penne cannot expresse   110
In theire Aray Did goe
to endlesse happinesse

Ioy In Ierusalem[10]
with Crownes of uictory
prepared Are for those   115
O christ that follow thee
thanks be to God
        Amen[11]

---

[9] With arrowes sharpe and thicke / shot through with mainie a wounde, in A.

[10] This stanza does not appear in A; instead, the poem ends with eighteen stanzas (to be found in the Appendix) describing the execution of four Catholic priests: Robert Nutter of Barnly and Edward Thwing of Yorkshire at Lancaster on 26 July 1600, and Robert Middleton and Thurston Hunt at Lancaster on 3 March 1601. J. H. Pollen comments that "the stanzas which deal specifically with the four English priests and the moral drawn from their execution must greatly have strengthened the hearts of Catholic singers and readers" (*English Martyrs*, 385). According to Rollins, this "quite remarkable ballad" began circulating in 1601, shortly after the described events (*Old English Ballads*, 70–71). By the time Fowler was copying poems in her book, these deaths probably did not seem as significant as they had more than thirty years earlier when the poem first circulated.

[11] In B these lines follow the poem:

In o^r great Jesus, was all wisdomes store,
yet did he live cõtemned here & poor
what pleasure had he, whome he loved best,
his mothe^r & Apostles neere could rest
Alwayes in troubles, of all mẽ thought worst,
dispisdd neglected suffering hūgo^r thirst
Surely yf worldly men ye right way goe,
Jesus would not have his frinds live soe.

[11]¹

The prodigall childs
soule wracke

[fol. 22v]   Disankered from A blissfull shore
             and lancht into the maine of cares
             growne rich in uice in uertue poore
             frō freedome falne In fatall snares

             I found my selfe on Euery syde   5
             enwraped In waues of woe
             And tossed with A toylsome tyde
             could to noe port for refuge goe

             The wrastling mindes wᵗh raging blasts
             still hold me in A cruell chase   10
             they breake my Anchors saile And mast
             permitting no repossing place

             The boysterous seas with swelling floods
             on Euery syde Did worke their spite
             heauens ouercast wᵗh stormy cloudes   15
             denide the plenets guiding light

             The hellish faries² lay In waite
             to win my soule into their power
             to make me bite At Euery baite
             wherin my bane I might deuoure   20

             Thus heauen & hell, thus sea And land
             thus stormes And tempests did conspire
             with Iust reuenge of scourging hand

---

¹ By Robert Southwell, in Gertrude Aston's hand. Printed in McDonald and Brown
(*Poems*, 43–45).
   The poem also appears in B, pp. 16–17, in Gertrude's hand. Textual variants from this
manuscript and McDonald and Brown are noted in the Appendix.
² I.e., furies.

to witnesse gods deserued Ire

I

[leaf torn out]

[fol. 23r] I plunged in this heauie plight   25
            found in my faults Iust cause to feare
            my darknes taught to know my light
            the losse therof enforced teares
            I[3]

            I felt my Inward bleeding sores[4]
            my festered wounds began to smart   30
            stopt far within deaths fatall dore
            the pangs therof went neare my hart

            I cryed truce, I craued peace
            A league with death I would conclude
            but uaine it was to sue release   35
            subdue I must or be subdude

            Death And defeit had pitcht their snares
            And put their wonted proofes in ure
            to sinke me in dispairing cares
            or make me stoope to pleasures lure   40

            They sought by their bewiching charms
            soe to enchant my erringe sence
            that when they sought my greatest harmes
            I might neglect my best Defence

            my dazled eyes could take no uew   45
            no heede of their Deceiuing shifts

---

[3] The letter that appears between the two stanzas is half formed. Obviously, the writer momentarily lost track of stanza spacing.

[4] In B, *smart* is written and crossed out between *bleeding* and *sores*.

soe often did they Alter hue
And practize new deuised drifts
                                        with

[fol. 23v]   with sirens songs they fed mine eares
             till luld Asleepe on errors lapp   50
             I found their tunes turnd into teares
             and short delights to long mishapps

             ffor I enticed to their lore
             And soothed with their Idle toyes
             was trained to their prison dore   55
             the end of all such flyting Ioyes

             where Chaind in sin I lay In thrall
             next to the Dungion of dispaire
             till mercy raisd me from my fall
             And grace my ruine did repaire   60
                        finis

[12]¹

Man to the wound
In christs syde

[fol. 23v] O pleasant port² O place of rest
O royall rest o worthy wound
Come harbor me A weary guest
that in the world no ease haue found

I ly lamenting at thy gate³   5
yet Dare I not Aduenture In
I bare with me A troubleous mate
And combred Am with heape of sinne
                        Discharge

[fol. 24r] Discharge me of this heauie loade
that easier passage I may find   10
within this bower to make Aboade
And in this glorious tombe be shrin'd

Here must I liue, here must I Dye
here would I utter all my griefe
here would I all those paines Discry   15
which here Did meete for my reliefe

Here would I uew that bloodye sore
which Dint of spitfull speare did breede
the bloodie wounds layd there in store
would force A stony hart to bleede   20

---

¹ In Gertrude Aston Thimelby's hand. By Robert Southwell (*Poems*, ed. McDonald and Brown, 72–73); this poem also appears in A and (in the same hand as in HM904) in B, fol. 15. The HM904 version follows *Mæoniæ* very closely compared to other manuscript versions of this poem. Variations among the McDonald and Brown text, HM904, and B are given in the Appendix.
² In B, "port" is inserted above the line.
³ This and every second stanza after are indented in B.

Here is the spring of trickling teares
the mirrour of all mourning weights
with dolfull tunes for dumpish eares
and solomne shewes for sorrowed sights

O happie soule that flies soe high   25
As to Attaine this sacred caue
Lord send me wings that I may fly
And in this harbour quiet haue
       sweete Iesus say Amen,[4]

---

[4] B ends "Amen."

[13]¹

The perfect Louer

[fol. 24v] Hee cañot worthelie be styl'd a louer,
That will his noble enterprize giue ouer
For any opposition; or who is
Too couetous of comforts, or of bliss;
For tis meane *lóúé* loue, meerly by fauors made,   5
That growes i'th sunshine, withers in the shade.
A true and perfect louer in distress
stands firme, nor is hee puft with happiness:
Hee aymes at no reward, nor uaynely'affects
Fauours, nor for disfauours disrespects: 10
Hee rather flyes his end's,² since by their gaine,
Hee looses all the pleasure of his paine.
Hee meanely loues whome accidents can moue
Or hath a reason but his loue, to loue;
For he that nobly loues doth not reflect   15
On his owne interest, but in effect
Transform'd so perfectly in what he loues,
That by her motions, not his owne he moues:
Hee hath no will but hers, and understands
All things as she conceaues them or comãnds: 20
Hee uallewes nothing but at her esteeme,
And so him selfe, nor striues he so to seeme
Allthough his owne in nothing, for his zeale
                    tis
Tells him merrit, merrit to conceale:³

---

¹ This is the first of several poems written by Constance Fowler's brother, Herbert
Aston. It is in Fowler's hand; a slightly different version appears in *TP* (268–70). These
variations are noted in the Appendix.
² Flees the ultimate goal of love, because, having achieved that, his pleasure would
lack the pain of unfilled anticipation.
³ In *TP*, the following lines are inserted:

Which makes him practise art to hide his paine,
But still his eyes make that ambition vaine;
For though false flames may be within suppresst,

Hee oft enjoyeth extasyes, and proues   25
An Alien to him *loue* selfe for what he loues;
His thoughts, words, actions, all are in excess
For true loue hath no measure,[4] which express
[fol. 25r]   Strange force in loue, but more that they should proue
Madnes to judgment, reason to his loue: 30
Hee aprehends no dangers, nor retreats
At any difficulties, no deceipts
Molest, nor injure him; for his owne fire
Is his owne happiness, and it's owne hire;
Yet he hath one desire nor <u>doth</u>[5] that staine   35
The purity of loue; tis loue againe
This the most perfectly refined[6] approue;
who rootes out y[s], añihelates his loue;
It being loue's uery essence to desire
T'engender the Idæa of his fire.   40
And ther's no compentent reward but this,
Nor Heauen, nor earth; which though he haue, or miss,
It neither rayseth nor putts out his flame,
That's constantly, essentially the same;
That happy accident doth only proue   45
His glorie may bee more, but not his loue;
Yet boast's not of his loue, nor doth pretend
A merrit of his suffrings, nor an end;
Hee wisheth them imõrtall as his loue,
which when his bodie dies, findes no remoue   50
Being rooted in his soule, but doth assend
with her, and like her, neuer hath an end.

True fires are not contained within a brest.
So that who loves must vent flames through his eyes,
Sigh, flame, or burn a smother'd sacrifice.

[4] In *TP*, "measures." Whether Clifford silently emended this word to make it agree
with the verb "express" or whoever copied it onto the paper Clifford found mistakenly
wrote "measures," "measure" in the singular makes more sense. The sentence is syntacti-
cally complicated but probably reads: His thoughts, words, and actions (which express
Love's strange force) are all excessive because Love has no measure (or boundaries) and,
even more, their excessiveness shows his judgement to be madness and his love to be
reasonable.

[5] The line beneath "doth" is somewhat ink blotted.

[6] A stray pen mark or malformed apostrophe appears between *e* and *d*.

[14]¹

[fol. 25v] whilest I here absente² languish out my time
wher those blest eyes x nere shone, accorsed clime,³
Eéuer contemplating your mind, or face
The meracle of natur, that of grace
Liuing methinks I sin against my loue   5
Discredit all my sofrings seames to aproue
Of this my exile or what greues me⁴ most
Apeare to underualue what I'ue lost
For who with comon reson can sopose
Although he nether loue nor goodnes knows   10
That seperated from my soule and throwne
From Heuin to Hell I liue to make it knowne.
Loue tis prophane, unher'd of tiranye
To worke a meracle to torture me.
But thou'art all goodnes and can'st nere intend   15
so great a worke to such a cruell end
No, tis thy greatest mercy to preserue
My life in torment that I may deserue.
For now I dayly ofer to her eyes
My hart an unconsumed sacrifice   20
when death were but one ofring, and might bee
with reason Iudg'd rash cowardice in mee,
Besides it tis in me iniustice growne

---

¹ Probably by Herbert Aston, since it concludes with one of Constance Fowler's emblems; in Constance Fowler's hand.

² "te" is blotted.

³ Herbert Aston probably composed this in conjunction with his 1635 journey to Spain, when he accompanied his father on Walter Aston's second diplomatic mission to that country. Arthur Clifford comments:

In 1635, he accompanied his father, on his second embassy to Madrid; before which time, he appears to have formed a strong attachment for Catherine Thimelby, sister of Sir John Thimelby, of Irnham, whom he afterwards married. During his absence from England, his youngest sister, Constantia ... who was tenderly attached to him, did all in her power to promote this union. Herbert Aston seems to have felt, very early, the inspirations of the muse. Perhaps, the passion of love, as has happened to many other poets, first warmed his breast to poetic raptures. ... (TP, xx)

⁴ Blot under "eues m."

To rob her of a life that's not my owne.
she may comaund me dead, tell then for me   25
T'anticipate her will, my destinye
If it were posible I doe distroy
By it all hope of any forther Ioy,
Thus is my loue with absence still at strife,
spight of my torments to preserue my life.   30
loue comforts me with hopes I may retorne
[fol. 26r]   To uew those too⁵ bright stars againe, which borne
Pure as the uestall fires, and so may haue
My paine redem'd by Heuin, not by the graue.
Absence objects then infinite dispares,   35
That For one hope of ioy, I'ue thousand cares.
But sence *it* tis the meridian of loue,
To couet life most, when by it *pro* I proue
The exquisitest torments I xxx inuoke
The worst of absence, fortunes deapest stroke,   40
loues sharpes't mischefe, that I may be come
A constant, an insesant matirdome,
since nothing now can kill me, though your eyes
Exhal'd my soule, loue that defect suplys,
so that were nature spent, senses at strife   45
I neuer changing loue, can nere change life.
But stay my hapy thoughts, t'were too much bliss
Hell driuen from her fayre eyes to thinke but this,
If there might be such extasyes in hell,
The diuell nere would know that e're he fell,   50
so my faire Heauin, while I contemplate thee,
I loose all meret, loosing mesery,
let me consider then my lost estate,
Dispare and the peruersnes of my fate
Thinke what may most aflict me, and procure   55
How with most sence, I mesery indure
But (loue) tis all in uaine since tis for her
Misfortune I aboue content prefer
Greefes I reioyce in paine for plesure take

---

⁵ Herbert puns on two/too.

so I can sofer nothing for your sake   60
This ~~this~~ (though nought else would kill me) but alone
Tis then my torture, that I suffer none.

[15]¹

The first Alter:

[fol. 26v]   Chast Flames of sacred virgins purely bright
            Like hallowed Tapers on the Alter; light
              My zelous loue: while heere confin'd
            | In this darke closett of my Minde
            | Obscur'd: my early uows I² pay   5
            | And make a thought of her my day:
            | Of her (faire Cælestina)   shee
              whose euery thought's a Deity
            | sprunge from the uertues of her soule
            | If parts bee taken for the whole: 10
            | And can I guide my penn to raise
              a stepp to her deserued praise
            | No I must needs those Merrits misse
            | that haue no part of what shee is.³
            | For if the⁄ sages understood   15
                    of
            | Loue to be want faire and good
            | How then cann I that loue (expresse
              her worth) that good nor faire possesse:
            | And both in her so Iust so sweet
            | with such exact proportions meete   20
            | As though in Heauen one did see
              Nature vow verginity:
            | He then (who blest) shall undertake
            | to say what Cælestina is: must make
            An Angells quill the penne: wisedome must thinke,   25
            The Heauens paper: and contrite teares the Inke.⁴

---

¹ By William Pershall, in Constance Fowler's hand. See Habington, "Elegie 5," one of the eight elegies written on the death of Habington's good friend George Talbot (*Poems*, ed. Allott 105–7).

² This and the preceding word are slightly blotted.

³ I.e., essentially. Those traits that are good but superfluous to her essential virtue.

⁴ I.e., he must make an angel's quill his pen, must think wisdom, must make the heavens his paper, and must make tears his ink.

[16]¹

On Celestinæs² goinge a
Iorney in wett-weather:

[fol. 27r] | weepe the Heauens? and not wee;
| Haue eyes the powre now to see
For³ teares; when celestinaes gone
| Must the weather not wee moane:⁴
| The Aire pours doune her gloomy raine   5
| And draws her clowdy curtaines; fayne
| would nature Ioyne to keepe her heere
| But goodnes will be euery-where:⁵
| And yeat no sooner did wee marke
| Her seated in her lether Arke⁶   10
| Ready to leaue the world alone
| Drown'd in theire teares when she was gone:
But Th'Relicks⁷ of her presence made
Faire weather; and the Tempest stayde:
As pleas'd to shew the Raynbows Fame   15
In the first letter of her Name:⁸
But who obseru'd not as shee went

---

¹ This unattributed poem is in Constance Aston Fowler's hand.
² The Latin *celes* is a small, fast boat.
³ In spite of.
⁴ "Must the weather moan, while we do not?"
⁵ It is in the nature of goodness (here in the form of Celestina) to be everywhere.
⁶ A coracle; see Marvell, "Upon Appleton House":

> But now the salmon-fishers moist
> Their Leathern boats begin to hoist,
> And like Antipodes in shoes,
> Have shod their heads in their canoes. (769–72)

⁷ Anything Celestina leaves behind, from physical belongings to her scent. "Relicks" gives the line a Catholic slant. See Donne, "The Relic," for the witty uses to which the word could be put in the seventeenth century.
⁸ I.e., "C."

How euery Blossom lost his sent
For t'was the springe, and so it[9] might
As grown maturer by her sight[10]   20
The early Hathorn vow'd to stay
His greene vntill the end of may;[11]
The fruitfull plant's now quick with sapp
Obortiue grew by this Mishapp[12]
And all the earth (resolu'd to mourne)   25
Vow'd barrenes till her retorne:
The Violett and primrose stole
A secrett meetinge to condole:

[fol. 27v] | But they were grac't aboue the rest
            | For her fayre hands had toucht and blest   30
            | Them; which because from her wee take
            | Must neuer perish for her sake
            | Besids with them a vnion meets
            | For shee and they are kynn in sweets:
            | But what avails the springe thus crost   35
            | To us in desolation lost:
            | That leane vpon our Elboes, full
            | Of saddest thoughts and sighs; like dull
            | Astronomers with heauy looks
            | That study starr-light by theire books:[13]   40
            | Blest Mayde retorn: (or if that Mayde)
            | To nature bee prophanely sayde[14]

---

[9] I.e., the blossom.

[10] The scent of spring flowers fades as they mature into the summer.

[11] The hawthorn, the may tree, should begin greening at the beginning of May.
Here, he delays leaf production until the end of May.

[12] Her leaving.

[13] That is, viewing the spring without her is comparable to astronomers looking at
pictures of stars instead of at the stars themselves. They study starlight by their books instead of studying their books by starlight.

[14] The closing parenthesis is misplaced. For the phrase to make sense, the final parenthesis should be placed after "sayde" in the next line. The line then means that the
term "blest Mayde" as applied to nature is too profane.

| Take any Ayde[15] that bears the sence
| Of saints or naturs Excellence
| looke back but with one gratious eye,   45
| Els wee, the springe, and all must Dye:

[15] If "Mayde" is too connotatively religious for nature, she should, the poet puns, take any "Ayde" that will bring her back; that is, she should take any help and she should take any designation ending in "ayde." The consistency in spelling is too unusual for this play not to have been deliberate.

[17]¹

on castaraes sittinge on
Primrose banks

[fol. 27v] | see how the little starrs in Azure nights
| when cynthia's present cast their tremblinge lights
| As fearfull least her² Numerous sparks might moue her
| And winke a welcome to the wakefull louer
| So when castara satt; The primrose banks   5
| shrunke up their odours in their yellow ranks³
| For what are all the sweets together mett

---

¹ Allott doubtfully attributes this poem, in Constance Fowler's hand, to Habington (*Poems*, 160). Allott's transcription from HM904 and mine differ only in a few accidentals. Allott says:

> These two poems [this and 19, "goinge A foote in the snow," fol. 28v] are from Huntington Library MS. H.M. 904 . . . The case against Habington's authorship on stylistic grounds is based chiefly on the first lyric, but both must be attributed to one author as they are both signed with the same cipher. Note that the first lyric [17] is developed more loosely and with more inconsequence than Habington allows; that it has uncharacteristic prettiness—the use of colour, the epithet 'little' for 'Starrs,' the phrase 'lilly sheppardesses in their bowre'; and that a feminine rhyme—'moue her /Louer'—is found here, but only once in *Castara*. (*Poems*, 204)

Allott is almost certainly correct that this poem is not one of Habington's; as he comments, the genuine Habington poem in the Huntington manuscript (51) ends with the initials W. H. (*Poems*, ed. Allott, lxi), whereas the two Castara poems in HM904 end with the same cipher—three vertical bars crossed by four horizontal bars.

The poem is not without its charm. Castara is like the moon, presumably in her chastity, but the poet stresses not that element but rather the intensity of Castara's scent as compared to the other flowers, which like the stars in Cynthia's presence grow faint in Castara's. The "lilly sheppardesses" (lilies, of course, having the potential to fester) scorn this new flower's scent, when in fact Castara is a plant from Eden.

Allott notes one instance of feminine rhyme, but in fact only two couplets are purely masculine in rhyme; two are feminine, and two are mixed, the latter two kinds of rhyme contributing to the gracefulness of the lines, as does the occasional use of alliteration (lines 4 and 12).

² The text clearly reads "her," but the analogy makes more sense with "their," i.e., the stars'.

³ With a possible pun on "rank odor," since Castara's scent outdoes all other flowers'.

| If but compared to the Violett:[4]
| yeat lilly sheppardesses in their bowre
| Mistake this sweete and call it gilly-flower   10
| what ere it be; it seems for worth and price
| A plant for princes out of paradice.

---

[4] Cf. "A Pregnant banke swel'd up, to rest / The violets reclining head," in John Donne's "The Extasie" (2–3).

[18]¹

An Elegy on the death of
The Lady Frances Draicott

[fol. 28r] To dye and to dye younge; and to dye full
Of freinds, of blessings, of renown, would pull
And stoope a giant heart; what then of her
whom losse of all at once could not deterr;
For when the holy warrant once was signd   5
That she must dye, how perfitely resignd
Her soule imbrast the news, as if the Doome;
were but remoouinge to another Roome;
Had death Assaulted some owld barren peece
shurnk² up and clouthed in a riueled Fleece   10
where death longe time a sentinell had bene
I'th trenches of an owld contracted skynn
such might haue well discharged natures Right
And thought it Iust to leaue the Earthe's Delight:
But happy soule, t'was noblenes in you   15
To pay the debt so longe before t'was due:
Death therefore glory not, thou can'st not Rayse
Thy tropheis heere, thy triumph is her praise,
It was no uuolgar desteny that cal'd
Her hence, whose lates³ Age was wal'd   20
with youth and strength; and might haue liu'd to bee

---

¹ This poem in Constance Fowler's hand was probably written by William Pershall
(La Belle, HAM 551), whose second wife was Frances Aston, Constance's sister. His first
wife was Mary Thimelby, Katherine Thimelby Aston's sister.

Lady Frances Draycott (or Drascot or Draycote) had several close connections with the
Aston family. She was the wife of Philip Draycott and the daughter of Richard Weston
(1577–1635), first Earl of Portland and Lord Treasurer of England, by his second wife
Frances Waldegrove. Lady Frances Draycott's half-sister Mary, Richard Weston's daughter by his first wife, married the second Walter Aston, Constance's brother. Frances's
husband Philip and Constance's husband Walter Fowler also had the same grandfather,
Walter Fowler of the Grange (d. 1622).

I have not been able to discover when Lady Draycott died.

² Shrunk.
³ Latest.

A cronicle to longe posterity:
No t'was decreed aboue, that she should teach
Youth how to dye, religiouse what to preach
she liu'd so good, as only those that knew   25
Her like (religion) thought it to bee true
For others whome their malice blinde did strike
Might thinke the sunn and candles all a like
[fol. 28v] But vertue soone all clowdy Aires had calm'd
And her bright soule with holy Acts imbalm'd   30
At last was grown to Angells thoughts so nigh
Except she had made Earth Heauen, shee needs[4] must Dye.
                                                              WP

---

[4] The *s* is partially obliterated by what seems to be a drop of water blotting the ink.

[19][1]

upon castaries and her sitters[2] goinge
A foote in the snow

[fol. 28v]   The Heauens knowinge that the tedious way
             Did rauish ease from fayre castara: lay
             Their sentence on the Earth, and thinke it meete
             It should doe pennance in a snow-white sheete
             As it hath done this morninge: for the last   5
             Enamel'd at your sights did sparkles cast
             Like hardest diamonds, and were proud to bee
                A pauement for your brightest eyes to see[3]
             This is my feare, least like faire phœbus Rays
             Your eyes might melt the snow, and make wett ways.   10

---

[1] Doubtfully Habington's; see Allott (*Poems*, 160). Allott's transcription of this poem in Constance Fowler's hand differs from mine only in accidentals.

[2] I.e., sister's.

[3] This line is written interlineally.

[20]¹

An Eglogne betweene
Melibeus and Amyntas:

[fol. 28v]   Melibeus: Tell me Amyntas why you looke,
                          so sadly on this murmuringe brooke,
                          As though you had some Distemper tooke:

                          Hope well; the fates may be Inclinde
                          propitious to your troobled minde,   5
                          And Cælestina will be kinde:

             Amyntas: O Melibeus   True I loue
                          Faire Cælestina, farr a boue
                          The thoughts that commen louers moue:

                         |
[fol. 29r] | Nor will I Ielous bee, or feare   10
                         | The brauest Bard that cann Appeare,
                         | More gratious *tó* in her eye or Eare,

                         | I know the gods my riualls are,
                         | And panns great heire² must court my faire,
                         | To loue her well is all my care: 15

                          My soule was buisied in the thought
                         | Of news, which from the gods was brought,
                         | when I theire resolutions sought:
                         |
                         |
                          For when their Answeare I did craue,
                         | How longe I should remaine a slaue,   20

---

¹ In Constance Aston Fowler's hand.
² The poet probably means Orpheus, Apollo's son, who could be considered in his
musical abilities the spiritual heir of Pan.

| Or what successe my loue should haue:

|

  Iust thus the oracle did say;
| When Riuers runne the other way
| Then looke to se that happy Day:

|

| Sad comfort, such poore Hopes doe proue   25
| Not to Inioy successe in loue
| Till streams and riuers backward moue:

Melibeus Lett Riuers runne which way they will,
| Cannot you loue as you doe still,
  Let fates the oracles fulfill   30

|

[fol. 29v] | A constant Faith all Feare Expells
| And hope subdues Impossibles:
| Loue often worketh Miracles:

|

|

Amyntas: Tis gold I know To'haue luckye Fate,
| But hopes expresse a poore estate,   35
  To those that are vnfortunate:

|

|

Melibeus: Take heede Amyntas, sett not free
| The raines of loue, at liberty,
  For rashnes is loues Enimy:

|

| Some motions back discreetely stept,   40
| At such a Distance should be kept,
| Not as your thoughts (but hers), Accepte:

|

| when passions are not well retir'd,
| But oftner uttered then Admir'd,

| It maks the Seruice lesse desir'd: 45

|
| Lett no uaine feares your̸ thoughts possesse,
| Or Malice others happines,
| Though her esteeme proue more or lesse:
|

[fol. 30r] | Canne you so simple be to thinke,
                | That all the world but you doth winke,   50
                  when they with your opinon linke:
                |

                | why should you? your own Ioyes preferre
                  Or thinke to be sole conquerer:³
                | That wer to loue your selfe not her:
                |

                | And say! what Madnes guides your minde   55
                  Still vext with what wee only finde;
                  To Accidents and form's Inclinde:
                |
                |
                  Loue you her person or those Arts,
                | which Heuen to her soule Imparts,
                | with both these, Hers, and your Death parts: 60
                |

                | If only vertues vnderstood
                  By all your loues, Tis Nobly good:
                  If otherwise t'may breede ill blood:

Amyntas: Lord, how discreete you fayne would show;
                | pray feare those dangers when you knowe,   65
                | The brooks and riuers back-ward flowe:

---

³ These two lines make more syntactic sense if the question mark follows "conquerer."

[fol. 30v] | Is there a loue with such pretence,
                               That dare's prophane (in any sence)
                              | The Alter of her Innocence:

                              |
                               I challenge Anchorites to be   70
                              | My Iudge: my loue's as faire and free
                              | As Flamines thoughts of Chastitye:

                              |
                               And tell me you that seeme so wise;
                              | Is nature prostituted if we prize,
                               The beawties of the spatious skyes: 75
                              |
                              |
                              | Ioue hath the soule so bright exprest,
                               That vgly forms it doth detest:
                              | And loues her own true coppy best:

                              |
                               Behold in Cælestinas Eyes
                              | where harts doe dayly sacrifice,   80
                              | A light that Mortalls glorifies:
                              |

[fol. 31r]   Her Motions such a gesture beare's
                               As Cynthia (when she full Appears)
                               Danct to the Musick of the sphæres:

                               Her speech Like Orpheus doth Intice   85
                               Her accents breathinge balme and spice
                               with all the sweets of paradice:

                               Her forms and graces may compare
                               with naturs skill: nay more I dare
                               say, They Incorporeall are;   90

                               For as the soule's in euery part
                               As in the whole; and doth Impart

Her risidence with equall Art:

soe her perfections beinge knowne
In euery place: Assign'd to none: 95
Makes her soule and body one:

[21]¹

Mʳˢ   A discourse of A dreame.   K T.

[fol. 31v] sleepe the best ease of the most troubled mind,
            Rest from our labors, Nurse of humankind,
            why soe unkind to me falce Ioyes to frame.~
            when the most true, pertake too much of dreame.²
            waking I see how extreame false they³ are   5
            which giue us Ioy, to purchase greater care⁴
            Or wast thou meanst this way my hart to take
            By giuing Ioyes I can not find a wake.~
            where pouerty hath dwelt (they are like one
            All wayes in pleasure) custome makes it none;⁵   10
            But those who halfe ther life had consolation
            Must needs haue greater sense of depriuation
            Then lett me wake, or euer haue such dreames
            And not by contradiction know th extreames.⁶

---

¹ Composed by Katherine Thimelby Aston, in Constance Aston Fowler's hand, this poem was probably written before 1638 because, according to Clifford, Katherine Thimelby married Herbert Aston "about that time" (*TP*, 294). See also La Belle (HAM 561). The first six and final two lines are printed in *TP* (294). Variations between the two versions are noted in the Appendix.

² The truest, most real joys seem to be a dream.

³ I.e., dreams.

⁴ To submit in real life to worldly cares.

⁵ For those with hearts deprived of joys, dreams create a sensation of being always in pleasure, which custom or use shows to be a false state of affairs.

⁶ The poet concludes by wishing that she may be ever in a state of wakeful poverty (never knowing the joys dreams offer) or that she may be ever dreaming, instead of having to experience the extremes of knowing the reality and dreaming the ideal.

[22]¹

Loue's Meritt

[fol. 31v] strange Alterations in my soule
Loue, thou hast made; thus to controule
synne, and ill Habitts: now I finde,
Thou˟ art a passion pure refinde:
when I walkt carelesse of a thought   5
of thee, or of thy power, I sought
Like a dull userer to Increase
My own content and stock of Ea'se:
Not once regardinge what esteeme
My Actions did produce or seeme: 10
since loue beseigh my heart, it stole
[fol. 32r] Heroike thoughts; within my soule:
I feele a noble ualour stirr
within my ueins, to fight for her:
And Arm's mee to Attempt and take   15
some faire Aduenturs for her sake:
I finde my minde apt to conferr
esteeme on those that honer her
And thinke my place, wher she doth come
belowe the meanest in the Roome: 20
I trooble not my brains with nwes²
Of scottish warrs, with turks or Iews:
only when I of battailes heare;
I pittye captiue prisoners there:
No thinge is busines now to mee,   25
Nor³ doe I ualue my Degree;

---

¹ In Constance Aston Fowler's hand.
² The *w* and *e* are transposed.
³ Ink blot precedes *Nor*.

what cloths I weare; or where I dwell,
so Cælestina thinke them well:

Beholde[4] the rare effects of loue,   30
How neere perfection it doth moue,
No Anchorite in carelesse dresse
More silent sadnes canne possesse
Then I: nor oftner sigh and weepe.
Besids a constant fast I keepe   35
For euer sence I feltx loues dart
My stomake went in to my heart:
My sleepe's so poore that I cann tell
All howers like a centinell:
with starts a wak't, least with her spies,   40
Disdaine my (enimye) should Rise:
Loue maks me perfitely resign'd,
with such Indifferency of minde,
[fol. 32v]   That it doth freely power giue,
As willingly to dye as liue: 45
For Iudge you what poore hopes remaine,
when her mistrust bespeakes disdaine:
Cann I a greater honor haue
Then Iustly wish a quiett graue:

---

4 Ink blot precedes lines 30, 31, and 32.

[23]¹

A congratalation For the happy
Retorne of ᵀL: A: From spaine

[fol. 32v] My Lord
When from Th'Antipodes Apollo brings
The gladd retorne of fayre and early springs
wee see how all the aires Musitions meete
And there² Accesse with seuerall carolls greete
The meaner uoices of the grou's³ will dare   5
To chirpe in presence of the queene of Aire
And cannot silenst bee with shame, though all
Their whisteling Accents are Apochrýphall
So I In Imitation of their quier
present you heere no Art, but meere desire   10
To expresse my Ioys: for when I saw at last
The clowdy winter of your absence past
your happy presence such a Ioy did bringe
I had no temper how to speake but singe,
Or ell's I might haue better come with those   15
who bidd your Lo:ⁱᵖ· wellcome-home in prose:
Tis boldly dune and rash I needs must say
To write; and write to you, and write this way
[fol. 33r] To offer Iuy leaues to you, who weare
Apolloes lawrell in our hemisphære   20
It shows as if grammarian pedants sought
To boast the Latin which their masters taught.
since not one haire of mine was euer yeat
In Aganippaës streams by muses wett,
Nor can my lines giue me a fame more high   25
Then liue a catechumen still in pöetry
yeat this may them to perfite faith preferr
If your aceptance prooue their god-father.

---

¹ In Constance Fowler's hand; probably by William Pershall, husband of Constance's
sister Frances, welcoming his father-in-law back from Spain in 1638. Also printed in Kay
("Poems," 202–3), where it differs from this version only in incidentals.
² They greet their own excess of music with more carols.
³ Groves.

[24]¹

[fol. 33r]   Ill busied man, why dost thou take such care
             To lenthen out thy lifes shorte callender
             when euery spectacle thou lookst uppon
             presents and actes thy execution.
             Each weethered station, and each flowor doth crie   5
             Foole as I fade, and weether thou must die
             The beating of thy pulce when thou art well
             Is Iust the Towling of thy passing bell²
             And all these earthly dewes that nightly fall
             Are but thy teares, shedd for thy funerall.   10
                                       B I

---

¹ "My Midnight Meditation," by Henry King, in Constance Fowler's hand. Printed in Crum's edition of King's poems. According to Crum, the poem, sometimes attributed to John King, Henry's brother, "was one of the best-liked of King's poems in his own time" (*Poems*, 157).

Fowler seemed to believe, given the initials at the end of the poem in HM904, that Ben Jonson was the poet.

² In Crum, the following lines are inserted: Night is thy Hearse, whose sable Canopy / Covers alike Deceased Day and Thee. Other variations from Crum's text are given in the Appendix.

[25]¹

To his Mʳˢ on her
outward Beauty

[fol. 33v] Iust (Seraphina) as a priest doth doubt,
If to the gods he truly be deuoute,
Each word each action in the sacrifice,
As if int'ention would not Heaue'n suffice
with what a trembling hand he comes to touch   5
The sacred offring, and his Zeale is such
In all the ceremonyes, it doth make
Him fearfull, and that feare makes him mistake
when yet another to whome doth adheare
Far lesse deuotion, as well as feare   10
May seeme xxx more holy to the vulgar eyes
Because he erres not in the sacrifice,
Hauing a toung deuouter then his heart,
That which he wants in Zeale, supplies with art
yet the eternall, and Iust powers of Heauen   15
prefer the offering deuoutely giuen,
They looke not on the sacrifice, nor art,
That doth adorne it, but upon the heart
So I a loue-deuine deuoute to you
My only Deyty, to whome is due   20
more honour then I can performe, doe bring
My heart for sacrifice, for offering
I doe present these lines unto your prayse
purely a Holocaust, only to rayse
[fol. 34r] your glory, that mortallity may see   25
How much they owe unto Deuinity:
Oh how my hand now trembles, my mind doubt
Each word I write, sometimes I doe blott out
what I before did Interline, and then

---

¹ Probably by Herbert Aston: *Seraphina* designates Katherine Thimelby in family poems and letters. This poem, however, is not followed by one of Fowler's ciphers proba- bly because the poem's ending is missing.

what I new blotted out strate like agen,   30
sometimes I thinke this uerse it doth not flow,
This word too common, this expression low
Feare which with true deuotion you'le find
Always united so orerules my mind,
That though what I haue uoluntary writt   35
hath bene by many men approued witt:
Now that I am most serious, and doe striue
To write what to eternity may liue,
Nothing but errours from my pen doe flow
And tis my too much care that make's it so   40
perhaps other yet whose minde is free
From loue's soule ouerawing slauery,
may write politer lines, and with more art
Though eu'ry word a stranger to his heart;
yet I am almost confident that you,   45
whose nature is deuine, your selfe as true,
And Iust as gods themselues, will prize no art
like to the true deuotion of a heart:
Fayre seraphina let your eyes then shine
gently upon this offering of minedé   50

[fol. 34v]   which to your outward Beauty I present,
of which your eyes are the chiefe ornament,
For t'was that Beauty that my soule first drewe
Although that uertue tyes me fast to you,
Iust as the sun by uertue of his heate   55
Draws exhalations from their propper seate
And as the fire doth always upward tende
where it tis in perfection to ascend,
Euen so my soule was drawne by your fayre eyes
And she as willing as the fire to rise,   60
which in its propper region is pure,
And only there from contra'yes secure:
so whilest my body did my soule Inclose
sinne Dayly did her purity opposse;
But being arriu'd unto her propper spheare   65
your body, purer then most soules are here;
Hath now no opposites, but liueth euen
As a small star, fixt in the selfe same heauen

with the bright sun, quite da<u>zel'd</u> with the light
                (yet rauisht with delight)tion
<u>of your fayre eyes,</u> which none ere saw sans prepara=   70
         \<u>those eyes</u>\[2]
That did not faint away in admirasion
There are no little cupids in those eyes,
not one lasciuious glance from hence ther flyes
by which may be conuay'd one wanton dart
to wounde with base affection any heart;   75
Instead of cupids in your heauenly eyes,
A legion of Angells houering flyes,[3]

---

[2] Fowler incorrectly copied this poem and then corrected it to read "with the bright sun, quite dazel'd with the light / of your fayr eyes, (yet rauisht with delight) / [of] those eyes which none ere saw sans preparation" ("tion" is written at the end of the line above).

[3] This image is reminiscent of Spenser's *Epithalamion*:

> Behold whiles she before the altar stands
> Hearing the holy priest that to her speakes
> . . . .
> That even th'Angels which continually,
> About the sacred Altare doe remaine,
> Forget their service and about her fly,
> Ofte peeping in her face that seemes more fayre,
> The more they on it stare. (223–33)

[26][1]

A Child my Choyse

[fol. 35r]   Let folly praise ~~wat~~ y^t fancy loues
I praise And loue that child
whose hart no thought whose tongue no word
whose hand no Deed Defild

I praise him most; I loue him best   5
All praise And loue is his
while him I loue in him I liue
And cannot liue Amisse

Loues sweetest marke lauds highest theame
mans most Desired light   10
to loue him life, to leaue him Death
to liue In him Delight

He mine by gift, I his by Dept
thus each to other Due
first friend he was, best friend he is   15
And time will try him true.

Though yong yet wise though small yet strong
though man yet god he is
As wise he knowes, As strong he can
As god he loues to blesse   20

His knowledge rules, his strength defends
his loue Doth chirish all
his birth our Ioy, his life our light

---

[1] "A Child my Choyse," Robert Southwell (*Poems*, ed. McDonald and Brown, 13).
In Gertrude Aston's hand. In Southwell manuscripts, the poem is written in fourteeners
in four-line stanzas or inpoulter's measure (four eight-line stanzas) (*Poems*, ed. McDonald
and Brown, 123). In HM904, it appears as eight four-line stanzas of poulter's measure.
Variations from McDonald and Brown are given in the Appendix.

his Death our end of thrall

Alas

[fol. 35v]   Alas he weeps, he sights he pants   25
yet Doth his Angells sing
out of his teares, his sights and throbs
Doth bud A Ioyfull spring

Almighty babe, whose tender Armes
Can force all foes to flye   30
correct my faults, protect my life
Direct me when I Dye

Amen,

[27]¹

Lifes Death, lous life²

[fol. 35v] Who liues in loue, loues best³ to liue
And long Delayes Doth rue
yf him he loue by whome he liues
to whome all loue is Due

Who for our loues did choose to liue   5
And was Content to Dye
who lou'd our loue more then ~~o'lif~~ his life
And loue wth life Did buy,

Let us In life, yea with our life
requite his liuinge loue   10
for best we loue when best we liue
yf loue our life remoue

Where loue is hot, life hatfull is
their grounds Do not Agree
loue where it lou's, life where it liues   15
Desireth most to be,
                                                    And

[fol. 36r] And sith loue is not where it liues
nor liueth where it loues,
loue hate'th life that holds it back
And Death it best Approues   20

---

¹ Written by Robert Southwell. In Gertrude Aston's hand, in HM904 and in B.
Variants among these and McDonald and Brown's edition of the poem (*Poems*, 54) are
noted in the Appendix.

² This poem is transcribed in stanzas only in one contemporary manuscript compila-
tion of Southwell's short lyrics (of the five copies) and in B (*Poems*, ed. McDonald and
Brown, 146). It is also divided into stanzas in HM904.

³ *Least*, in McDonald and Brown, although two of the five Southwell manuscripts
(B.L. Add. MS. 10422, B.L. MS. Harl. 6921) give *best* as does B.

ffor seldome is he wonne In life
whome loue doth most Desire
yf wonne by loue yet not enioy'd
till mortall life expire

life out of oath, hath not Abode   25
In earth loue hath no place
loue setled hath her Ioyes in heauen
In earth, life all her grace

mourne therfore no true louers death
life onely him Annoyes   30
And when he taketh leaue of life
then loue begins his Ioyes,
              finis

[28]¹

[fol. 36v]   In meditation where I sate
thinkinge of my soules estate
beholdinge with Attentiue eye
christ his picture that stood me by
me thought christs speaches I did heere   5
thus uttered in my Inward eare
O how much do I loue thee
why should I lose thee²
sith I haue bought thee so deere

I say mans soule, my hart my doue   10
my onely darlinge And my loue
do thou not lose for sinnes short pleasure
me thy lord And endlesse treasure
I that Am thy surest friend
who for thy sake my life did end   15
O how much do I loue thee, &ᵗ

Thinke what I haue endured for thee
All in this uaile of misery
passinge my time in toile And paine
to bringe my lost sheep home Againe   20
thinke how in bethlem borne I was
And poorely layd betweene oxe & Asse
O how much do I loue thee &ᵗ

Thinke how my mother fled with mee
for feare of herods crueltee   25
In

---

¹ This poem, in Gertrude Aston Thimelby's hand, can be found copied in the same hand in B, pp. 12–13. Variations between the two texts are given in the Appendix.
² This and the preceding line are written as one line in B; also the refrain is written out at the end of each stanza.

[fol. 37r] In Egypt seauen yeares I we³ stayd
            the text doth tell oʳ foes were dead
            therfore for my sake be thou content
            to suffer flight or bannishment
                O how much do I loue thee, &ᵗ   30

            Thinke how I fasted forty Dayes
            And tempted was three maner of wayes
            to fast therfore learne thou of mee
            for to resist thy Enemy
            fast thou I say though Epicure   35
            do scorne thee with new breathren pure
                O how much do I loue thee &ᵗ
            Think what I left to be thy foode
            in sacrament my flesh And bloud
            such was my loue such was my will   40
            old Iewish figures to fullfill
            therfore hold thou thy Auncient faith
            whatsoeuer the bare figure sayth
                O how much do I loue thee &ᵗ

            Thinke on my whipps, my crowne of thorne   45
            wherwith my head And flesh was torne
            my robe, my reede, my Isall⁴ And gall
            my crosse, my nayles, And torments All
            thinke how at last I lost my life
            to winne thee to my spouse And wife   50
                O how much do I loue thee &ᵗ

            Thinke how in soule I went to hell
            to fetch out soules that lou'd me well
                                    the

---

³ For meter and sense, the word should be either "I" or "we." In B, "I we" is written in, crossed out, and replaced by "we," reinforcing the argument that B was copied from HM904.

⁴ Thimelby's spelling of "ysell," a variant of "eisell," i.e., vinegar.

[fol. 37v] the third day After my death most dolorous
            I rose Again In brightnesse glorious   55
            And those that proue till death them end
            Like Resurrection sure shall finde
                O how much do I loue thee &ᵗ

            And thus my sweete lords speaches ended
            thinkinge my selfe most highly freended   60
            I bade All fadeinge Ioyes Adue
            fixinge my minde on louers true
            And now I finde my selfe At ease
            sweete Iesu grant I may thee please
                O how, now I do loue thee   65
            let me not lose thee
            sith thou hast bought me so deere
                thanks be to god

[29]¹

[fol. 37v]   O Blessed God O sauiour sweete
O Iesu thinke on mee
refuse me not that Am uniust
though late I come to thee

I come to thee confounded quite   5
In sorrow griefe And paine
when I behold thy bitter smart
And know I Did the same

                    crowned
I Am the wretch that w̶o̶u̶n̶d̶e̶d̶ t̶h̶ee
I made those wounds so wide   10
                    I

[fol. 38r]   I nailed thee upon the crosse
with speare I perst thy syde

Thy back, thy syde, thy belly eke
I rent with cruell rod
twas I yᵗ wrought thee all this woe   15
forgiue me my good God

ffor the pryde of seraphims
how many thousands fell
from pleasure to perpetuall paine
from heauen to hatefull hell   20

more then A thousand, thousand times
haue I Deseru'd thine Ire
yet doe I mizer still remaine
yet feele I not hell fire

---

¹ In Gertrude Aston Thimelby's hand, here and in B (where every other stanza is indented). The poem also appears in A, pp. 114–18. Variations among the three are given in the Appendix.

Yet doe I still thy fauour finde   25
yet dost thou keepe me still
Against the force of All my foes
that seeke my soule to spill

And more then that, that I should liue
thou Dyedst on the roode   30
And for to saue my sinfull soule
thou shedst thy Dearest bloud

That precious bloud, wch frō thy hart
came gushing out Amaine
                                            was

[fol. 38v]   was spild to saue my sinfull soule   35
from endlesse woe And shame

O god, my god most mercifull
what haue I done or wrought
what moued thee o Iudge most Iust
                    said
what haue I dóńé or thought   40

what didst thou see in me o god
O god what Didst thou see
what moued thee o Iudge most Iust
to take such ruth on mee

Come Angels come Arke Angels eke   45
come soules And saints Diuine
come martyres And confessors both
your Ayde to me Assigne

Lend me yor helpe, yor Comfort giue
O tell me how I may   50
requite my lord that lou'd me soe
that Am but earth And clay

All worldly honor now farwell,

All couetousnesse A Due
pryd And uaine glory pack yoᵂ hence   55
to long I haue serued you²

In yoᵂ I had thought my Ioyes had beene
but I Deceiued was,

                    but

[fol. 39r] but now broad wakinge I do see
that he hangs on the crosse   60

Upon the crosse betwene two theeues
stark naked Alas he hangs
for me uild wretch of endlesse woes
he suffered these grieuous paines

O that it were once granted mee   65
to kisse those wounds so wide
or that it might be my good happ
to harbour in his syde³

Or that I might with magdalen
Imbrace his blessed feete   70
or with the good theefe hang by him
A thinge for me most meete

---

² In A:

    All wicked welth adous
    Pryde and uaine glorie packe you hence
    too longe I serued you

³ In A:

    O that it once were my good chance
    to kisse those woundes soe wyde
    O that my hart had once the happe
    to harbour in his syde

Then durst I then be bold to say
that neither rope nor Cord
nor Any torment of the Diuell   75
should Draw me from my lord

The knyght marshall wth all his craft
should neuer make me moue
neither turke nor tyrant nor ye diuell
should draw me from my loue⁴   80

Grant Blessed God, grant sauiour sweet
grant Iesu king of Blisse
that in thy loue we liue And Dye
sweet Iesu grant us this
                   Amen,

---

⁴ In A:

Then would I bouldlie dare to say
that neither racke nor coard
Nor any torments in the world
Do barre me from my lord

Then machavell with all his sleights
should not once make me mone
Noe Turke, nor Tyrany, noe nor Divell
should make me leave my lord.

[30]¹

[fol. 39v]   When Abraham was An old man
             And sarah wax'd In yeares
             two Angels there Approched
             And to them did Appeare
             And when he did behold them   5
             he runne In all the hast
             Desiringe them to tarry
             his meate And drinke to tast

             Att whose request they granted
             And then full glad was hee   10
             Desiringe them to tarry
             A little under A tree
             And he would bringe Incontinent
             A morcell of good meate
             for to refresh their hunger   15
             yf they would please to eate

             Then went he unto sarah
             who in the tent did stay
             Desiringe her to bake him
             some cakes without Delay   20
             then gaue he to his seruant
             A tender calfe to kill
             who made it ready quickly
             According to his will

             Then tooke he milke And butter   25
             And eke that calfe so good
             And carried it to the Angels
             In place whereas they stood
                                         And

---

¹ In Gertrude Aston Thimelby's hand. Also found in B (35–38), in the same hand.
In B, the last two lines of each stanza are indented. Variations are given in the Appendix.
    For the story of Abraham, Sarah, and Isaac, see Genesis 18:1–16, 21, and 22. The
poem omits the story of Sodom and Gomorrah.

[fol. 40r] And he himselfe In Company
         most Ioyfull was to see   30
         that they did eate so sweetly
         under A goodly tree

         The Angels Asked Abraham
         where sarah Did Abyde
         who Answered And sayde   35
         In the tent A little beside
         then spake these heauenly Angels
         within the time of life
         A child shall be conceiued
         by sarah thy owne wife   40

         Then sarah standinge hereinge this
         within the tent behind
         to here these words pronounced
         Did laugh all in her mind
         And to her selfe she sayd   45
         my lord And I Am old
         how should I then beare Childeren
         when nature waxeth cold

         Then spake those heauenly Angels
         wherefore doth sarah smile   50
         is not oʳ lord sufficient
         mans reason to beguile
         looke what we haue pronounced
         shall certainly be Done
         And at the time Appointed   55
         shall sarah haue A sonne
                             Then

[fol. 40v] Then sarah beinge fearefull
         Did Answer presently
         And to excuse her folly
         the Deede she did Deny   60
         then spake these Angels sadly
         the certaine trueth to show

sayinge thou laughedst sarah
And therfore say not noe

when that the time drew neere   65
And was expired cleane
our lord remembred sarah
And she with child was seene
A sonne o^r lord he sent her
which made them glad And faine   70
wch Abraham his father Deare
Did Isaack call by name

And when eight dayes was ended
the child was Circumcised
Accordinge to the ordinance   75
which God himselfe Deuised
when that o^r lord on Abraham
this Blessinge Did bestow
And hundred yeares of Age he was
As holy scripture showes   80

This child did Daylie prosper
And grew In stature great
And Abraham And sarah
Did greatly Ioy thereat
                                        but

[fol. 41r]   but when this Child was weaned   85
his father then Did make
A great And sumptuous banquet
for his sonne Isaack sake

They loued Isaack Dearely
And therfore sarah shee   90
could not Abide in Any wise
misused he should bee
with that shee wisht her husband
all quarell for to shunne
to put Away Incontenent   95

the band maide[2] And her sonne

Which thinge was uery grieuous
In good old Abrahams sight
for in his yong sonne Ishmaell
he tooke A great Delight   100
but God spake unto Abraham
And bade him to Agree
for in his yong sonne Isaack
all men should blessed bee

Then early in the morninge   105
good Abraham Did not stay
but put Away the handmaide
And her yong sonne Away
Away they went together
In sorrow And Destresse   110
And up & down they wandered, w^t^hin ye wilde^r^nes
                                              w^t^hin

[fol. 41v]   Within A short time After
              Our lord from heauen soe high
              sent Abraham strict commandēmet   115
              his faithfull hart to try
              sayinge take thy yong sonne Isaack
              whome thou soe dearly lou'st
              And make of him A sacrifice
              unto our lord Aboue   120

              Then good old Abraham hearing this
              he did no longer stay
              but to the place Appointed
              he tooke the ready way
              when that he did come neere it   125
              he bid his seruants stay

---

[2] I.e., bondmaid (Hagar); hand maide, in B.

while he And his sonnne Isaack
went further for to pray

And then tooke he the fagott
that should this offeringe burne   130
And layd it upon Isaack
his yong And Dearest sonne
And he himselfe did carry
the fier And the knife
And soe they went together   135
without all further strife

The child said to his father
A long As they Did goe

                      O here

[fol. 42r] O here is fier father
And here is wood Alsoe   140
but yet my louing father
I pray you shew to mee
where is the lambe y^t by And by
must sacrificed bee

my owne Deare sonne sayd Abraham   145
set all thy care A syde
A lambe for this burnt offeringe
Our lord will sure prouide
And soe they went together
unto the place they come   150
And then he tooke his wood knife
And would haue slaine his sonne

with that bespake An Angell
from heauen there soe high
sayinge hold thy weapon Abraham   155
for Isaack must not Dye
And then our lord prepared
A ram when this was Done
for Abraham to sacrifice

In sted of his Deare sonne   160
  thankes be to god
    Amen,

[31]¹

[fol. 42v] A certaine king married A sonne
             And he prepar'd A feast
             At his cōmand All things were done
             And he bade ~~made~~ many A guest
             he sent for those whome he had bade   5
             And they therof were nothing glad
             but they the messenger did deny
             from highest unto the lowest
             they did refuse And would not come
             unto the marriage of his sonne   10
             but marke you what the king hath done
             As saint matthew Doth expresse

             And like A lord most louingly
             he sent for them Againe
             And like A king most royally   15
             he would them entertaine
             to eate with me it is my will
             now let my weding feast be fild
             my calues and fatlings they Are kild
             And All things ready Drest   20
             goe bid them come And not refuse
             my banquet is to heauenely newes
             which first was offered to the Iewes
             yet they did it Deny

             They went Away And made light of it   25
             As many doe now A Dayes
             some went About their marchandize
             some to their farmes likewise
             such excuses then As there was rife
             As each man hath now in this life   30
                                              And

---

¹ In Gertrude Aston Thimelby's hand; also copied in B, pp. 38–39, in the same hand.
See the Appendix for variations. For the parable, see Matthew 22:1–14.

[fol. 43r]   And he that had married A wife
             he sayd he could not come
             some of them did fume And fret
             And some his seruants did Euill entreat
             some they kild, And some they beate   35
             thus working their owne woe
                       that
             When ʌ the king he hard of this

             he was not well content
             All in his fury waxing wrath
             to see how they were bent   40
             he called for his men of warre
             for to destroy those murtherers
             wᶜh to his feast were hinderors
             when he for them had sent
             He bid his warriors them Destroy   45
             looke in the text it Doth not lye
             but also that their faire Cittie
             with fire it should be brent

             This feast it was prepared
             And all things readye drest   50
             not one for it that cared
             that there would be A guest
                       he
             behold quoth, who bidden were
             they Are not worthy to come heere
             therefore goe forth now Euery where   55
             As I shall you entreat
             goe bid Accordinge to my mind
             in euery place where yoʷ shall find
             the poore yᵉ lame yᵉ deafe, the blinde
             to furnish up my feast   60
                                                  This

[fol. 43v]   This feast it was full furnished
             with many A guest I wis
             the king came in As he thought fitt

And uew'd out euery messe
And finding there Amongst them one   65
haueing not on his wedding gowne
And unto him he sayd Anon
my friend how happeneth this
how durst thou here for to presume
here at my table to sitt Downe   70
haueing not on A wedding gowne
As now the order is

This man he was speechles and dumbe
And could he Answer to nothinge
because he did there to presume   75
to banquet with the king
hauinge not on his garment fitt
where at the table he did sitt
therefore example take by it
And marke well this weddinge   80
he called for his men in hast
he bid them take And bind him fast
And into utter darknes cast
In paine without endinge
Now let us all make garments newe   85
Against that weddinge Day
that we may sitt with christ Iesu
In garments that be gay
he hath bid us soe willingly
so curteous And so louingly   90
                                        That

[fol. 44r]   That we his messenger cannot deny
nor eke this feast refuse
for many Called Are indeede
but few Are Chosen As wee reade
therfore thereto lets make good speede   95
And make noe long Delay
                      finis[2]

---

[2] In B replaced by "God grant us y^r grace Amen."

[32]¹

[fol. 44r] My wretched soule with sinne opprest
        to thee o lord Doth Cry for ease
        uouchsafe o christ to giue me rest
        wᶜh may my mournfull plaints Appease
        strech forth therfore thy mighty hand   5
        And ease me of my Cruell bands

        Thy mercye lord which boundlesse is
        made thee leaue heauen And man to bee
        to bringe All Adams seede to Blisse
        wᶜh hell Did chalenge for his fee   10
        now sith that I Am one of those
        let not my soule thy mercy lose

        Thy death /o christ/ thou didest take
        Although it were ere I was borne
        I know twas partly for my sake   15
        my sinne in part did make thee torne
        grant mercy lord And take to thee
        that wᶜh thy Death Did ransome free
                           yf

[fol. 44v] yf Iustice, it, /o lord/ require
        that I should suffer for my fault   20
        then whip me lord And scourge me heere
        that hell hereafter chalenge nought
        but when my body needs must Dye
        my soule may liue eternally

        Pricke /lord/ my head wᵗh thornes of care 25
        And let my eyes sheed bloudy teares

---

¹ In Gertrude Aston Thimelby's hand. At least two versions of this poem exist, beyond the copy in HM904, both in Gertrude's hand in B. One version (designated B¹)
appears before the manuscript's main text, in what the copyist seems to regard as the pre-
face to the volume; the other (designated B²) begins on fol. 42. Variations among the
three are given in the Appendix.

let slanderous buffits beate mine eares
my face let tyrants scrat[2] And teare
And let me suffer All for thee
who shed thy precious bloud for mee   30

Let speare of pennance pierce my heart[3]
let nayles of labour rent my hands
whipp me with famine till I smart
let prison wrap my feete And hands
After these paines I thee Desire   35
that heauen may be thy finall hire

yf therfore /lord/ thou me refuse
because I Daily sinne And fall
let frailty /lord/ some faults excuse
And let thy promise cut of[4] All   40
that is when sinners truly repent
thy minde to mercy streight is bent

The scripture sayes thy mercyes greate
more greater then all thy works be side
when my misdeeds will weigh Amisse   45
yf w'h my good they should be tryde
                                        let

[fol. 45r]   let mercy /lord/ thy weights unite
when my good Deeds will be to light

The theefe that hanged on the crosse
by humble suite did grace obtaine   50
And peter whome had thee Denyde
by repentance came to grace Againe
my sinnes sweete /lord/ do greeue me sore
turne not thy face from me therfore

---

[2] Variant of "scratch." Spelled *scrat* also in B¹ and B²; B¹ reverses lines 27 and 28.
[3] This stanza is omitted in B¹.
[4] I.e., off. *Of* in both versions of B.

Although my sinnes Are soe Increast   55
that I may neuer reckon All
yet still to craue I will not cease
till thou giu'st pardon for them all
And then I hope to get through grace
In heauen to haue A Dwelling place   60
               Good god Amen,

[33]¹

[fol. 45r]   O christ that Art the highest
              And sits In heauen Aboue
              upon thy downecast seruant spread
              the figure of thy loue
              I doe confesse my folly   5
              Deserues eternall paine
              O saue me And releeue mee
              I faine would liue, to die to die
              and Die to liue Againe

              ~~My will my hart is prone to uice~~
              ~~corruption keepes the sinfull keye~~²
                                          ~~And~~ my

[fol. 45v]   My will my hart Doth kill   10
              my flesh is prone to uice
              corruption keepes the sinfull key
              And Doth my hart entice
              it makes me headlong runne
              my soule it hath halfe slaine   15
              befreend me comfort send mee
              I faine would liue to die to die
              And Die to liue Againe

              My minde was much Inclin'd
              to lewde And guilefull Deallinge   20
              hath now A true to chast we tast
              And comfortable feellinge
              from saule to paul Ile turne
              Ile mourne no more with cayne
              to uex me And preplex mee   25

---

¹ This poem also is copied in B (13–14) in Gertrude Aston Thimelby's hand. Variations are in the Appendix.

² The verse appears in B without the crossed-through lines.

I faine would liue to die to die
And Die to liue Againe

Now I haue Clearst Espide
my faults Deseru'd full well
the difference twext good And bad   30
the ods twext heauen And hell
the one is full of Blisse
the other of greater paine
heauens chewes mee, hell refuse me
I faine would liue to die to die   35
And Die to liue Againe
                                             The

                         place
[fol. 46r]   The ∧ to end my race
             I chewese fayre syon hill
             Against that gate wrought sinners death
             can meditate none Ill   40
             the true Eternall rest
             be Euer my soules gaine
             I craue it I would haue it
             I faine would liue to die to die
             And Die to liue Againe³   45

             Not I for my selfe Cry
             but for our noble king
             oʳ king & queene & royall buds
             that from oʳ garden springe
             the nobles of the land   50
             that wickednesse Disdaine
             God gard them And reward them
             that faine would liue to die to die
             And Die to liue Againe
                         finis

---

³ In B, "finis" follows, and the poem ends; between 1649 and 1660 when this poem
was probably copied into B, England was not being ruled by a king.

[34]¹

1

[fol. 46v]   whilst here eclipsed From those hapy beames
              I liue by dreames
      Absence the certaine bane of cõmon loue
              Apt to remoue
      Oft traytor-like inuades with Fayre pretence   5
              my partiall sence
      To leaue this seruitude in which I sterue
      And here take present pay before I serue
              2
      To sensuallists this stroung temptation proues
              Butt wher fath loues   10
      It liues and Feeds upon the inward sight
              Refin'd delight
      By which I uiew my heart thy forme my flame
              euer the same
      Though shades of absence reach my Earth, those lights   15
      Doe neuer know corruption nor nights
              3
      By which when I compare their faces here
              To thy Forme there
[fol. 47r]   And waigh the sacraledge I shuld cõmitt
              Defacing itt   20
      As soone to sell my knowledge dearly bought
              I may be wrought
      As This False Fruite can me againe intise
      To loose my inosence and paradice.

---

¹ In Constance Aston Fowler's hand; followed by Fowler's cipher, designating this as one of Herbert Aston's poems.

[35]¹

The Complemement

[fol. 47r]   Cupid did crye his mother chidd him so
              And all, because the child had lost his bow
              But how? with no Intente that she should haue it
              Hee mett my M^rs and to her hee gaue it
              Excusing it: one was soe like the other   5
              That hee mistooke and tooke her for his mother:

[fol. 47v]   Blank

---

¹ This poem, in Constance Fowler's hand, has been attributed to William Habington, but his modern editor Allott does not print it, even as a doubtful poem.

[36]¹

[fol. 48r]   I striue to loue with out reward in vaine
                          for loue is gayne
             Fayne would I suffer But my soule's disease
                          It selfe doth please
             And my loue soares so emminent a height   5
             That I am scrupulous of this delight

             I couet death but in this bold desire
                          Loue doth inspire
             New reasons that perswade me death is vice
                          And cowardize   10
             To dare to liue is louers boldest height
             so that I fly from death as from delight

             But if I liue my torments I discreddit
                          which plead some merrit
             If die my soule must from this Heau'n remoue   15
                          And change her loue
[fol. 48v]   so that nor life nor death my soule can please
             For death's inconstancy and life seemes ease

             This new found mischiefe intricate distress
                          strangely possesse   20
             A soule that's trulie touch't: it doth repriue²
                          Makes me suruiue
             A paine that's infinite; yet t'can't suffice
             Although I fall a dayly sacrifice.

---

¹ In Constance Fowler's hand; the end cipher designates it as one of Herbert Aston's
compositions.
² Variant of *reprieve* (*OED*).

[37]¹

[fol. 48v] Eyes gaze no more; as yet you may
            in time forbeare, but if you stay
            And linger on, although I would
            you will forgett to bee contrould,
            And lett in such hott glowinge beam's   5
            As quench you cannot with your stream's
            Though you would weepe as many teares
            As I haue known both hopes and feares:

            But since mine eyes will not obay
            Hast gentle uerse in to her way   ʼ   10
            yeat see my name thou not unfold
            But bidd, when she shall next behold
            A face that's pale and wann as death
            wher many a broken sleepe and sigh
            Is well exprest; she notice take   15
            That all that sorrow's for her sake.

            ----

[38]¹

on the Death of the Duke
of Bucchingham

[fol. 49r] Death come thy selfe and let thy Image sleepe
Her quiet face and comick² action keepe
Nor with strain'd lookes and gestures night by night
Thy trajedyes ere thou canst act recite:³
Let us not blindefold search the booke of fate   5
And sleeping our misfortunes antidate
Grow'st thou so feeble men must now ly still
And thou strike twice before thy dart can kill
must shadowes and dumb showes in ambush lye
To wound the spirrit ere the body dye   10
Then men most wretched and of men muchmorᵉ
Then all the rest, the depriued poore
ours was the night though rich men gott the day
And must sweet sleepe our bedfellow betray
our secret store and all times isue see   15
our mortall foes and leaue no minuet free
the morning dreames and midnight uisions plye
A soule prepar'd for any trajedy.
[fol. 49v] something mee thought did some thing to my eyes
That made mee sleeping see the destinyes   20
sett in an Amphitheater design'd
By no mans hands, nor by a wall confin'de
But free and open as the æthereall skye
Bounded alone by the beholders eye⁴

---

¹ In Constance Aston Fowler's hand; La Belle tentatively attributes this poem to
Aurelian Townshend because it ends with "Mr A T" (HAM 553), but Cedric Brown
does not include the poem in his 1983 edition of Townshend.
Significant bleed-through of the ink on ff. 49 and 49v makes the first 37 lines of this
poem difficult to read.
² The comic action of sleep is opposed to the tragic action of death.
³ What looks like an ampersand is bleed-through.
⁴ The poet may be alluding to the anecdote (as related in Bulfinch's Mythology) that
when the poet Aeschylus presented the Furies in a performance, many spectators were
overcome by their terrifying appearance and fainted. The theater described in this poem

Clowdes were[5] their cloathing here and there made fast   25
with a small starr that sullen beames forth cast
The plannetts lent their aery actors light
And for ther sceanes they borrowd blackes of night
A shewer of threads each to a spindle ty'd[6]
Like a small rayne fell thicke on ery side   30
which neuer left twisting and turning round
Till most made clewes[7] as they aproacht the ground
Some, broke before some att the uery touch
Some scarce halfe full some that were fil'd to much
All that lay still and soe forbore to spin   35
our mother earth strayt gap't and tooke them in
Amoung the rest one[8] lookt so cleare so bright
[fol. 50r]   As round aboute it cast a liberall light
on whose out side no æquall eye could looke
But euery turne and eu'ry motion tooke   40
Soe gentle too as toucht one would haue thought
The silkworme onely on that web had wrought
And yet soe firme as felt one might bee bould
Rather then thread to say t'was wire of gold[9]
Nice virgins fear'd t'was part of that same shewer   45
That onrebuickd[10] once pierct a golden tower
Mirsers[11] beleeu'd theire mammon did descend

---

is the prototypical Greek amphitheater, although in ancient Greece plays were performed
during the day.

    [5] I.e., *wear*.

    [6] The poet elaborates on the classical notion of human life as a thread, spun out and
then cut by Atropos, one of the three Fates (see line 67). In line 34, "full" and "fil'd"
refer to the spindles: some lives are destined to end prematurely; others go on longer than
expected. Those threads that refuse to "spin" (line 35) (with a punning reference to the
lilies of the field, which neither toil nor spin, and to the twisting and turning that these
threads make as they fall from their spindles) represent those unremarkable lives that are
merely consumed in their graves by the earth.

    [7] That is, they twisted into balls.

    [8] I.e., Buckingham's thread.

    [9] The poet continues to play with the concept of spinning threads, in this instance to
make cloth. In Buckingham's case, the spun cloth may feel like silk but is as firm as spun
gold.

    [10] Unrebuked. The allusion is to Jupiter and Danaë.

    [11] Misers.

And chimists welcom'd their long lookt for frind
Trauellers thought the fam'd fleece scarce so fayre
And louers tooke it for their mistrisse hayre   50
Poets would wright upon no other Theame
Supposing it a flexible Sun beame
Not what, but whose ambitious now to know
The Fates that seldome such a secrett show
[fol. 50v]   open their bookes and in their lists of names   55
That louely thread I found was Buckingams
Million of harts and myriads of eyes
Lighting upon it couerd it like flyes
Till one¹² a sodayne one could hardly tell
why ore wherefore thousands dropt of and fell   60
Transform'd to snakes biting wher once they kist
Aloft they bus'd, but now beloy¹³ they hist
Rays'd by this spell out of the stygian lake
Swifter then thought a fourth fell fury¹⁴ brake

---

¹² On.
¹³ Below.
¹⁴ The three Furies punished unavenged crimes; however, since the poet is sympathetic to Buckingham, he is probably using Furies loosely to signify destroyers of human life. Also, the poet tends to conflate the Furies and the Fates (see line 24, note).
The fourth fury is John Felton (with *fell* punning on his name), who stabbed Buckingham in 1628. Henry Wotton describes the assassination:

There was a younger Brother of mean fortunes, born in the County of Suffolk, by name John Felton, by nature of a deep melancholy, silent and gloomy constitution, but bred in the active way of Souldier: and thereby raised to the place of Lieutenant, to a Foot-Company, in the Regiment of Sir James Ramsey. This was the man that closely within himself had conceived the Dukes death.
. . . . he made shift, partly, as it is said, on Horse back, and partly on foot, to get to Portsmouth; for he was indigent and low in money, which perhaps might have a little edged his desperation. At Portsmouth on Saturday, being the 23. of August of that current year, he pressed without any suspicion in such a time of so many pretenders to Imployment, into an inward Chamber, where the Duk was at breakfast (the last of his repasts in this world) accompanied with men of quality and action, with Monseur de Soubes, and Sir Thomas Fryer. And there a little before the Dukes rising from the Table, he went and stood expecting till he should pass through a kind of Lobby between that Room and the next, where divers attending him. Towards which passage, as I conceive, somewhat darker then the Chamber which he voided, while the Duke came with Sir Thomas Fryer close at his ear, in the very moment as the said Knight withdrew himself from the Duke, this Assasinate gave him with a back blow a deep wound into his left

Arm'd with a blade that in a trice dispatcht   65
That web the world must longing leaue unmatcht
Atropos scorning her prefix't decrees
Should stoupe to human mutabilityes
Snatch't up her sheeres intending in a rage
For that one stroake to leaue an empty stage[15]   70
Cinthia drew back; and mercury let fall
His charming rod as of no use at all
Venus afresh bewayld Adonis slaine
As twice a liue and now new dead againe
[fol. 51r] The sun rose slowly and made hast to bedd   75
And fiery mars neuer apear'd so redd
Tost[16] lightning flasht out of the thunderers eye
And saturne walkt like a sad mourner bye
Nature cry'd out and up sterne justice stept
Ceres lay doune Heauen and the graces wept   80
An uniuersall compound shrieke and shoute
As if the worlds great soule were new breath'd out
Startle'd my senses then a sodayne ill
Apear'd as dismall as the sound was shrill
With sad presages frighted from my bed   85

---

side, leaving the knife in his body. Which the Duke himself pulling out, on a
sudden effusion of spirits, he sunk down under the Table in the next Room, and
immediately expired. ("Reliquiæ Wottonianæ," 1651; 3rd ed., 1672, 231–33)

Roger Lockyer cites a note Felton was discovered to have written, which was found
stitched into his hat, that read:

"that man is cowardly, base, and deserveth not the name of a gentleman or sol-
dier, that is not willing to sacrifice his life for the honour of his God, his King
and his country. Let no man commend me for doing of it, but rather discom-
mend themselves as the cause of it. For if God had not taken away our hearts for
our sins, he [Buckingham] would not have gone so long unpunished." (*Buckingham*, 458–59)

Felton was executed on 29 November 1628. Although Charles I was extremely dis-
tressed at the death of Buckingham, his good friend, most of the English were delighted.
See Fairholt (*Poems and Songs*, xxx–xxxi) for a discussion of the satirical and derisive
poems written about Buckingham after his death.
    [15] Enraged at Felton's deed, Atropos, who cuts the thread of life, threatens to end the
lives of everyone.
    [16] Troubled.

A rumour rays'd confusd of Duke and dead
Looking and lisoning I walkt on perplext
Till I had heard such comments on that text
As made me wish Deucalions[17] race of men
Rays'd out of stones newly reuiu'd againe   90
ore thoese men monsters which though armed sprung
From dragons teeth wanted a killing toungue[18]
Some wer to that excesse of bounty growne
They freely gaue him faults that were their owne
[fol. 51v]   And some to shame him with such slips began   95
As to haue mist hee had bin more then man
Some were so æquall to his actions still
They would condemme whether good or ill
And some were so with uigilance possest
when hee was dead they would not let him rest   100
But did (like Anthropophagi) entreate
His uery corps as if they kill'd to eate
Amoung these weeds some eares of corne were found
That hung their heads after his fell to ground
some Flowers soe full of Heauenly dew they bent   105
Vnder their load though they retayn'd their sent
some tempers taken from the truest steele
That still the touch of the lou'd loadstone feele
But that faire mirrour[19] in whose spotlesse breast

---

[17] Son of Prometheus. He and his wife Pyrrha survived a great flood sent by Zeus and produced all mankind by throwing stones, their Mother's bones, over their shoulders.

[18] Cadmus, searching for his sister Europa, killed a dragon who had devoured his companions. From the dragon's teeth tossed onto a plain, arose armed men, who turned against each other. All but five were killed.

[19] Katherine Manners, daughter of Francis Manners, sixth earl of Rutland, married George Villiers in 1620. According to Roger Lockyer, religion complicated the Buckingham-Manners marriage negotiations:

Katherine was, like her father, a Roman Catholic, and would not abandon her faith even for the most handsome man in England. This might not have deterred Buckingham, for he was tolerant in matters of religion, and his mother was on the verge of becoming a catholic [sic] herself. But James, as head of the protestant [sic] Church of England, would never consent to an alliance between his favourite and a papist. Either Katherine must renounce her faith, or she must give up all hope of marrying Buckingham. (*Buckingham*, 58–59)

Hee left an Image of himselfe impreast   110
To whome all trees that in the garden grow
sett by that cædar are meere shrubbs in show
All corne but chaff all flowers in garden sett
smelt but like crowfoote[20] to that Violet
[fol. 52r] What hands held up what folded armes a crosse   115
What sighes breathes she after her Deare lords losse
Mee thinkes I see her like an Alpe of snow
Melt till her teares in to a torrent grow
Then by degrees the calme resemblance take
Not of a riuer but a standing lake   120
Which if no frindly Diety bee bent
To turne in to a christall monument
Like Arethusa[21] she will slyly run
To worlds unknowne and meete the new sett sun
Ore the mayne sea striue with her teares to swell   125
Like sad cornelia[22] when her pompey fell.
I like poore codrus[23] that can onely picke
Vp here a stone and ther a litle sticke
To build an Alter and to make a blaze
That a rude winde may soone put out ore rayse   130
wish him a pile that sett on fire may light
His darkend fame thorough detractions night
And obeliske that might his urne conuay

She eventually chose the former course, at least nominally. Buckingham's marriage no doubt intensified his sympathy towards English Catholics like the Astons.

[20] A member of the buttercup family, characterized by lobed leaves resembling a crow's foot or any plant resembling a crow's foot, the wild hyacinth, for example, which, according to *Gerard's Herball* (1597), "hath long narrow leaves leaning towards the ground, among the which spring up naked or bare stalks loden with many hollow blew floures, of a strong sweet smell somewhat stuffing the head" (Woodward, *Gerard's Herball*, 54–55).

[21] Arethusa was turned into a river to escape a would-be lover.

[22] Plutarch describes Pompey's wife Cornelia as being quite distraught when Pompey was reduced to one ship from his former five hundred (trans. North, *Lives*, 4:286).

[23] King of Athens. Before attacking Athens, the Peloponnesians consulted the Delphic Oracle to determine their success and were told that they would take the city as long as they did not kill the Athenian king. Upon learning this, Codrus dressed as a beggar and began gathering sticks outside Athens. When two enemy soldiers approached, he provoked them, killed one, and was himself killed by the other, thus saving Athens.

shining in gold up to the gods halfe way
And when his tombe shall like a Trophy rise   135
glorious enough to putt out enuyes eyes
such Epitaphs and Elegies as sung
By a sweet muse may silence slanders toungue

M^r

A T

[39]¹

[fol. 52v]   To weepe were poore, thy most unhappy fate
             is far more great then teares cann expiate
             such short expressions of a sorrowed mind
             In watry eyes wee see are oft confind
             when Th'heart's oppression ouer layd with care   5
             Dissolus all sorrow in a Cristall teare
             The limitts of which grife so farr extends
             That when the eyes are drye the sorrow ends
             Must then so poore a memory Interr
             And lay thy sighs and tears Intomb'd with her   10
             No let thy resolution still be this
             neuer to entertaine a thought of Blisse
             In earths contentment more since she is gone
             In whome consisted all thy Ioys alone.

[fol. 53r–fol. 135v]   Blank

---

¹ In Constance Fowler's hand.

[40]^1

of uncontancy

[fol. 136r]   Why did you fayne both sight's^2 and teares to gayne
              My hart frome mee and afteward disdayne
              To thinke upon those oth's you did protest
                                              in
              As if men soules were to be pauned Iest.
              I could not thinke soe liuely any art   5
              Could frame a passon so far frome the hart.
              Did not your hart know what your tounge did say
              or did ~~your~~ they both agree for to betray
              poore wemen that beleeue, that fathlesse you
              speake what you thinke, because themselues are true   10
              when you like to an echo doe I feare
              Repeate the wordes which you from others heare
              And neare^3 speake that which from your hart proceedes
              Like noble mindes whose wordes fall shorte there deedes
              But lett theese lines this fauore frome you gaine   15
              ether to loue or not att all to fayne
[fol. 136v]   This is but that which honer tyes you tow
              Tis for your owne sake I would haue you true
              For if your worth, you ownce with fallshood staine
              When you speake truth all will beleeue you fayne   20
                        The L: D: S:

---

^{1} Probably by Lady Dorothy Shirley, given that the phrase "The L. D. S." ends the poem as it appears in HM904. The poem is recorded in Constance Fowler's hand. New-digate printed this poem in 1942, as part of his study of the relationship between Lady Dorothy Shirley, her husband William Stafford, and the poet Thomas Randolph (see Introduction, xlvi).

Newdigate says that he has silently emended punctuation; he has also added missing letters, and in one case, he changed what in the manuscript is clearly *truth* (although the final two letters are traced over several times) to *true* (l. 20).

^{2} Probably *sighs*, as Newdigate has emended it.

^{3} Never.

[41][1]

[fol. 136v] If you would know the reason why
             I hate you now once held soe deare
             Vpon the glasse but cast your eie
             And' you shalle find ~~the~~ it written there
             For as in that behoulde you may   5
             Your fayre false eyes and louely face
             But nothinge in the glasse will stay
             When you are parted frome the place
             soe when I loue did first pretend
             Methought I saw my selfe in thee   10
[fol. 137r] And the'fore chouse thee as a friend
             Which ought another selfe to be
             All uows and othes I made of loue
             Thou wouldest repeate when I had don
             And by a sweet reflection proue   15
             Though seming too wee were but one,
             But when I absent were a while
             And others came to looke in thee
             As they would laughfe so wouldest thou smile
             But no impression left of me,   20
             If Then to haue a friend wer best
             which might reflect thoughts as the pas
             my mind shall rather goe undrest
             Then mend it selfe in such a glasse

---

[1] This unattributed poem is in Constance Aston Fowler's hand. A slightly different
version appears in B.L. MS. Eg. 2725, fol. 92b.

[42]¹

An Elegie on the Lady Iane
Paulet marchionesse of winchester.

[fol. 137r]   what goodly ghost besprinckt with Aprill dew
Hales me so sollemly to younder yeugh
And beckning woes me from the fatall tree
To pluck a garland for her selfe ore mee
[fol. 137v]   I doe obay you beauty for in death   5
you seeme a faire one, o that you had breath
To giue your shade aname stay stay I feele
A horrour in me all my blood is steele
stiffe starke my joynts gainst one another knock
whose daughter, ha! great sauage of the rocke   10
Hee's good as great I am almost a stone
And ere I can aske more of her she's gone.
Alasse I am all marble wright the rest
Thou wouldst haue written fame upon my brest
It is a large fayre table and a true   15
And the disposure will be somethinge new
when I who would her poet haue become
At least might beare the inscription to her tombe
She was the Lady Iane and marchionesse
of winchester the Heraulds can tell this   20
Earle Riuers grandchild serue not titles fame
sound thou her uirtues giue her soule a name
Had I a thousand mouthes as many toungues
And uoyce to rayse them from my brazen loungues
I durst not aime at that the dotes were such   25
no motion euer could expresse how much
Theire carract was, I ore my Troumpe must breake
But rather I, should I of that part speake
[fol. 138r]   it tis to neere of kinne to god the soule

---

¹ By Ben Jonson, in Constance Fowler's hand; printed in Donaldson (*Ben Jonson*, 413) and elsewhere. Variations between HM904 and Donaldson are given in the Appendix.

To be discrib'd, fames fingers are too foule   30
To touch those misteryes wee may admire
The heate and splendour but not handle fire
What shee did here by great example well
To'inline posterity her fame may tell
And calling truth to wittnesse make it good   35
From the inherent graces xxx in her blood
Else who doth prayse a person by a new
But a fam'd way, doth spoyle it of the true
Her sweetnesse softnesse her fayre courtesy
Her warie guards her wise simplicity   40
were like a ring of uertues bout her sett
And piety the center where all mett
A reuerend state she had, an awfull eye
A dazling yet inuiting majesty
What nature, fortune, institution, fact,   45
Could heape to a perfection was her act.
How did she leaue the world with what contempt
Iust as she in it liu'd and so exempt
From all affection, when they urg'd the cure
of her disease, how did her soule assure   50
Her suffrings; áas her body had bin a way
And to the torturers her doctors say
[fol. 138v]   sticke on your cupping glasses, feare not, put
                                            or
your hottest canstickes to burne, lance, cut
Tis but a body that you can torment   55
And I in to the world all soule was sent
Then comforted her Lord and blest soone
Chear'd her fayre sisters in her course to run
with gladnesse temperd her sad parents teares
made her frinds joyes to gett aboue their feares   60
And in her last act taught the standers by
with admiration and applause to dy
Let Angells sing her gloryes who did call
Her spirrit home to her originall
That saw the way was made it and were sent   65
To carry and conduckt the complement
Twix death and life. wher her mortality

Became her birth-day to æternity
And now through circumfused lights she lookes
on natures secrets ther as her owne bookes   70
speakes Heauens language and discourseth free
To euery order euery Hyrarchie
Beholds her maker and in him doth see
what the beginning of all beautyes bee
And all beatitudes that hence doe flow   75
which the Elect of god are sure to know
goe now her happy parents and bee sadd
[fol. 139r] If you not understa^{n}d what child you had.
If you dare quarrell with Heauen and repent
T'haue paid againe a blessing was but lent   80
And trusted so as it deposited lay
At pleasure to bee cal'd for ere day,
If you can enuy your owne daughters blisse
And wish her state lesse happy then it is.
If you can cast about your either eye   85
And see all dead here ore about to dye
The starrs that are the Iewells of the night
The day deceasing with the prince of light
The sun, great Kings and mightest kingdomes fall
whole nations nay mankind the world and all   90
That euer had beginning to haue end
with what injustice can one soule pretend
To escape this common knowne necessity,
when wee were all borne wee began to dy
       braue
And but for that contention and strife   95
The christian hath to'enjoy a future life
Hee were the wretchedst of the race of men
But as hee soares att that he bruiseth then
The serpents head, getts aboue death and sinne
And sure of Heauen rides triumphing in. B I   100

[fol. 139v–fol. 143]   Blank

[43]¹

Q

[fol. 143v] Tell me (Lucinda) since my fate
And thy more powerfull forme decrees
my heart an imolation to thy shrine
where I am only to incline
How I may loue and at what rate   5
By what Dispaires and what degrees
I may my hopes enlarge and my desires confine

A

First when thy flames begin
see they burne all with in
And so as lookers on may not discry   10
smoake in a sight, or sparcles in an Eye
I would haue had my loue a good while ther
Ere thine owne heart had bin a ware
[fol. 144r] And I my selfe would choose to know it
First by thy care and cunning not to shew it   15

Q

When my loue is your owne way thus betray'd
must it be still affraid
May it not bee sharpe sighted too as well
And finde you know that which it durst not tell
And from that knowledge thinke it may   20
Tell it selfe ore a louder way

A

Let mee a lone a while
And so thou maist beguile
My heart perhaps to a consent
Long ere it be meant   25
[fol. 144v] For whilst it dares not dissaproue

---

¹ In Constance Fowler's hand. Probably written by Thomas Carey. Variations between HM904 and Saintsbury's text are given in the Appendix.

Least it betray a knowledge of thy loue
It will be so accustom'd to allow
    That I shall scearce know how
To be displeas'd when thou shalt it a uow   30

          Q
When by loues powerfull silent sympathy
        our hearts are got thus nigh
And that by one a nother seene
Ther need's no breath to go betweene;
Though, in the maine agreement of our brests   35
only our hearts subscribe us interests,
        yet it will need
our toungues siyne too as witneese to the deed

         A
[fol. 145r] speake then, but when you whisper out the tale
         of what you ayle   40
Let it be so dissorderd as I may
Guesse only thence what you would say
Then to be able to speake sence
        were an offence
And t'will thy passions tell the subtliest way   45
        Not to know what to say.

M^r T C

[44]¹

on the Departure of two
Louers in Teares:

[fol. 145r]   why should I hide my sorrow & why these feares
                to bee seene weepe: loue doth discourse in teares:
                And as the sunne moist uapours doth Exhall
                so loue doth draw up teares, and lets them fale
[fol. 145v]   sad loue Appears in gesturs, speech, and Th'Eye   5
                only Ingeinouse in symplicty.
                          Mr G B

---

¹ In Constance Fowler's hand. Mr. G. B. is unidentified.

[45]¹

on Louers Teares

[fol. 145v] canne Teares meete with affections flame
           And both continue still the same
           Canne fyer and water freindly greete
           And feele no combate when they meete
           Then Honour loue: for loue Inuents   5
           To reconsile the Elements: ~~S W P~~

---

¹ In Constance Fowler's hand and probably initialed S. W. P., for Sir William Pershall, but the initials are partly scribbled-through. See the Introduction (lxxxi) and Poem
66, note 1, for La Belle's explanation and analysis of these scribbled-through initials.

[46]¹

on black paches

so

[fol. 145v] I know your hart cannot guilty bee,
             That you shuld ware those spots, for uanity,
             or as your beautyes trophyes put on one
             For euery murder that your eyes haue done,
             No theyr your morning weedes for harts forlorn,   5
                                    you
             which though you must not loue canot scorne,
[fol. 146r] To xwhome though cruel fortune did denye,
             That Blis could onely cure theyr mesery,
             yet you to grace thy'r death, this wae haue found,²
             while this your grefe theyr martirdume hath crownd   10
             But yet take heed you proue not prodigall,
             For if to euery comon funerall,
             of your eyes marters such grace were a low'd
             your face would were no paches, but a clow'd.
             Mʳ   H T

---

¹ In Constance Fowler's hand; this poem is initialed Mʳ HT, probably for Mr. Henry
Thimelby. Hamilton Thompson (*The Works of Sir John Suckling*, 1964) does not print this
poem; however, Thomas Clayton (*The Works of Sir John Suckling*, 1971) prints it under
"Dubia" (92). Variations are given in the Appendix.
    ² "Those joyes could onely cure theyr mesery, / Yet you this noble way to grace them
found," in Clayton.

[47]¹

[fol. 146r] Mistres godmorow, tell you please to Rise
             wee are in darknes, for from your fayre Eyes
             The sunne has light, the day cannot Apeare
             Tell with your lookes, you make the Heauen's cleare

[48]¹

[fol. 146r] A louer if beloue'd, is such a state
             Hee cannot wish him selfe more fortunate,
             But if disdained, then his state is such
             He'd chainge with Hell, and thinke hee gained much

---

¹ In Constance Aston Fowler's hand.
¹ This unattributed poem is in Constance Fowler's hand.

[49]¹

D K on the Death of
his Wife

[fol. 146v]   Accept thou shrine of my dead saint
             Insteade of dirges this complaint
             And for sweete flowers to crown thy Herse
             Receue a strew of weeping uerse
             From thy greiu'd freind' whom thou maist see   5
             Quite melted in to teares for thee.
             Deere losse since thy untimely Fate
             My taske hath bene to meditate,
             on thee; on thee thou art the booke
             The library where on I looke   10
             Thought all most lost for thee loued clay
             I languist out not liue the day
             vsing no other Excersies
             Then what I practise with my eyes
             By which wett glasses I find out   15
[fol. 147r]   How lasely time creeps a bout
             To one that morns: this onely this
             My Excercies and practies is
             I doe compute the weary howrs
             with sights dissolued in to showrs   20
             Nor wonder though my time runis thus
             Backwards and most preposterouse
             Thou hast benighted mee, thy sett
             This Eue of darkenesse did beegett
             who wert my morn thought ouercast   25
             Before thou hadst the noone tide past
             And I remeber, must in tears
             Thou scarce had sene so many years
             As day tell's howrs, by thy blest sunne

---

¹ Henry King's "The Exequy," in Constance Fowler's hand. La Belle (HAM 549–50)
lists "interesting variants" from Crum's edition, pointing out that in two cases, the end
rhyme is more perfect than in Crum. These variations are given in the Appendix. Titled
"An Exequy To his Matchlesse never to be forgotten Freind," in Crum.

My loue and fortune first did runne   30
But thou wilt neuer more Appeare
Folded with in my Hemisphere
[fol. 147v] since both thy light and motion
Like a fledd starr is faln and gone
And twixt mee and my souls deere blisse   35
An Earth now interposed is
which such a strange Ecclipse doth make
As neer was read in Almanake.
I could allow thee for a time
To darken mee and my sadd clime   40
were it a month a yeare or tenne
I would thy Exile waite till then
And all this space my mirth adioxurne
so thou wouldest promise a retorne
And puttinge ofe thy ashes shrowde   45
At last disperse my sorrws clowde,
But woe is mee the longest date
Tw narrow is to calculate
such empty hopes, neuer shall I
[fol. 148r] Bee so much blest as to descrye   50
Ax glimpse of thee till that day come
That shall the world to cinders doome
And a ferice feauour shall calsine
The body of this world like thine
My lettel world: this fitt of fyer   55
once ouer ~~ouer~~ our bodyes shall Aspire
To our soule's Blisse where wee shall rise
And ueiw our selues with clearer eyes
In that calme region where no night
Can hide us from each other sight   60
Meane while thou hast her Earth, much good
May my harme doe thee, since it stoode
with Heauens will I should not call
Her longer mine, I giue thee all
My sad lou'd life and interest   65
In her, whome liueing I loued best
[fol. 148v] And freely though thou see mee weepe
I giue thee that I could not keepe

Bee kinde to her and preethee looke
Thou write with in thy doomesday booke   70
Each parcell of this rarity
That in thy caskets shrine doth lye
see that thou make thy recking straight
And yeald her back a gaine by waight
For thou must audite on thy trust   75
Each graine and atome of her dust
As thou will ansure him that lent
Not gaue thee my deere monument,
So clos'd the grownde, and bout her shade
Black curtines drawne my bride is lay'd   80
sleepe on my deere in thy col'd bedd
Neuer to bee disquieted
My last good night I will not wake
[fol. 149r] Till I thy fate shall ouer take
Till age ore greife ore sorrow must   85
Marry my body to that dust
It so much lou's, and fill the roome
My hart keeps empty in thy tooume
stay for mee there I will not faile
To meete thee in that hollow uale   90
And thinke not much on my delay
I am allready on the way
To follow thee with all the speede
Desire can bring or sorrow breede[2]
At night when I betake to rest   95
Next morne I rise neerer my west
of life: allmost by eight howrs saile
Then when sleepe brought his drowsy gale
Thus from the morne my botome steares
And my days compasse downward beares.   100
[fol. 149v] Nor wonder thought I steume the tide
By which towards thee I swftly glide
Tis true with shame and greife I yeild
Thou like the uann first tooke the feild

---

[2] "Each minute is a short degree / And e'ry Howre a stepp towards Thee," in Crum.

And gotten hast the uictory   105
By thus aduentaring to dye
Before mee, whose more years might carue[3]
A iust precedeince in the graue
Hark how my pulse like a soft drume
Beats my approch tells thee I come   110
And slow so'ere my marchys bee
I shall at last sitt downe by thee
The hope of this bids mee goe one
And waite my dissolution
with feare and comfort, deere for giue   115
The crime I am content to liue
Deuied but with halfe a hart
Till wee shall meete and neuer part. / finis

---

[3] I.e., *crave*.

[50]¹

To the Lady Mary Aston.

[fol. 150r]   Euer most Honour'd Sister tis' to you,
              Tis to your forme; tis to your uertues too
              That I wright this, from all vaine glory free,
              Full of deuotion uoy'd of flattery:
              Tis true y'are fitter for man's contemplation,   5
              Then for a weake poeticall relation;
              But were it so that ther were none did liue
              The actiue life all the contemplatiue
              vertue in thousands would obcured² lye,
              wanting expression too forgotten dye;   10
              which being reueal'd would cause first admiration
              That loue, and loue would force an imitation:
              Hee's blest contemplate's you, yet at the most
              Hee seemes to others but a kind of ghost;
              This thought hath forced me to wright, though I   15
              Enioy'd a more sublime felicity
              Still to contemplate what Ieie³ seene in you
[fol. 150v]   which is farr more perfection, and more true
              vertue, then all your Sexe enioyes, or can
              Enough be honour'd or exprest by man   20
              All that are uertous else are by reflection
              Of that pure light that shines from your perfection
              And you as liberall as the Heauen's bright eye
              Scatter your beames on all mortality
              vertue is so inærent in your blood   25
              you can not thinke a thought that is not good

---

¹ In Constance Fowler's hand. This poem ends with Fowler's emblem designating poems by her brother Herbert Aston. The addressee of the poem is no doubt Mary Weston Aston, the wife of Herbert's and Constance's oldest sibling, Walter. Mary Weston was the second daughter of Elizabeth Pincheon and Sir Richard Weston, first Earl of Portland and Lord High Treasurer of England. She married Walter Aston in 1629. Her half-sister was Frances Weston Draycott, whose death is mourned in Poem 18.

² I.e., *obscured*.

³ Probably *I've*.

oh that some long liu'd chronicle would tell
what good you practice, how much you excell
All others, that our after times might bee
Taught and instructed by your Historry,   30
All uertues now you by examble giue,
you are the uery forme by which they liue:
And times before us to perfection grew
By reading prophesyes long writt of you
As that by petrarck so deuinely writt   35
[fol. 151r] Title'd his Laura, so admired yet,
Draytons Idæa, and the loue=sick lines
of daniells delia, hee too who refines
our language sedney, whilst hee stella prayseth
Her glory, and his fame together rayseth   40
with CællcA⁴ most elegantly writt
In æmulation of braue Sedney's witt
all theese were shaddowes and meere prophesyes
of some true sun, that after should arise.⁵
Immagin then if such be sidney's starr   45
what the sune, you that by't prefigur'd are
The Heauens are beautifull, yet when the sun
Guilds our Horizon, all their gloryes dunne
The starrs their ornament uanish't, are gon,
Like weake eyes not being able to looke on   50
So glorious an obiect, but are fayne
To close their lidds till night op'e them a gayne:
So whilst you heere like to a sun a rise
All petty beautyes uanish from our eyes;
Perhapps when you shall sett, that you may rise   55
[fol. 151v] To higher gloryes greater dignityes;
Wher all the Angells haue expected longe
your coming at the which with ioy theyle thronge,
who shall imbrace you first, who in a uoyce

---

⁴ A sonnet cycle written by Fulke Greville, Lord Brooke, Sidney's friend and Elizabethan and Jacobean statesman.
⁵ Lines 43 and 44 are penned into the margin but are clearly intended to follow line
42.

Most like your owne, can sing your happy choyce;   60
The world being left in darknesse like sad night
some beautyes else will shew a glimmiring light,
A faint weake loue of uertue which yet too
They haue but by reflection of you:[6]
which sad night may I neuer liue to see,   65
I can scearce thinke how it can euer bee:
For can the sun be weary of his spheare,
Or starrs forsake that spatious Heauen, wher
They haue so long bin fixed, or else can
Princes be weary of their courts, wher man   70
Like godds on earth a dore them; had not sin
Lost man the paradice that hee was in,
[fol. 152r]   Had hee not bin by force of them bereft
Such deere delights hee neuer would haue left,
How can your soule then leaue her happy spheare   75
The blessed Heauen wherein she doth appeare
In so much glory, and that stately court
To which our eyes and then our herats[7] resort
To doe her homage, and that paradice
Full of all uertue, ignorant of uice: 80
It cannot, since your soule can neuer sin,
How should it loose the paradice 'tis in:
vnlesse your selfe weary 'oth world desire
To mend the tunes of the cælestiall quire,
wher you æternally may glorious liue   85
which your soule merrits and which heauen can giue
                                        can
And no place else, and you be deny'd

---

[6] Lines 55–64 echo John Donne's *First Anniversarie*: the dead Elizabeth Drury's

> ... Ghost doth walke; that is, a glimmering light,
> A faint weake love of vertue and of good
> Reflects from her, in them which understood
> Her worth. ... (70–73)

See my essay "John Donne and the Astons" (636) for a discussion of echoes of Donne in HM904 poetry.

[7] I.e., *hearts*.

Nothing 'you aske, and so y'are Deiffy'd.
Yet may wee long enioy you heere and liue
Blest by the blest examble that you giue   90
[fol. 152v] For nothing more then this drawes soules to heauen
vertous example that by beautyes giuen
How blest is then your family in you
How happy are those eyes that daily view
Those two life giuing lights, and heare your voyce   95
By which man knowes how Angells doe reioyce.
But stay, what extasy is this, my zeale
                my
Drawes mee beyound self doe I reueale
Dare I describe with my poore humble pen
A subiect fit for Angells, not for men.   100
All I aspire to is it may expresse
A true deuotion, which loues nothing lesse
Then flattery, in all that's written I
Beeleeue my selfe, and then I cannot lye

[51]¹

To the honourable G T

[fol. 152v] Lett not thy grones force eccho from her caue,
            ore interrupt her weeping o're that waue,
[fol. 153r] which last narcissus kist; Let no darke groue
            Be taught to whisper stories of thy loue
            what though the wind be turn'd; canst thou not saile   5
            By uertue of a cleane contrary gale,
            in to some other port; wher thou wilt find,
            it was thy better genius chang'd the wind,
            To steere thee to some iland in the west,
            For wealth and pleasure, that transcends thy east,   10
            Though Astrodoro,² like a sullen starre
            Eclipse her selfe, ith' sky of beauty are
            Ten thousand other fires, some bright as she.
            And who with milder beames, may shine on thee;
            Nor yet doth this eclipse beare a portent,   15
            That should affright the world: the firmament
            Enioyes the light it did, a sunne as cleare,
            And the young spring doth like a bride appeare
            As fairely wed to the thessalian groue
            As e're it was; though she and you not loue.   20
            And we two, who like two bright stars haue shin'd
[fol. 153v] Ith heauen of friendship, are as firmely joyn'd
            As bloud and loue first fram'd us, and to be
            Lou'd and thought worthy to be lou'd by thee
            is to be glorious. since fame cannot lend   25
            An honour equals that of talbots friend.
            Nor enuie me that my castara's flame
            yeelds me a constant warmeth: though first I came

---

¹ This poem in Constance Fowler's hand is by William Habington. (See *Poems*, ed. Allott, 81–82.) The only variations between the versions in HM904 and Allott are accidentals.

² From *aster* (star) and *doron* (gift), this was the fictional name of the woman Talbot unsuccessfully wooed (*Poems*, ed. Allott, xxvi).

To marriage happy ilands; seas to thee
will yeeld as smooth a way, and winds as free.   30
which shall conduct thee xif hope may deuine;
To this delicious port: and make loue thine.
M M W H

[52]¹

The ansure to these uerses
Made by Mʳˢ K T

[fol. 153v] sʳ since you are profest to dwell
I'th Heauen of frindship, you shuld tell
what tis to loue and ualew well

I nere conseau'd t'was to perswade
our frind to be unconstant made   5
if that a womans loue should fade

[fol. 154r] I rather thought t'was frendship part
To setle uertue in the hart
Not let it dye by womans art

if uertue place loue tis secure   10
cros fortunes it can well indure
Nothing but change it doth obiure²

But one must first loue³ who you proue
Vnconstant, she did neuer loue
If ownce she doe thers no remoue   15

But if unconstancy be held
worthy a frind unparaleld
No wonder wemen in't exceld⁴

---

¹ Written by Katherine Thimelby; copied in Constance Fowler's hand, presumably before 1638 when Katherine married Herbert Aston. Printed in Allott (*Poems*, 188).

² I.e., *abjure*.

³ Full stops after *Love* in lines 13 and 14 make sense of these three lines.

⁴ If such a valued, unparalleled friend like Talbot is not tarnished by unconstancy, then it should come as no surprise that women, the unparalleled gender, excel in it.

Nor ist more strange that you shuld say
A ladys changed since no decay   20
of uertue you thinke comes that way[5]

[fol. 154v]   No since tis to perfection brought
you may call't hers from your owne thought
though neuer in her nature wrought[6]

For this new uertue you thought best   25
To shew your frind the wealthy west[7]
As if transending what is best

But I beleue your frind will find
No better ienious torn'd the wind
The west's no treasure for a mind   30

yet if your counsell can preuale
Tis best for him else where to sayle
Although with an unconstant gaile

For where hopes canot liue tis uaine
To shew a loue to a disdaine   35
Though trewest loue admits that paine

Yet I admire ther hapy state
who can seeke for a better fate
Though I shuld neuer imetate

For if I lou'd who now am free   40
shuld he retorne no loue to me
I must loue ther eternally.   M K T

---

[5] Given that unconstancy does not rule out virtue, I can understand why you can say that a lady, in this case Talbot's friend, changed, since in doing so she retained her virtue, and we know that women are virtuous.

[6] Indeed, since you've brought unconstancy to the level of a virtue, you can say that women are unconstant, even though this is not part of their nature.

[7] West Indian gold mines, as opposed to East Indian spice mines.

[53]¹

To My Honer'd sister G A

[fol. 155r] Infuse in to me all your choycest straines,
You Heliconian sisters, wash my Braines
In Aganippes well, that stupid I,
May sing your great Queenes prayse; in uerse as high,
As strong lin'd donne; the soule óf of poetry   5
Exprest his progresse; and Anatomy:
Descend thy selfe Apolo with thy lire,
For thy deare Daphne's' sake I thee desire,
And for the loue thou bear'st her sacred tree,
The crowne of true deseruing poetry,   10
That thou deuinly may'st her praises sing,
And be her seruant though thou be our King.
But you deserue more honnour; and more loue;
Then men can pay on Eearth; or gods aboue;
which makes men pine away; the gods to greeue;   15
Because you mirit more then they can giue:
if gods fall short; what can I then expect;
[fol. 155v] These lines can mirritt nothinge but neglect;
Though nere so much I write; nere so much prayse.
Your boundlesse mirrit, t'will your glory rayse   20
As one smalle dropp the ocean, as one starr,
would make the Heaueñs' seeme brighter then the are,²
Ther's no proportion twixt you, and my pen;
were ther as many gods as ther are men;
Aánd were they all enamour'd of your face,   25
And all turn'd poets; cause you please to grace
That happy name; were the large Heauens their booke,
The starrs their pens; and had the sea forsooke.
His coulour and were inke, all would not serue

---

¹ Probably by Herbert Aston; the poem ends with his initials enclosed in Constance Fowler's cipher. In the manuscript, G A (for Gertrude Aston) was clumsily altered to G T to reflect her married name, Thimelby. Since Gertrude married between 1651 and 1654, Constance continued to modify her book twenty years after she had begun it. (See also Poem 66.)

² *Than they are* makes contextual sense.

To expresse what your perfections doe deserue,   30
Vnlesse your selfe like beningne Heauen smile
propitiwsly on us: and your owne stille
which gods doe tremble at) to us expresse
your selfe; which will be double happines
First blest in hearing your phebean lines   35
which all our Iugements and our witts refines
[fol. 156r] And by them to the happy knowlege grow
Of you; which we did quite despayre to know
By any other meanes, no subIect's fitt
For you to write of but your selfe, no witt   40
Able to comprehend you but your owne;
To write none worthy but your selfe alone:
I doe confesse that this my contemplation
Is not my owne; tis but an inspiration,
which I receaue from you; tis you that giue   45
my lines the worth they haue; by you they liue.
You are the soule of them; and of all uerse.
That witt, or goodnesse; euer did reherse,
of lesse perfection, and lesse worthynes
Then yours; the Heathens made them goddesses;³   50
Each had one uertue for the which they were
A dor'd, in you they all vnited are.
For first which most attracts mens minds your beauty
To which the gods them selues doe owe a duty
men adoration) in your Heuuenly face;   55
[fol. 156v] Your courtly carriage, and your wining⁴ grace;
Bright Cytherea would no more compare;
Then starres, to phebus, ore to Heauen the ayre:
what disputation, wonder, and what feare;
The trepidation of the starry sphære   60
Hath Caus'd moungst men, yet none hath had the witt
To reach the reason; anx true ground of it,⁵

---

³ Lines 48–50 echo Donne's "Elegie: Death":

For from lesse vertue, and lesse beautiousnesse,
    The Gentiles fram'd them Gods and Goddesses. (54–55)

⁴ I.e., *winning*.
⁵ Lines 59–62 echo John Donne's "A Valediction: forbidding mourning":

Tis only this the starrs dance in the skyes
For ioy that they are likend to your eyes:
Your Hayre resembles; but excelleth farr   65
Those beames that periwigg a bla[s]ing starre;
Vnder these fayre beames loue him selfe abides
And lyes in ambush; in each curle he hides[6]
Thousands of darts; which secretly hee throwes,
And wounds mens harts; but how thers no man knowes;   70

                              u
which hayre successiuely in crious rings
like cristall Beades upon pure christall strings
hang ore your face; and doe eclipse apart
of that bright luster; but tis with such art;
[fol. 157r]   And they themselues are so pure christaline,   75
Methinkes your face they rather doe refine,
Or as the Heauens Diaphnous and pure;
Conceale the sun so they your face obscure:
Being taken all together you doe shrine;
In human flesh; so true; and so deuine   80
A diety, methinkes that it should mooue
Vertue it selfe to be with you in loue:
And so she is, and therfore as t'was fitt
Vertue's stransform'd[7] to you, you in to it.
In you's all goodnesse; wisdome; Iugement; witt;   85
Man e're conceau'd, or pen hath euer writt;
All this when I consider; though I know
Loue is a tribute; which all men doe owe
To Beauty, to your uertue then far more;

Moving of th'earth brings harmes and feares,
Men reckon what it did and meant,
But trepidation of the spheres,
Though greater farre, is innocent. (9–12)

A. J. Smith in *John Donne: The Critical Heritage* records no pre-1660 echoes of "A Valediction: forbidding mourning." These lines in Fowler's book are thus a rare imitation and reveal a thorough knowledge of Donne's poetry on the part of Herbert Aston and probably of the whole family.

[6] Fanshawe also comments on Gertrude's curly blonde hair (61.6–15).

[7] I.e., *transformed.*

This they affect, the other they adore;   90
And that t'were in me not not to affect
You, for both these; and most in this respect,
That wee to one a nother are nigh,
wee both haue had one wombe our nursery;
[fol. 157v] Yet nether Beauty, uertue; nor the name   95
of brother; doth so much my mind inflame
To honour you; as doth that witt, and skill
By which you guide your high poetique quills
I loue you for the rest, this I admire;
in nothinge more then this doe I desire   100
To imitate you in; by this you tye
Etternall luster to our familye:
How short's Ioue borne minerua of your will,
How short are all of us in honoring it;
How blest were one to dye if on his herse,   105
As others dropp a teare, you sticke a uerse:
For nothinge you can write, But will suruiue
when the world's ashes, it will be aliue.
persue deare sister then what y'haue begun
with so much splendour; like the glorious sun   110
neuer denye us that inspiring light,
which we receau'd, with such a high delight
from your pierian straines; but still inspire,
Vs, with the heate of your poetique fire;
[fol. 158r] For as the sun by uertue of his great   115
Masculin luster and his quieckning heate;
Of slime; and Mud, produceth liuing creatures;
Diffring in nature; and of seuerall features;
Acording to the mould from which they'r made,
so your lines heate; and splendour; doth inuade   120
Our dul, dead, muddy, minds; and doth create
New Creatures; of what seem'd inanimate:
As euen these lines though creatures of my minde,
By your poetique fire they are refin'd;
From there dull mould, you on them life bestow;   125
Ther's nothinge in them from my witt doth flow:
By you they moue; all prayse to you is due
For tis not I haue written this tis you.

[54]¹

upon the L D saying K T
could be sad in her company

[fol. 158r] Madem you say I am sad I ansure noe
vnlesse it be because you say I am soe
I know some prays'd For ~~pke~~ speaking what is truee
[fol. 158v] But mores your wright whoes truth doth wate of you.²
Before you spoke I found no cause of grife   5
But in your speach you tooke all wished releife
From me your seruant place'd me in want
of meaner to shew my pouerty and scant³
For I had now atayn'd what I desire'd
And consequently happy now's require'd⁴   10
why I am sad oh worde of most hiegh powre
To torne me misserable with in the howre
For I am griued that my exteriour Ishow
shuld contradick the joy I haue From you.
For madam doe me wright I doe protest   15
Ther is no Ioy if not by me possest.
when in your conuersation I can find
Ther be all treasures to delight the mind
                     I
And I unworthy shuld this possesse
which might rewarde the worthyes,⁵ and blesse   20
Those that had uenter'éd most for your Deare sake
And I receaue this From you, and not take

---

¹ By Katherine Thimelby, in Constance Fowler's hand. The *L. D.* is Lady Dorothy Shirley, friend to Constance and daughter of Frances Walsingham, Sir Philip Sidney's widow, and Robert Devereux, second Earl of Essex. This poem was written and copied before 1638, when Katherine Thimelby married Herbert Aston.
² But more is your right to be praised because truth (i.e., that I am sad) only comes when you pronounce that that is what I am.
³ Now I am in want of or lack a lower expression to show my sadness, since my present countenance seems to indicate to you that I am sad.
⁴ Presumably, the poet's desire, which she has attained, is being in the Lady Dorothy's company; therefore, happiness is "require'd."
⁵ I.e., *worthiest*.

It as a blessing giuen to me by you
That from this time I should no sorrow know
wer I in this in doubt I would bequeth   25
my place to others weare the willow reath[6]
Therfore by these your fauors I intreate
you will beleeue my Ioy in you compleate   M K T

---

[6] A symbol of unrequited grief or the loss of a mate (*OED*).

[55]¹

The L. D. ansure

[fol. 158v]   A Deare cosen pardon me if I mistowke
I thought the face had bin the truest booke
To reade the hart in, but A face that's good
It seames by dull witts is not understood
[fol. 159r]   since curious lines that's drawne by Art and skill   5
study they may yet ignorant be still
I feare'd you sad because that smileing² grace
which oft hath Ioye'd me was not in your face
Ioy me it did, because it made me see
you please'd to tollerate this place³ and mee   10
But in this act your fauors doth not end
you doe not onely like, but doe comend
Frindship ocassions this, and you alasse
Doe uiew me threw a multipling glasse⁴
But what I can be unto you I will   15
And wish increase in me for your sake still
which by your company I hope that I
shall gaine soe much I shall you satisfye
But thinke not like a thefe I will conceale
From whome I stole, the truth I will reueale   20
And say tis you that haue inriched mee
For whoes sake I did wish to steale From thee
But this beleeue you canot fauore shew
To one more yours and will be euer soe.   The L. D. S.

[fol. 159v–fol. 182r]   Blank

---

¹ By Lady Dorothy Shirley, in Constance Fowler's hand.
² The second *i* was written as an *l* and then shortened and dotted.
³ According to Newdigate, " 'This place,' at which Katherine was on a visit to Doro-thy when the two poems were written, was doubtless either Staunton Harold [Hall] or Ragdale" ("Constant Lovers," 2:216). These are 8 miles and 14 miles east of Tixall, re-spectively. Dorothy Shirley was the widow of Sir Henry Shirley, second Baronet of Staunton Harold and Ragdale Hall, Leicester (Newdigate, "Constant Lovers," 1:204).
⁴ I.e., a magnifying glass.

[56][1]

Mrs
An elegie on his death

[fol. 182v]   with bowed thoughts lowe as this hollow cell
wher thy warme youth eternally must dwell,
with eyes out-uying this curl'd marbles sweat
My treasures proud usurping cabinet,
with the poore hart which once thou gau'st releife   5
And that poore hart fir'd with all zealous greife
I come to parley with thy sacred clay
And with thy ghost keepe mournfull holy-day:
To offer on the place thou art inshrin'd
This sight more churlish then the southerne wind,   10
whoes perfume that mount Heuuen and ther controule
The swift departur of thy winged soule.
Pale mayd, farre whiter then the milkye way
which now thou treadst or (if I all may say
white as thou liuing wert, what erring hand   15
Hath carried thee in to this silent land?
who Cropt the rose and ~~xx~~ cherry from thy face
To plant in this same dull and barrent place
where nothing like thy selfe will euer rise
Allthough I dayly water't with my eyes   20
[fol. 183r]   say thou, who didst to me of late Appeare
Brighter then tytan in our Hemispheare
What sullen chance hath thus eclipsed thee,
And throwne this earth betwixt thy^{ne} eyes and me?
Adultrous feauer, worse then tarquins brood,   25
That mixt thy lustfull heate with her chast blood
who sent who fann'd thy flame to such a height
within her ueynes that it must d'out her light
T'was not thy worke great loue thy actiue darts
Conuey not burning Agues to our harts,   30
But moue in blood warme fires whoes liuelyhood

---

[1] In Constance Fowler's hand. La Belle attributes this poem to Philip King based on the attribution in B.L. Harl. 6917 and B.L. Add. MS. 25707 (HAM 567).

By calme degrees ripen's the tender bud
Of true afection if the rule be sure
That our soules follow our bodyes temprature,
                                    soule
Then by her purest I may conclude   35
That not the least distemper durst intrude
Vpon her body, nor cracis² dare to bee;
But that there was such perfect harmoine³
In her blest fabricke as if nature had
weigh'd out the sweet materialls ere she clad   40
Her in her fleshie robe. I oft haue read

[fol. 183v] gods haue their heauenly Throne abandoned,
And feign'd mortalitie to compasse soe
our brighter shining Heauen here below
(weomen) sure loue t'was so, some higher powre   45
looking from aft his all commanding towre
First on our constant loues then on thy face,
Grewe proud to riuall mee enuyde my place.
Hee came clad all in flames and courted thee,
As once the thunderer did semele⁴   50
laying on thee her fate, to dye in place,
And bee consumed in the hott imbrace.
whilst I that once injoy'd a libertie
Kinges durst not clayme to loue and Honer thee,
And by this knewe my selfe ×aboue the strayne   55
of our best mortalls cause thou lou'dst a gayne.
Now rest of all may unto nought aspire
But these sad reliques of the former fire;
These ashes in this leaden sheet inroll'd
cold as my frozen hopes, o bitter cold!   60
pretty corruption, that my sighing cou'd
Breath life in thee, or weeping showre warme blood

---

² According to the *OED*, *crasis* means "the combination of 'humours' or qualities constituting a state of health or disease; (healthy or diseased) condition." It seems to be used here in the more general sense of disease.

³ I.e., *harmony*.

⁴ Daughter of Cadmus and mother of Dionysus; consumed in Zeus' lightning when she saw him in his full glory.

Into thy bosome, for I enuye thee
Thy crowne of blisse now thou art tane from mee.
My greife runns high and my distracted brayne   65
like the wing'd billowes of the angre mayne
when hee attempts to flye in to the Ayre
Falls in to thousand streames of moyst dispare.
Tis true thou liuing wert most gentle, calme
As louers whispers or the steame of balme: 70
yet when I thinke that all this now is dust
The fancy breakes upon me like *áń* gust
or a high-going sea, whoes fury threats
more then my reason can well brooke and beats
Her wounded ribbs, this must a wracke portend   75
[fol. 184r]   Or sure some promise to a uiolent end.
It calls mee coward and to that doth adde
Falce harted louer at least that neuer had
sparke of a turtles fire whose patience
Can brooke the world now thou art fled from hence,   80
It wrongs my breast, giues my true heart the lye,
And sayes I neuer lou'd and dare not dye.
And yet I dare, I dare an inrode make
vpon the tedious breath which now I take,
I dare out-worke times sickle, I could moue   85
My bloming youth to dust eue'n at a blowe,
which hee hath *ít* labor'd at (but not yet done,
soe many birth's of the reuiuing sune.
I haue keene steele, and a resolue'd arme,
Back't by dispare and greife to any harme.   90
But shuld I strike (Deare) thou wouldst uayle thy face
with thy white robes and blush me to a place
where nought is euer heard but chreikes and howles
of the condemned and tormented soules.
No, when mine eyes behold and view how still   95
This sprightly peece now lyes, the sight doth chill
                              a
My desprate fury, and cristian feare
Commands me quench this wild fire with a teare.
This uery touch of thy cold hand does swage
My hott designe and inreligious rage   100

But tis no manners thus to keepe thee frome
The silent quiets of eliziume.
I will butx adde a word ~~dered~~ ore tw, and then
Cast thee in to thy long dead sleepe agane.
[fol. 184v]   your fauor holy linen, happy shrowde,   105
For I must take away this snowie[5] cloud
From off thy whiter face; and wittnesse now
yee gods unto an orphan louer's uow.

                                                n

By these blind Cupids, these two sprigs of light
Now hoodwinkt in the maske of endlesse night,   110
By this well-shapen promont[6] whoes streight end
Like to a mount of Iuory doth bend
Vpon this red sea, on whose corrall shore
I had rich traficke which I neuer more
Must deale in, by thy selfe, ~~xxx~~ and if ther were   115
A worthier pledge for me, by that I'de sweare
That thou shalt not like others lye and rott
with thy fayre name, fayre as thy selfe, forgott:
But thy Idea shall informe my braynes
Like the intelligences who hould the reines   120
of all the orbes, I will not know the day
But a[7] it hath a lustre like the ray
of thy bright eye, and when the night is come
Tis like the darkenesse of thy silent Tombe.
Last I will x liue only to greife, and bee   125
Thyne epitaph unto posteritie,
That who so sees me reades, yonder shee lyes
For whom this widdow'd louer howrly dyes.
And wittnesse Heauen now I this oath haue tooke,
I kisse, and shut the alablaster booke.[8]   130

---

[5] Originally *showie*, the stem of the *h* is scratched out to form an *n*.

[6] I.e., *promontory*.

[7] The upward stroke of the *a* has a dot at the top, indicating an ill-formed *s*.

[8] The poet's metaphor seems to have gotten out of hand. Having asked his readers to treat him as a book (125–28), the poet then turns the metaphor around and closes "the alablaster book" of her body, giving her up to the grave.

[57]¹

[fol. 185r] O loue whoes powre and might could neuer be wthstood
Thou forcest me to wright come turne about robinhood²
Her tresses that were wrought most like the golden snare
My loueing hart hath cought as mosse did catch him mare³
grant pittie elce I dye loue soe my hart bewitches   5
with griefe I'd houle and crie oh how my elbow itches⁴
      flow
Teares ouer my sight with flouds of daily weepinge
That in the silent night I canot rest for sleeping
What is't I would not doe to purchase but one smile
Bid me to china goe faith ile sit still the while   10
But sence that all releife and comfort doth forsake-me
I'le kill my selfe for with griefe nay then thex diuell
take me.

---

¹ In Fowler's hand. See Crum, *First-Line Index*, O669 and *Wit and Drolery*, 32–34. Although in Constance Fowler's hand, this poem, with its abundant colloquialisms, has a different tone from the others in her commonplace book.

² See Tilley, *Proverbs*, R148; "Many speak (talk) of Robin Hood that never shot in [with] his bow."

³ Tilley, *Proverbs*, M1185; "To take one napping, as Mosse took his mare."

⁴ Tilley, *Proverbs*, E98; "My Elbow itches, I must change my bedfellow."

[58]¹

A Epitaph on ben Iohnson

[fol. 185r] | The muses fayrest light, in no darke time
             | The wonder of a lerned age, the line
             | which none can pas, the most proportion'd wit
             | To nature, the best iudge of what was fit,
             | The deepest, plainest, highest, clearest pen   5
             | The uoyce most echoed by consenting men,
             | The soule which ansur'd best to all well say'd
             | By others, and which most requitall made,
             | Tun'd to the highest key of antiant rome,
             | Retorning all her musick, with his owne,   10
             | In whome with nature, study claim'd a part,²
             | And yet who to him selfe, owe'd all his art,
             | Here lyes Ben Iohn euery age will looke
             | with sorrow here, with wonder, on his booke.   M.S.C.

---

¹ In Constance Fowler's hand; this poem has been associated with Jasper Mayne and
Sidney Godolphin. Whom the closing initials, M. S. C., represent is not clear.

² Reminiscent of Jonson's epitaph on Shakespeare:

> Yet must I not give nature all: thy art,
>   My gentle Shakespeare, must enjoy a part.
> For though the poet's matter nature be,
>   His art doth give the fashion . . . (55–58)

[59]¹

A dreame²

[fol. 185v] I saw two swans come proudly downe the streame
Of Trent, as I his siluer curles beheld,
To which the doues that drawe fayre venus Teame,
And venus selfe must beauties scepter yeild:

Ioue was not halfe so white when hee was one   5
And courted Leda in a snowie plume,
Nor euer such a taking shape put on
of all that loue compell'd him to assume.

Fayre Birds, allide to him that sett on fire
The world, why doe yee so delight in floods,   10
And kindling in a thousand hearts desire

Quench his soft moouings in your gentle³ bloods?
[fol. 186r] Ah! since so many liue in flames for you,
Leaue to bee swans; growe salamanders too.
Mʳ R F

---

¹ By Richard Fanshawe, in Constance Fowler's hand. Printed in Bawcutt (*Shorter Poems*, 77). Clifford first printed this and poem 61 in *TP* (213–15). Variations are given in the Appendix.

² "Of two most beautifull Sisters rowed on the Trent; under the allegorie of swans," probably an imitation or inaccurate version of Fanshawe's poem, appears in HM116:

> Two stately swans sayle downe yᵉ Trent I saw
> Like spotlesse Ermynes charg'd on silver feilds
> To wᶜʰ yᵉ ores wᶜʰ venus chariot drawe
> And Venus selfe, must Beauty as [a] scepter yeild
> Jove was not halfe so white wⁿ he was one
> And courted Leda, in a snowy plume
> Nor ever such a taking(?) shape putt on
> Of all wᶜʰ Love compell'd him to assume
> Faire kinne of Phaeton, who set on fire
> The world, why doe yee so delight in floods
> And bridling in a Thousands hearts desire
> Quench his soft moonings wᵗʰ your maydes
> Ah! since so many dwell in flames for bloode you
> Leave to be swans: turne salamanders too. (161)

³ The *n* in *gentle* was originally an *h*; the upper stem is crossed through.

[60]¹

A true loues knott that was giuen
As a fancy for a newyears gift.,

[fol. 186r]   make mee thy fancy and if I proue not
                        A true loues knott
            That neuer faides, then cast mee of a gaine
                        with more disdayne
            Then with loue you receau'd mee, but if I   5
                        doe neuer dy
            or slacken in my strettnees,² lett mee still
                        Inioy my fill
[fol. 186v]   Elce wher I cannot hope so sweet a rest
                        As in your breast   10
            There I'le discouer all that thinke to knitt
                        A counterfitt
            Thus then it must bee drawne by hand deuine
                        to be like mine

---

¹ In Fowler's hand. Although Constance Fowler has initialed this poem *H. T.*,
Henry Thimelby, it was probably written, as La Belle notes, by Herbert Aston (HAM
559). In verifying Herbert's poetic abilities, Clifford, in *TP*, quotes from "a half sheet of
letter-paper, in his [Herbert's] handwriting" (the original of this note has apparently been
lost):

> My Mrs havinge nothinge els to doe this winter, hath made a slight collec-
> tion of all my workes. Wherfore you must make an inquiry into all your
> papers, and if you find any of mine that beginn not as this note, you must
> send them her by the first opertunity, that is, by Cannal to us. (*TP*, xxii)

Clifford notes that "My Mrs" probably refers to Katherine Thimelby Aston, Herbert's
wife, and that " 'Cannal' is Canwell, near Lichfield, then the seat of Sir William Persall,
brother-in-law to Herbert Aston. This 'Note' was probably addressed to one of the
Thimelbyes, at Irnham; between which place, and Herbert Aston's residence, Canwell
was situated" (*TP*, xxii).
Among the thirty-seven poems that Herbert lists is "Make mee thy fancye" (*TP*, xxiii),
the first line of "A true Loves knott" in Constance's book. Clifford believed none of these
poems to be extant.
La Belle also argues convincingly on stylistic grounds that the poem is Herbert Aston's
(HAM 559).
² Straightness.

For t'were in uayne for mortalls to indeauour   15
        what last's for euer
And that's a true loues knott all other date
        s'adulterate³
Next looke it bee not made to loose, too fast
        for nether last   20
The looser ty'd at fortunes harder stroake
        doe slipp the yoake
And what are drawne together by a force
        Breake or doe worse
[fol. 187r] They only hold that in a golden meane   25
        A uoy'd extreame
Last it must haue no endes, for such a Tye
        is pollicy⁴
True loue could neuer tell how't came to passe
        But so it was   30
ore if compell'd to answeare to a why
        T'was I am I
Thus much for forme, the matters not forgott,
The hart stringes only tye a true loues knott   Mʳ
              H   T

³ Is adulterate.
⁴ I.e., *cunning*.

[61]¹

[fol. 187r]   Celia hath for a brothers absence sworne
              (Rash oath) that since her tresses cannot mourne
              In blacke, because uncutt Apollos hayre
              Darts not a greater splender² through the ayre³
              shee'l make them droope in her neglect; forgett   5
              Those rings which her white hande in order sett;
              And curiously did euery morning Curle
[fol. 187v]   Into a thousand snares the siluer⁴ purle.
              But they are disobedient to cõmand,
              And sweare they owe noe homage to her hand.   10
              That nature is their mistresse, in her name
              The priueledge that they were borne to clayme,
              scorning to haue it said the hayre gaue place
              to the perfections that all parts doe grace
              so weaue themselues in loopes; and curle now more   15
              By carelesnesse, then by her care before.
              Like a crisp't comet which the starres persue
              In throngs, and mortalls with pale horror uiew
              Threatning some great ones death: such light displayes

---

¹ By Richard Fanshawe, in Constance Fowler's hand. Printed in *Shorter Poems*, ed. Bawcutt, 77.

Except for occasional differences in accidentals, the poem as printed in *TP* (214–15) is identical to that in HM904.

This poem also appears in HM116 (163) with the title "Of one of yᵉ same sisters, having made a vow not to curle her hayre (wᶜʰ was extreame fayre) untill a brother of hers returned frõ Trauayle"; it immediately follows "Of two most beautifull Sisters rowed on the Trent; under the allegorie of swans." Variations among Bawcutt's text, HM904, and HM116 are given in the Appendix.

For the circumstances surrounding the writing of this poem, see Poem 59, note 1.

² *Splender* appears to have been first written *sleender* and then written over and crossed out to form the appropriate word.

³ Celia's hair, blonde like the sun god Apollo's, though outshining his, obviously cannot mourn in black.

⁴ In HM116 followed by:

> Wᶜʰ makes yᵉ silver base, & doth behould
> As a lesse Treasure yᵉ despised gold.

her face, or Like a saint that's crownd with rayes.   20
Lady, what bootes neglect of face or hayre?
you must use art if you would growe lesse fayre
M^r R F

[62]¹

A stranslation

[fol. 188r] somtimes by Aprill arrogantly deckt
Th'enameld mountaine shewes her curled head
And somtimes by Nou^embers rigors check'd
Appeares as naked desolate and dead
her desert bosome Iuly sets on fire   5
which Ianuiaries frosts² and snowes doe fill
But though she uary in her state and tire
In her true nature she is mountaine still
Euen so my bosome by thy changes tride
still in one state of heauenly loue remaines³   10
though sometimes sadd and somtimes satisfied
For what inports thy fauours or disdaines
Loue beinge the true essence of my brest
And but exteriur accidents the rest.   L
W A

---

¹ In Constance Fowler's hand; this poem by her father Walter Aston is probably a translation of a Spanish poem (Clifford, *TL*, 1:89). In a long letter to her brother Herbert, Constance writes:

> Sence I receved this letter from you, which I have now writ to you of, I have receaved another from you, some five days agoe, which you writ to my sister, and me together; and in it sent us most admirable verses of my lord's [i.e., their father's] translating, which are justly admired by all here. (Clifford, *TL*, 1:89)

Also printed in Kay ("Poems," 201–2). Kay's version differs from this only in incidentals.
² *fr* blotted.
³ Whole line is blotted from bleed through.

[63]¹

[fol. 188v] When by sad fate from hence I summon'd am
Call it not absence, that's tow mild a name:
Beeleeue it (derest soule)² I can not part,
For who can liue two regions from his heart;³
No, say I am dissolu'd, for as a cloud   5
By the suns uigour melted is, and strow'd
on the earth's lapp, to be exáhal'd a gaine
By the sun's beames that turn'd it in to rayne,
so absent, thinke me but a scatter'd dew
Till vertue re=exhale me that is you.⁴   10

---

¹ By Owen Felltham, in Constance Fowler's hand; printed in Pebworth and Summers as "A Farewell" (*Poems*, 18). Variations are given in the Appendix.
The closest link between the Astons and Owen Felltham seems to be that Felltham wrote a primarily complimentary poem on George Villiers, Duke of Buckingham, after Buckingham's death (see poem 38 and L-4 in *Poems*, ed. Pebworth and Summers).
² The *e* in *soule* is written over a partially obliterated *l*.
³ Followed in Pebworth and Summers by "Unlesse as stars direct our humane sense,
/ I live by your more powerful influence."
⁴ The last line of the poem as it appears in HM904 is found, with variations, in a number of manuscript editions, including Bodl. MSS. b. 1, Malone 16, Eng. poet c. 50, and Furth e. 4 and B.L. Add. MSS. 25707 and 44963 (see *Poems*, ed. Pebworth and Summers, 18n).

[64]¹

The nightingall

[fol. 188v] With such variety and dainty skill
            yond nightingale deuids her mournefull song,
            As if ten thousand others through one bill
            Did sing in parts, the story of their wrong:
[fol. 189r] yea she accuses with that life and flame   5
            Her rauisher, I thinke she would incline²
            The conscious groues to register his name
            vpon the leaues, and barke of yᵗ tall pine:
            But happy she that may her sorrow leaue,
            since hauing wings to wander though the woods,   10
            And bill to publish it shee may deceaue
            Her payne: but let him powre forth silent floods
            whom his medusa turn'd in to a stone
            That he might neither change, nor make his moane

¹ By Richard Fanshawe, in Constance Fowler's hand; a printed variation appears in *Poems*, ed. Bawcutt, 35, and variations are given in the Appendix.

The poem is Fanshawe's somewhat loose translation of Luis de Góngora's sonnet "Con differencia tal, con gracia tanta" (*Obras Poéticas*, 1:55). The subject of both sonnets is Philomela's rape by her brother-in-law Tereus and her subsequent transformation to a nightingale.

² The next six lines appear in *Poems*, ed. Bawcutt as follows:

            The conscious grove thereof to have a sence
            And print it on the leaves of that tall pine
            Yet happy she who may her pain declare
            In moving notes and wandering though the woods,
            With uncut wings, by change divert her care!
            But Let him melt away in silent floods

[65]¹

[fol. 189r]   Mʳ   The Constant Louers   R F

A
pastorall Eglogne
Laura Amintas, and Chorus

MWS   Laura   LDS

[fol. 189v] The halfe staru'd lambe warm'd in her mothers wooll
Feeles not a ioy so perfect and so full
As this my soule conceaues; now I behold
Longe sought Amintas; hether driue his fould,
A sickly flocke (alas) poore, weake and leane   5
As death or famine had there keeper beene,
And such are mine, for t'would be wondred att
By all the swaines if louers Ewes were fatt,
We know to prise our nobler thoughts, and proue
There needes no other weald,² where there's true loue   10
Lett Clownes feede thousand Ewes uppon the hills
And thousand kine, and euery one that fills
The milkmaides paile, with each a younglinge too
Though they in wooll, and creame and butter flow
They are poore churles, had they But eyes to see   15
The wealth and treasure heau'n lock'd upp in thee
[fol. 190r] yet my deare shepheard wee our flockes will ioyne
Ile goe with thee, and goe thy flockes with mine

a
Ile truell all the meades and as I passe

---

¹ Written by Thomas Randolph, in Constance Fowler's hand. Printed in Newdigate
("Constant Lovers," 1:204). Variations are given in the Appendix.

Randolph was a close friend of William Stafford and lived with Stafford and Stafford's
wife Dorothy during the last year of his life. Dorothy Stafford, formerly Lady Dorothy
Shirley, was Constance's close friend. The poem concerns the difficulties the lovers en-
countered when family and friends opposed the marriage of the Catholic Shirley and the
Protestant Stafford. See Introduction, xlv–xlvi.

² Riches or wealth.

marke where's the sweetest of the three leau'd grasse   20
Feed and increase deare lambes, that when you goe
ouer yon hills you couer 'em like snow
meane while doe thou pipe forth the forepast thrall
And sweeten sorrowes in a madrigall
While I with all the nimphes, the field ore treade   25
To cull the choicest flowers to crowne thy head
And when that faire and odorous wreath is donne
o're runne 'em all that I may put it on

                         Amintas
The sun parch'd Earth, lieke's not a new fallne shower
As I sweet Laura; shepheards saint this hower   30
All other Festwals³ growne needelesse are
[fol. 190v]   This hower a lone, will blesse our calendar
What alteration through each place there flies
since you and I shott soules through others Eyes
Day has growne upp to noone; noone has declin'd   35
To nights darke raigne; and shee againe resign'd
The moone haz wax'd and wan'd, the glorious sunne
with his bright beames through seuerall tropickes runne
springes haue bin parch'd a way with summers heate
And summers drown'd in wealthy Autummes sweate   40
                          u
winter chain'd Autumme in his gives⁴ of frost
And his redde aples now are turn'd to rost
y'on Lusty rãmme whose head's so fairely sett
with knotted hornes, was yean'd⁵ when we two mett
These sycamores scarce then begun to sprout   45
That now so lordly spred their branches out
younge phillis but a girle the to'ther day
[fol. 191r]   Is this yeare Chosen lady of the may
And Cælia then the subiect of all witts

---

³ I.e., *festivals*.
⁴ *Gyves* or *fetters* and *guise*, as in *disguise*.
⁵ I.e., just born.

unuisited now, Close at her distafe sits[6]   50
what ioy with in this speculation moues
To find a change in all thinges But our loues
Though oft the sickle filld the reapers hand
since we at mutuall gazs[7] might freely stand
To the same height still our affections Climbe   55
                                       time
Hee loues by the howerglasse that is chang'd with

                 Laura
Ō flockes secure, and our dogges wachfull bee
vnder yon mirtle it is venus tree,
sittinge uppon the primrose banke relate
what iorney thou hast taine through thy sadd fate   60
                          e
my t'eares shall paint thy spach, when thou hast donne
Ile pay thee for thy tale as sadd a one

[fol. 191v]   Amintas
When my sad Eyes lost thee, they scorn'd to keepe
Their needlesse sight and only serue to weepe
A climse[8] they had with which to sea they went   65
A horrid sea, the sea of discontent
Nor mast nor saile had I, nor could I find
A pilot but the billow and the wind
Noe sooner driuen from uiew of any land
But my poore barke unfurnish and unman'd   70
was by a tempest tost from heauen to hell
such aduerse stromes from my owne bosom swell
Att last a courteous starre there did appeare
By whose faire glitteringe beames I hop'd to steare
But as in mockage) it with drew it's light   75
And left me nothinge for my giude but night

---

[6] Caelia, that is, is unmarried.
[7] I.e., *gaze*.
[8] In context, this obscure word would seem to designate a kind of boat. Newdigate incorrectly transcribes the word as *glimse*. However, *glimpse* continues the sight metaphor.

Next mornninge was a calme the waues did fall
smooth as the pauement of a well laid hall
[fol. 192r] Syrens with Iuory combes, and cristall glasses
Courted with songes my loue: But their bright faces   80
Could neuer moue a nother thought in mee
Then only this, how short they came of thee
Deliuered hence a whirlewind rapt me ore
Insencibly, and left mee on the shoare
wal'd round with thousand rockes, cragged and high   85
whose tops I could not clamber nor descry
with out loues aide; great loue where hee doth goe
marble doth melte like wax, and rockes like snow
The countrey, as if Curs'd for some offence
Had nothinge in't but what offeñdes the sence   90
The aire was foggy drawne from corrupt lakes
A quier of Croakinge toades the musicke makes
And what was there; that could the Eye possesse:
But noisome weedes, and ugly barrennesse
when hot desires search'd me through euery bone   95
[fol. 192v] I was conuai'd streight to the torrid zone
And thence o'th sudden borne with hopelesse care
To the cold North, and frozen with despaire
vntill from thence some wild and sauage thought
my stepps in to the Araibian desert brought   100
And Libian sandes, that thousand serpents breede.
Noe number to the griefes my soule did feede
I pas'd the cold Alps and the Agiptian Fenne
Fedd in darke groue's; and slep't in many a denne
And that inhumane ground my feet did beate   105
where carres⁹ like canibals, on men doe Eath

                 n

I haue seen Aetꭓa and uosuuius¹⁰ burne
And all the neighbouringe fields to Cinders turne
Tw louers that inflam'd with hot desire
Had heate enough to sett whole worlds on fire   110

---

⁹ There, cares eat men.
¹⁰ Mount Vesuvius.

I haue beheld the hesperian orchard too
[fol. 193r]   Canaries and Cannpania, bathes that flow
with all delights, I'ue seene the Eastearn spice
And westerne gold; and past by paradice
yet curiously those landes I did not uiew   115
In hope to find'em all richer in you
Att lengh ore hills and dales and uncouth way
my weary steps brought mee at last to sea
where through stromes through darkenes waues and wind
Cupid doth steaire me, and by night doth finde   120
Though tost from coast to coast where I may Rest
In a safe harbour beauteous Laura's brest
Loue steares not by the needle, card[11] nor starre
By his owne rules, his Nauegations are

Thus my deare Laura my sad tale is donne   125
                             rr
But you will wonder I so faxxe haue gone
[fol. 193v]   know all these passions that our soules doe moue.
Are seuerall climates in the world of loue

                        Laura
what absolute powers in braue affections bee
That you all this should'st suffer, and for me   130

                      Amintas
The quest of precious thinges through danger driues
who lookes for pearles uentures to sea and diues
Had'st thou bin easily wonne, and in a trice
T'were underualewinge thee, heau'n knew thy price

                        Laura
And thou wert highly pris'd: fate made me stray   135
Through many an untrode walke, and pathes a way
[fol. 194r]   And Then one glareinge with an hundred Eyes
set 'em 'ore all my stepps, soe many spies

---

[11] A map or chart.

And after him a crowde of monsters thronges
And each of these fraught with a thousand tongues   140
yet on I went beinge conscions of no wronge
And nether stoode in feare of eye nor tongue
I trauel'd still, and had no torch by night
But the faint glimmeringe of the glowewormes light
And when by that I spide some flowry bedde   145
where on I purpos'd to repose my head
Malice would flie before e'áre I came thither
And with his breath blast all; y^t all would whither
                       toade
For flowres lay there; the spawne of ye foule
Adders and scorpions, all the Lærnean[12] broode.   150
That place I left with courser turfe content
wher sadly all my howers, and slowly went
A thousand horrid fancies test my braine
[fol. 194v] Distemperinge reason with their horrid traine
untill ye holier shaddow did appeare   155
And chas'd um thence, as if some god were there
stocke doues[13] and turtles as if they had sence
of griefe with me, till they were driuen thence
were my companions: but some rauenous kite
castrell[14] or buzard, forc'd my birds to flight   160
They gone the rauen and that omnious name
The screech-owle; and the fatall mandrake came
I wak'd and labour'd on, fork'd snakes would shoot
From some close bush, and backward fright my foote
yet when my fancy did most horror heare   165
of thee I thought, and bainsh'd all my feare
I still persist my robes the brambles teare
And still those remmants they for trophees weare
The thornes haue pierc'd my feete, and scŕathc'd my
            thyes

---

[12] Inhabitants of Lerna, a marshy region near Argos in Greece and the mythical home of the Hydras.
[13] Wild pigeons.
[14] There is a blotted or scribbled line under *castrell*.

[fol. 195r]   The blood my limbes in Crimson tincture dyes   170
which should loue please to know; he would preferre
Noe other for his martirs[15] register
Thus many stopps many a thousand lett
Fate' laid to part our loues yet we are mett
Of labourinthes it may be truely sed   175
There's none but loue can wisely use the thred
so is poore Isis[16] oft constrain'd to winde
Through thousand crosse meanders ere shee finde
Leaue for her streame; the swellinge mountaines cheeke
Forces her through, many a turrning creeke   180
To looke a channell downe the uaile she creepes
And where the ground lyes humblest, that way keepes
And yet at last she meete's her louely Tame
And to him weds her waters and her name

               u
Where thosand swans doe welcome in her tide   185
And thousand proud ships on her bosome ride
[fol. 195v]   That now she only is trunnphant seene

                     queen
The Tweede's the Trent's seuernn's and Humber's
so shall these ebs and flouds of our chast blood
make constant tides, and an eternall flood.   190

               Chorus
That flame is borne of Earthly fires
That soone enioyes, or soone expires
His loue with winges ill feathered flies
That cannot reach beyond his Eyes
Though Alpes and oceans should deuide   195
The sheppheard from his sweet harts side
Loue hath a tricke a pretty art
To carry newes twixt hart and heart
Where hope doth fanne the idle fire

---

[15] Given the religious tension between the Shirley and the Stafford families, *martirs*
and the preceding lines provide an interesting Catholic flavor for the poem.
[16] The Thames, especially at and west of Oxford.

Tis easy to maintaine desire   200
But that's the noble loue that dare
Continue Constant in dispaire
Then Crowne this paire of louers Browes
with Iuy wreathes ore laurell boughes
For fadinge flowers that soone are dead   205
Become the fickle louers d heads

T. R

[66]¹

A Pastorall Egloune on
the death of Lawra:
Amyntas: Dorus: Chorus:

[fol. 196r]

Amyntas   But tell mee Dorus since no Obiecte heere
           Speaks any thinge but sorrow did'st e're heare
           A Fate like mine; Cann any Mortall say
           his greifs Inioyd not once an Holy-day
           My seldome smiles which as but lightninge broken   5
           were but as Heralds of a Thunder-stroke
           And all my Increase of Stock did but Create
           Mee a poore Tenant to my own estate
           while Coridon enioys his flocks secure

---

¹ Probably by William Pershall, in Gertrude Aston's hand. Newdigate rather tentatively attributes the poem to Pershall, noting that in one other poem in HM904 his initials are also crossed through. In fact, Constance tried to expunge her brother-in-law's
initials after this and his four other poems (15, 18, 23, 45). In 1980, La Belle discovered
Constance's motives:

> In Vol II, part 1, of *The History and Antiquities of Staffordshire*, compiled by the
> Revd. Stebbing Shaw, London 1801, 22, the compiler quotes from Sir Simon
> Degge's brief history of the priory of Canwell. At the end of his account, Degge
> writes, "In this last age Sir John Pershall bought and gave it to Sir William
> Pershall, his younger son, who not long after sold it to Sir Francis Lawley, after
> he had filled it with incumbrances, and likewise sold all the rest of his estate, and
> became as bad as a beggar, if not worse." Further, according to MS. 8253 in the
> William Salt Library, Stafford, Pershall brought a land suit against the second
> Lord Aston in 1656. Apparently then Pershall disgraced himself in the eyes of his
> family and friends, and thus Constance, at some time after writing out these
> poems and indicating authorship, returned to them and partially obliterated the
> offender's initials (HAM 551).

La Belle's discovery, as well as Gertrude's changed initials in Poem 53, emphasizes
how important Constance Fowler's book was to her and for how long she continued to
tinker with the poems. Lady Dorothy and William Stafford married in 1634; Dorothy
died in March or April, 1636. William died a little more than a year later (Newdigate,
"Constant Lovers," 2:216). This poem was probably written, then, between the spring of
1636 and autumn of 1637; twenty years later, Constance was still intimate enough with
her book that she made a conscious effort to obliterate acknowledgement of her brother-
in-law's contributions to it.

And prospers with his lovs and thoughts Impure   10
Ah Dorus had you seene when but of Late
I and my Lawra did Capitulate²
Our past Affections how shee made mee tell³
The Iourny of my Love and how I fell

                     (plaine
from hopes to feares how from the Torrid   15
I straight was Carried to the frozen maine

                    How

[fol. 196v]   How nothinge but my Eyes my thoughts durst breake
Tis free to Looke when tis not free to speake:
How even in Despaire I Lov'd, Then shee⁴
Did my Amyntas doe this, And for mee,   20
when I a sleepy peece, like a dull Mann
thought of no other Deity but our Pann
Shee streight Inspir'd mee with deviner Love
And brought mee to the Alter of great Iove:

Dorus   And will you then Amyntas though you must   25
weepe o're her Ashes, turn your self to dust
Alredy you a Statúa Represent
and you Appeare but as her Monument
whereon without an Epitaph exprest
wee reade who Lye's Intomb't within yʳ breast   30
And when you know by her departed breath
you had a Losse, yeat shee a gaine by Death
Abridge your sighes, 'els 'twill bee understood
you more esteeme your own then Lawräes' good;
But you'l Obiect and with Impatience Ask   35
              Síx
why Nature did Impose so hard a task

                  On
[fol. 197r]   On Humane wills, why should the Faculty

---

   ² "Laura's" and "Amyntas's" love had been capitulated, or specified, in the preceding poem in the commonplace book.

   ³ In "The Constant Louers," the preceding poem, ll. 59–60.

   ⁴ I.e., then she said; see "The Constant Louers," ll. 129–30.

Of Ioyes bee Allowd, and not their Contrary
For when wee are gladd, that state wee not decline
Let Crosses fall,⁵ wee are Counseld to resigne,⁶   40
But (deere Amyntas) know, our better part
The soule I meane, is given to Impart
A knowledge to vs to bee ever free
and (Like it self) doth teach æternity
That to bee greivd for what wee know must fall   45
is to repaire the House and burne yᵉ wall:

Amyn: Would God and Nature then make such a warr
To Ioyne a Rebell with a Governorr,
Counsels for patience (Dorus) needs must err
True Love was never good Philosopher: 50

Dorus: But (deere Amyntas) since this sad excesse
of Losse to Goodnes and your happines
I heard you had a vision, bee so free
To Lett mee know if none shall witnes bee:
                                          It
[fol. 197v]
Amynt: It was that time when in their Autumne dayes   55
They bidd God-morrow in Th'Antipodes
Our Hemispha're the nights Coole shade possest
And every Creature (but my thoughts) at rest
I to a darksome Cave my self betooke
in a thick grove, Close by a murmuringe brook   60
where in a sleepy traunce I was Convayd

---

⁵ Let misfortunes happen (Tilley, *Proverbs*, L457).
⁶ See Donne's "Song" (Sweetest love, I do not goe):

O how feeble is mans power,
    That if good fortune fall,
Cannot adde another houre,
    Nor a lost houre recall!
    But come bad chance,
And wee joyne to'it our strength
And wee teach it art and length,
    It selfe o'r us to'advance. (17–24)

by Cupid, through a misty Aire; and Layd
Close by a River side, as black as Styx
And neere a Maze; Love hath such pretty tricks
whence if retorn'd, twas drowninge in despaire   65
If forwards to a Labourinth of Care
There left alone, I rather ventured on
Then certaine drowning in dark Acheron
And after severall wandrings in the Maze
At last I Light vpon the middle place   70
where did Appeare a gloriouse Palace built
A house for Gods not Menn, for twas all guilt:
The Gatehouse like a beawteous face did shew
The Inward Graces which it Lett into:
And on the topp in wreaths like mirtle bonds⁷   75

Fortune 'd Amor: was writt in Diamonds:
No

[fol. 198r]   No gates to shutt, the Porters only were
A Guard of Amarous statuäes fixed there
In the first Court, I saw a Crowd of Clownes
possest of beawties Cause they were rich in Crowns   80
Others their Mistres portions Leadinge forth
Could sooner tell their monies, then their worth
And one thad⁸ did their vgly Loves behold   th
might sweare they Longd for Patience bought w Gold
Another Obiect presently begunne   85
A rich old Gallant Tuteringe his sonne
his only heire of hopes, and hee had Layd
his heart before vpon a Chamber-maide:
Proceedinge farther thence I thought I spyde
A spright-full youth Courtinge his new made bride   90
And death a distance of⁹ ready to burst
his Ioyes a'-sunder: Him I Iudg'd Accurst:
Next a Deserving suitor did Commend
his service to his (Faire) who did pretende

---

⁷ Venus's tree; see "The Constant Louers," line 58.
⁸ That.
⁹ Off.

Excuses but so poore as one might see   95
Shee seemd half angry at her Modesty
when on a Sodaine Iust dislike of freinds[10]
did part ye match, and brought on both their Ends:
                                        I

[fol. 198v]   I saw distracted Lovers in a strife
whether[11] should soonest sacrifice his life   100
for such as in my thoughts Love never ment
Scarce worthy of a Courtiers Complement
I saw Admired beawties all alone
Led Captives to a Choice not of their own
so sweetely bearinge the Inforced doome   105
As if they went to holy Martyrdome
Thus gazinge (as I thought) a grave old Mann
encountred with mee, whose discourse beganne
with Curteouse mildnes to Invite mee in
And entred thus ye good mann did beginne   110
S^r, what ye have seene in those exteriour parts
are but mechanick Lovers to those Arts
and Ornaments with in: where you shall see
A Cleere discovery of Loves mistery:
Then vp faire Marble Staires exceeding high   115
Hee ledd mee to a Sumptuouse Gallery:
Furnisht with Statuäes Curiously-Contrivd
As ~Ligl~ Like Pigmaleon's Image seemed Liv'd
Proportions so exact as Iustly movd
A Passion in mee to esteeme them Lov'd   120
                                     Then

[fol. 199r]   Then on a sodaine would appeare a Light
as twere behinde ye Images so bright
As Ravisht all my sences, and would bee
in severall places of each Imagry
Sometims in th Eye of one it would Appeare   125

---

[10] According to Newdigate, Lady Dorothy's friends roundly opposed her marriage to William Stafford (1.204).
[11] Which of the two.

and then my thoughts were only fixed there
In others 'twould ye Face alone possesse
and then I thought that peece my happines
And though it Came in parts, yeat where it hitt
I Could not Chuce but love ye whole for it: 130
This (sayd ye good old Mann) doth aptly shew
the way that Lovers to Affection grow
That flame you see so bright, is part of that
Of which all Creatures doe participate,
A Light Devinely bredd, which doth direct   135
Their Loves as severall natures doe Affect
And when they see it, it doth firmly tye
Their hearts to Love that Creature: Aske not why:
Sometimes (as heere you see) it only shews
It's brightnes in the Eye, and thence it goës   140
In others to the lipps, ye Cheeke, ye Chinne
And where it shews itself, it draws Love in:
                         From

[fol. 199v]   From thence I was directed to the Ende
Of this Faire Gallery, where did Attend
A quier of witts Like to the Muses nine   145
All writinge Elegies for Lawräes Shrine
which I too eager Catchinge at, did misse
The best and tooke ye worst, and this it is:

                    Epitaph:
Looke; and every Eye will tell
who Lyes in this Marble Cell   150
How if Lawra Livd Could Rise
Such a Deluge in all Eyes
Happy Ground in such a Guest
Thou hast in thy Earthy Chest
Treasure, that no Eye Cann see   155
Till the Earth a Taper bee
Lawra Livd but 'twas to show
How an Angell Livs below
Lawra died to tell that shee
Could not heere Immortall bee   160

Shee had on this earthly Stage
Nothinge youthfull but her Age
Nothinge Obvious; doe not call-t
An Error to bee Lovd of all:
                              Reader

[fol. 200r] Reader, know this Monument-s   165
Not placed heere to Represent
A Livinge fame to her that must
Live after this hard Marble's dust
Tis but to tell thee; If thou bee
Amyntas: Lawra prays for thee: 170

Heere wakt my thoughts grew restles as before
And sorrow now prevents my sayinge more:

                    Chorus
That flame is fruitles that prepares
Passions in Springe in Autumne Cares: 175
His Loves not worth the thought of Ioyes
That use or Accident destroyes
And only then Canne make him Gladd
when 'tis desired and not hadd
Though kingedomes should bee sold to buy   180
A Love that faine would never Dye,
Time has a trick a sullen Art
To Seperate both Life and heart:
                              Those

[fol. 200v] Those Loves which earthly Flames begett
Have visibly their noones and Sett,   185
But thats the Love that doth Expresse
No East and west of Happines
Then fix vpon Amyntas head
A Crown of Patience Hallowed:
For wreaths of Laurels which Th Earth givs   190
Are Ornaments but while hee Livs: || :
                    SWP

Appendix

Poem	Lines	Text / Patrick
6	1	at / in
	2	T'was / Tis
	3	For / But
	4	are / were
	5	then / now
	6	then / and
	8	much / cold
	9	white / pure
		as time canot / as fate can nere
	10	With Fath / But truth

Poem	Lines	Text / Bodl. Eng. poet b. 5 / BL 15225
9	4	christ / christ / God
	7	the flesh, the deuill / y^e flesh, y^e / the devill, the flesh
	8	my / my / thy
	11	A pilgrime till that thou Depart / A pilgrime till $^{\wedge that}$ thou depart / A pilgrim poore till thou Depart
	14	upon the sand / upon the sands / on sand
	15	minstrills play / minstrills play / minstrill plays
	16	thy wedinge / thy wedinge / the mariage
	17	ffor here A weding thou must haue / ffor here a Weding thou must haue / A weddinge garment thou must have I say

19	uane / uane / gay
21	all / all / this
	worldly / earthly / earthly
26	statures / statures / structures
28	of building passinge faire / of building passinge fayre / for costlie buildings faire
29	this / this / the
31	pearles Are fram'd / pearles Are fram'd / stones is wald
32	the / the / And
33	walls / walls / gates
	made / made / framed
34	And / And / There
36	therin Are / therin Are / Are there in
37	Thorowe / Quite thorowe / amidst
	floud / floud / well
38	siluer / siluer / goulden
45	This / This / The
46	In / And / And
47	there / there / For
49	bodies / bodies / bodie
50	Are / Are / is
53	shalt thou / shalt thou / thou shalt
55	the Angells / the Angells / there Angells
56	where / where / and
57	remaine / remaine / do dwell
58	Doth / do / Doe
59	Doe there / Doe there / there doe
61	prophets / prophets / marters
63	liue / liue / wait
	there they doe giue / and there they giue / there they doe give
64	Euery way / Euery way / Night & day
70	siths / siths / sihts
71	And sith her plaints And teares be gone / And sith her plaints And teares be gone / And since the teares and plaints are gone
72	Blisse / Blisse / peace
73	Where / Where / There

	dwell / dwell / bee
75	reioyce / rejiyce / doth joy
76	his / his / their
78	endlesse / endlesse / restles
79	now / now / here
80	his / his / this
81	expresse / expresse / expound
83	perfect / perfect / passing
	Remaine / Remaine / abound
84	with their Delights / with their Delights / that doe delight
85	There do / There do / Here all
86	there / there / here
87	And / And / Here
89	blissefull / speechless / speechless
91	blisse / blisse / life
92	thou lou'dst / thou lou'dst / we loved
93	doth / doth / all
94	wish And waite / wish And waite / watch and wish
98	which man Doth / which man Doth / that man may
99	braue nor fine / braue nor fine / joy nor brave
100	request or / request or / desire to
103	there / there / here
	canst desire / canst require / wilt require
107	of / of / and
	beaten / beaten / better
108	that / that / than
111	dwell / dwell / rest
112	blisse / blisse / life
115	is / is / are
116	which / which / that
119	there / there / here
122	case / case / cause
123	his louinge / his louinge / Here all his
128	Rewarded / Remembered / Rewarded
129	there reward / there reward / here rewards
130	cold / cold / could
	wants no / wants no / want not
133	The glorious Ioyes which thou shalt see / The glorious

Ioyes which thou shalt see / The pleasures thou shalt
there behould

134   siluer / siluer / treasure
135   or pearle or / or pearle or / nor pearle nor
136   Are things which / Are things which / or things that
138   these / these / the
      thou hast / thou hast / are heere
141   may / may / shall
      esteem'd / esteem'd / deemde
142   sweete how uery / sweete how uery / great and passing
143   that / y^t / which
144   o^r sweete saviours / our sweete saviours / our saviours
145   w^{c}h / which / that
146   those / those / their
147   the / the / their
150   liuinge / earthly / livinge
153   out / out / forth
155   speech / speech / speare
158   not torment / then torment / terrify
160   shall / shall / will
161   blaspheamers there remaine / blaspheamer there remains
      / blaspheamers there remaine
163   do liue / do liue / doth raigne
164   weight / weight / wight
172   wholy / wholy / fullie
175   Doth rest / Doth rest / Dare roote
176   that triumphant place / that triumphant place / thy
      triumphant peace
177   purged /purged / purified
179   they receiue / they receiue / thou possesse
180   Ioy / Joy / Joys
      fades / fades / fade
181   up the / up the / thou thy
182   of / of / &
185   time / time / day
187   no / no / what
188   prepard / prepard / remaine
189   Almighty / Almighty / O mighty
      my / my / one

| | 190 | which I Doe / which I Doe / that I shall |
| | 191 | soule in heaven / soule in heaven / suit is there |

Poem	Lines	Text / Bodl. Eng. poet b. 5 / BL 15225
10	7	may / may / doth
	8	is fraile / is fraile / doth faint
	13	faith / faith / feight
	14	rewards Doth / rewards Doth / reward we
	16	In midst of / In midst of / Strongly in
	19	saith / sith / saith
	20	thy / thy / my
	24	towards mount / towards mount / to mount of
	26	when she this / when she this / This dolfull
	27	when she her sonne / when she her sonne / with her sonne she
	28	Loaded Soe heauily / Loaded Soe heauily / Laden soe cruellie
	34	showeth / showeth / telleth
	35	with / with / by
	39	those grieuous / those grieuous / the wonderful
	40	these / these / those
	41	uerily pierce / uerily pierce / thoroughly foarce
	44	From gods / from gods / Christ his
	48	his crosse was content / their crosse was content / their crosse content
	49	walkinge on willingly / walkinge on willingly / but walked on lovinglie
	50	doth / doth / did
	51	because / because / that
	52	Another / Another / the latter
	53	Iust / Iust / great
	56	lew^{d}ly / lowdly / lewdlie
	57	herods / herods / heroldes
	58	what / what / so
	62	lots were / lots were / lot was
	63	painfull Crosses bore / painfull Crosses bore / weightie Crosses bare
	68	god was / god was / Christ were
	69	Blessed / Blessed / bessed

74	with sword he / with sword he / By the sword
76	his / Gods / In plantinge of Christ's faith his sacred bload was shedd
77	by / by / with
79	quoth hee / quoth hee / he sayd
87	downe from A tower was thrust / downe from A tower was thrust / from a tower he was thrust
93	likewise / likewise / also
94	he lost / he lost / did lose
95	to / toe / toe
100	Did Dye / to dye / to dye
102	stake / stake / tree
106	or wᵗh tongue who can show / or wᵗh tongue who can show / Or yet what tongue can show
107	these / these / there
108	to christ our lord Did owe / to christ our lord Did owe / Did to their maker owe
110	whome / whome / which
111	In their Aray / In their Aray / In this same way

In BL 15225, the poem ends with the following stanzas:
With merie hart, and cheere in their most deepe distresse
for god would not for beare to leave them comfortless

And such as martyrdome kild not with violence
to their conflict did come in Austeare penitance
In praier to entreat in fast and discipline
In workes of mercie great, and so they spent their time

Thus Christ hath gonne before & thou hath followed fast
All his saints evermore whose Crosses now are past
Ragninge in heaven above crowned with glorie great
In measure of their love eich hath his kinglie seat

Gods grace it was that made the saints soe well to doe
let us not be affraid for that is oures alsoe
I we will seeke therefore by fervant prair still
Though our crosse greeve us sore godes grace shall
                                 strength our will

Was ever blessed wight since man first came to loose
that wonne eternall bliss without bearing his crosse
All of necessitie as St Paule doth repeate
walke to felicitie with toiles and trouble greate

Wor[l]dlinges hereat will muse in their voluptuousnesse
and thinke those words I use nothinge but foolishnesse
gods wisdome as wee reade amongst the worldlie wise
is follie dremd indeede unto their veiled eies.

But let the flesh repine let worldlie wittes say nay
let us beginne in time to walk this blessed way
As manie marters doe in these our present daies
many confessors too gods name have all the prayse

In this our English coast much blessed blood is shed
two hundred priests almost in our time martered
And manie lay men dye with joyfull sufferance
manie moe in prison lie gods cause for to advance

Amongst those gratious troupe that follow Christ his traine
to cause the Devill stoupe foure priestes were latelie slaine
Nutters bould constantie with his sweete fellow Thwinge
Of whose most meeke modestie Angells & saints may singe.

Huntes heartie courage staut w[it]h godlie zeale soe true
Myld Middleton o what tonge can halfe thy virtues shew
At Lancaster lovingly these marters tooke their end
In glorious victorie true faith for to defend

And thus hath Lancashyre offered her sacrifice
to daunt their lowde desyre & please our saviors eies
For by this meanes I trust truth shall have victorie
when as that number just, of such saints compleat bee

Whoe the holie ghost doth move unto his Deitie
In fervant flaimes of love thus sacrificed to bee
whose faith and fortitude whose grace and constantie
with mildness meeke indude confoundeth heresie

Whose sacred members rent & quarters set on hye
caused moe to be content in the same cause to Dye
whose lives whyle they did live whose blessed deaths also
doe admonition give what waie we ought to goe.

If we should them dispise as manie wretches doe
we should contempne likewise our blessed Saviour too
Let their examples then move our hartes to relent
these were most blessed men whom god to us hath sent

Gods holie truth they taught & seald it with their blood
Dyinge with torments fraught and all to doe us good
Let lyinge heresie with how false lyebellis lout
truth will have victorie through such mild champions stout

Praise be to gods good will whoe deeth his truth defend
lord to thy Vineard still such worthie workmen send
And good lord grant us grace that we may constant bee
with our Crosse in each place to please thy majestie

On[e] thinge here I request and still of thee implore
in thy house to aspire to dwell for evermore
Ther for to see thy will in virtue all our daiys
and visit thy temple still to thyne eternall praise

All laud & glorie great be to the Trinitie
In his eternall seat one god and persons three.
And to the virgin mild the Queene of heaven the hye
With Jesus her lovinge Child in all eternitie

Unto all prophetes meeke to Christs Apostles deere
marters confessors eke and to all virgins cleare
And unto each of them Crowned in their degree
With joy in Jerusalem gods blessed face to see.
                              (fol. 31v–32v)

Poem   *Lines*   *Text / Bod MS, Eng. poet b. 5 / McDonald & Brown*
  11   6   In waues / In waues / in the waves

9	mindes / winds / winds
11	breake / breake / broke
15	heauens / heauens / heaven
26	to feare / to feare / of feares
31	stopt far within / stopt far w^thin / Stept far within
	dore / dores / dores
32	pangs / paines / pangs
	went / went / were
37	defeit / defeit / deceit
38	wonted / wonted / wicked
41	sought / thought / sought
46	heede / keele / heed
50	on / on / in
51	their / their / these
52	mishapps / mishapps / mishap
53	lore / lure / lore
56	flyting / fleeting / flying

Poem	Lines	Text / Bod MS. Eng. poet b. 5. / McDonald & Brown
12	2	rest / rest / rifte
	19	there / here / there
	22	weights / wights / wights

Poem	Lines	Text / Tixall Poetry
13	12	pleasure / glory
	13	meanely loues / doth not love
	15	nobly / truly
		doth not / can ne're
	28	measure / measures

Poem	Lines	Text / Tixall Poetry
21	Title	A discourse of A dreame. / To Sleep
	2	from / of

Poem	Lines	Text / Crum
24	1	dost / should'st
	5	weethered station / drooping season
	10	thy / the

Poem	*Lines*	*Text / McDonald & Brown*
26	9	lauds / Lawdes
	13	Dept / debt
	16	And time / all times
	20	blesse / blisse
	25	sights / sighs
	26	Doth / do
	27	sights / sighs

Poem	*Lines*	*Text / Bodl. MS. Eng. poet b. 5 / McDonald & Brown*
27	1	best / best / least
	5	loues / loue / love
	11	loue / loue / live
		best / best / least
	25	oath / earth / earth

Poem	*Lines*	*Text / Bodl. MS. Eng. poet b. 5*
28	2	of / on
	6	thus / ths
	13	endlesse / onely
	34	thy / thine
	56	till / tell

Poem	*Lines*	*Text / Bodl. MS. Eng. poet b. 5 / BL 15225*
29	2	thinke / looke / looke
	3	refuse me not that am uniust / refuse me not that am uniust / O Christ my kinge refuse me not
	6	In sorrow griefe And paine / In sorrow griefe And paine / wth sorrowe and wth shame
	7	smart / smart / wounds
	13–14	Thy back, thy syde, / same / Thy syde thy bellie thy belly eke eike I rent
		I rent with cruell rod / same / with whix and cruell rod
	15	this / thy / that
	17	ffor the pryde of seraphims / ffor the pryd of seraphins / For onelie pryd of Cherubines
	24	yet feele I not / yet feele I not / and feel not yet

29	And / And / Yea
	then / then / than
	that / y^t / this
	should / should / might
30	the / the / thy
31–32	And for to saue my / same / And to redeeme my
	sinfull soule soule from hell
	thou shedst thy / same / thou speandst thy
	Dearest bloud deerest blood
33	hart / hart / syde
35	spild / spild / spent
36	shame / shame / paine
37	O god, my god / O god, my god / Alas my lord
39	what moued thee o Iudge most Iust / what moued thee
	o Iudge most Iust / that thou should'st like soe well of
	mee
41	o god / o god / vile woretry
45	Come Angels come Arke Angels eke / Come Angels
	come Arke angles eke / O come Angells, come Arch-
	angells
46	soules and saints / soules and saints / saints and soules
47	both / both / eke
49	Lend / Lend / Let
51	requite / requite / release
52	that / that / which
57	had thought / had thought / dream'd
	Ioyes / Ioyes / joy
60	he / he / it
62	naked Alas / naked Alas / dead Alack
63	uild wretch / uild wretch / the child
	woes / woes / death
64	suffered / suffered / felt
	grieuous paines / grieuous paines / bitter panges
68	his / thy / *see note, p. 77*
69	Or / Or / O
70	blessed / blessed / fathened
71	the / the / that
72	most / most / more
83	we / we / I

Poem	Lines	Text / Bodl. MS. Eng. poet b. 5
30	6	runne / ran
	21	his / A
	52	reason / nature
	88	Isaack / Isaacks
	91	could / cold
	96	band / hand
	102	bade / bid
	107	handmaide / band mayd
	118	soe / dost
	129	And then tooke he / then Abraham tooke
	151	And then he tooke his / then Abram took a

Poem	Lines	Text / Bodl. MS. Eng. poet b. 5
31	4	bade / bid
	25	Away / their way
	33	fume / frowne
	42	murtherers / murderors
	48	fire it should be brent / fire should be burnt
	54	they Are not / Are not
	55	where / were
	66	his / a
	77	on his / a
	92	this / that

Poem	Lines	Text / Bodl. MS. Eng. poet b. 5 B^1 / B^2
32	3	o / sweet / sweet
	10	his / her / her
	27	let / and / let
	28	teare / teare / tare
	43	sayes / saith / saith
	44	greater / great / great
	45	misdeeds / good deeds / good deeds
	46	good / sinnes / sinnes
	61	Amen / finis / amen

Poem	Lines	Text / Bodl. MS. Eng. poet b. 5
33	8	liue, to die to die / liue to die, to die
	17	liue to die to die / liue to die, to die

	19	was much / much was
	20	And guilefull / And And gainefull
	26	liue to die to die / liue to die, to die
	40	none / no
	44	to die to die / to die to die,

Poem	*Lines*	*Text / Cutts*
37	3	I / you
	7	Though / If
	8	known / seen

Poem	*Lines*	*Text / Donaldson*
42	*Title*	marchionesse of winchester / Marchion of Winton
	1	goodly / gentle
		besprinckt / besprent
	18	might / may
	21	titles fame / forms, good fame,
	26	no motion euer could / Thereof, no notion can
	29	god / heaven
	31	those / these
	32	heate / blaze
	34	inline / enlive
	35	it / that
	38	fam'd / feigned
		spoyl / rob
	46	heape / sum
	51	her / the
	54	canstickes / caustics
	55	that / which
	57	blest soone / blessed her son
	58	course / race
	65	That / Who
	69	lights / light
	74	beginning / beginnings
	75	hence / thence
	76	the Elect of god / they that have the crown
	79	quarrell / grudge
	82	ere / every
	88	The / And

	90	and / with
	91	beginning to / beginning there, to
	92	can / should
	96	a / the

Poem	*Lines*	*Text / Saintsbury*
43	*Headings*	A / Mistress
		Q / Lover
	7	enlarge / dilate
	11	sight / sigh
	13	thine / thy
	21	way / way?
	24	consent / {consent
		respect
	25	Long ere / Long time ere
	26	whilst it dares / while I dare
	27	Least / Lest
	28	It will / I shall
	29	That / As
	31	loues / this
	33	seene / soon
	35–36	Not in Saintsbury

Poem	*Lines*	*Text / Clayton*
46	5	theyr / th'are
	6	canot / could not
	7	though / since
		fortune / honor
	8	That Blis / Those joyes
	9	yet you to grace thy'r / Yet you this noble
		death this wae haue way to grace them
	10	this / thus
	11	But yet / Of which

Poem	*Lines*	*Text / Crum*
49	5	maist / might'st
	11	lost / blind
	14	Then / But
	18	practies / bus'nes
	19	I doe / So I

20	sights / sighs
21	though my time runis thus / if my time goes thus
24	darkenesse / blackness
25	wert my morn thought / wast my day though
26	the / thy
28	had / hadst
35	blisse / wish
42	waite / live
43	this / that
44	a / to
46	Last / length
	my / this
49	such / these
52	That / which
	world / Earth
53	shall / must
56	ouer / off
57	where / then
60	other / other's
61	while / time
63	should / might
65	sad lou'd Life / short Liv'd right
67	And freely though thou see mee weepe / With a most free and bounteous grief
68	that / what
70	write with in / write into
72	That in thy caskets shrine / Which in thy Caskett shrin'd
76	her / this
79	clos'd / close
80	drawne / draw
81	deere / Love
83	I will / thou wilt
91	on / of
98	brought / breath'd
99	morne / sunne
101	Nor wonder thought I / Nor labour I to
102	By which towards / Through which to
106	By / In
107	carue / crave

109	Hark how / But hark!
111	so'ere / howe're
115	feare / hope
117	but with / with but

Poem	*Lines*	*Text / Tixall Poetry (Bawcutt prints from* Tixall Poetry)
59	7	euer / neuer
	9	allide / allied

Poem	*Lines*	*Text / Bawcutt / HM116*
61	3	uncutt / unshorne / unshorne
	5	forgett / forgett / forgott
	8	siluer / wanton / bosted
	10	noe / noe / not
	12	that / which / which
		to / too / too
	14	that all parts / which all parts / which each part
	15	weaue / winde / winde
		loopes / wreaths / wreaths
	20	face / brow / brow
		saint that's crownd / saint crowned / saint crownst
	22	would / will / will

Poem	*Lines*	*Text / Pebworth and Summers*
63	7	lapp / face
	8	By the sun's / To the same
	10	Till vertue re=exhale me that is you / Till re-exhal'd again to Vertue; You.

Poem	*Lines*	*Text / Bawcutt*
64	3	others / of them
	5	yea / Nay
		that life and flame / such vehemence

Poem	*Lines*	*Text / Newdigate*
65	25	ore / doe
	53	sickle / sickle's
	65	climse / glimse
	70	unfurnish / unfurnisht

Works Consulted

PRIMARY SOURCES

Anon. B.L. Add. MS. 15225. c. 1616. British Library, London.

Aston family correspondence. B.L. Add. MS. 36444–36452. c. 1600–1750. British Library, London.

Aston, Walter. Commonplace book. Aston D988. 1635. Staffordshire Record Office, Stafford, England, fol. 18.

————. Letter to Katherine Thimelby Aston. B.L. Add. MS. 36452. c. 1638. *Aston Papers, Vol. IX, Private Correspondence, 1613–1703.* British Library, London.

Collection of recusant poetry. Bodl. MS. Eng. poet. b. 5. Mid-seventeenth century. Bodleian Library, Oxford, England.

Fowler, Constance Aston. Commonplace book. HM904. c. 1630–1660. Huntington Library, San Marino, Calif.

Fowler, Walter. Marriage renegotiation. Bundle 20, doc. 20. 1649. William Salt Library, Stafford, England.

Shirley, [Thomas]. *The Geneological History of the House of Shirley: by Thomastos Calaeimon.* Harl. 4928. 1733. British Library, London.

Staffordshire Record Book. Account of the second Walter Aston's Civil War experiences. 25 December 1644. Staffordshire Record Office, Stafford, England.

Villiers, George, First Duke of Buckingham. Letter to Walter Aston. B.L. Add. MS. 36446. 7 January 1622. British Library, London.

SECONDARY WORKS

Akrigg, J. P. V. *Letters of King James VI & I*. Berkeley: University of California Press, 1984.

Alexander, Michael Van Cleave. *Charles I's Lord Treasurer: Sir Richard Weston, Earl of Portland (1577–1635)*. Chapel Hill: University of North Carolina Press, 1975.

Aubrey, John. *"Brief Lives," chiefly of Contemporaries, set down by John Aubrey, between the Years 1669 & 1696*. Ed. Andrew Clark. Vol. 2. Oxford: Clarendon Press, 1898.

Bald, R. C. *John Donne: A Life*. Oxford: Clarendon Press, 1970.

Berman, Ronald. *Henry King and the Seventeenth Century*. London: Chatto & Windus, 1964.

Bibliotheca Staffordiensis; or a Bibliographical Account of Books and Other Printed Matter. Comp. Rupert Simms. Lichfield: A. C. Lomax, 1894.

Birch, Thomas, ed. *The Court and Times of Charles the First*. 2 vols. London: Henry Colburn, 1848.

Brink, Jean S. *Michael Drayton Revisited*. Boston: Twayne, 1990.

Bullen, A. H., ed. *A Collection of Old English Plays in Four Volumes*. Vol. 1. London: Wymans and Sons, 1882.

Bullough, Geoffrey. "The Early Poems of Sir Richard Fanshawe." *Wiener Beiträge zur Englischen Philologie* 62 (1952): 27–36.

Burner, Sandra A. *James Shirley: A Study of Literary Coteries and Patronage in Seventeenth-Century England*. Lanham: University Press of America, 1988.

Burton, Edwin H., and J. H. Pollen. *Lives of the English Martyrs*. 2nd series. Vol. 1. *The Martyrs Declared Venerable*. London: Longmans, Green and Co., 1914.

Camden, William. *The Visitation of the County of Leicester in the Year 1619*. Vol. 2. Ed. John Fetherston. London: Harleian Society, 1870.

Carew, Thomas. *The Poems and Masque of Thomas Carew*. Ed. Joseph Woodfall Ebsworth. London: Reeves and Turner, 1893.

———. *The Works of Thomas Carew, Sewer in Ordinary to Charles the First*. 1640. Edinburgh: W. and C. Tait, 1824.

Charles, Amy M., and Mario A. Di Cesare, intro. *The Bodleian Manuscript of George Herbert's Poems: A Facsimile of Tanner 307*. Delmar, N.Y.: Scholars' Facsimiles & Reprints, 1984.

Cherry, J. L., and Karl Cherry. *Historical Studies Relating Chiefly to Staffordshire*. Stafford: J. & C. Mort, Ltd., 1908.

Clifford, Arthur, ed. *The State Papers and Letters of Sir Ralph Sadler.* 2 vols. Edinburgh: Archibald Constable and Co., 1809.

———. *Tixall Letters; or the Correspondence of the Aston Family, and their Friends, during the Seventeenth Century.* London: Longman, Hurst, Rees, Orme and Brown, 1815.

———. *Tixall Poetry; with Notes and Illustrations.* Edinburgh: John Ballantyne and Co., 1813.

Clifford, Arthur, and Sir Thomas Clifford. *A Topographical and Historical Description of the Parish of Tixall, in the County of Stafford.* Paris: M. Nouzou, 1817.

Crum, Margaret. *First-Line Index of English Poetry 1500–1800 in Manuscripts of the Bodleian Library, Oxford.* 2 vols. New York: Index Committee of the MLA, 1969.

Cutler, W. H. R. "Political History." *A History of the County of Stafford.* Vol. 1. Ed. William Page. London: Archibald & Co., Ltd., 1908.

Cutts, John P. *Seventeenth Century Songs and Lyrics.* Columbia, Mo.: University of Missouri Press, 1959.

Douglas, Sir Robert. *Peerage of Scotland.* Edinburgh: R. Fleming, 1764.

Doughtie, Edward, ed. *Liber Lilliati: Elizabethan Verse and Song.* Bodleian MS. Rawlinson Poetry 148. Newark: University of Delaware Press, 1985.

Duncan-Jones, Katherine. *Sir Philip Sidney: Courtier Poet.* New Haven: Yale University Press, 1991.

Estcourt, Edgar E., and John Orlebar Payne, eds. *The English Catholic Nonjurors of 1715: Being a Summary Register of their Estates, with Genealogical and Other Notes, and an Appendix of Unpublished Documents in the Public Record Office.* London: Burns and Oates, 1969.

Ezell, Margaret J. M. *The Patriarch's Wife: Literary Evidence and the History of the Family.* Chapel Hill: University of North Carolina Press, 1987.

———. "The Myth of Judith Shakespeare: Creating the Canon of Women's Literature." *New Literary History* 21 (1990): 579–92.

Fairholt, Frederick W., ed. *Poems and Songs Relating To George Villiers, Duke of Buckingham; and His Assassination by John Felton.* Vol. 29. London: The Percy Society, 1850.

Fanshawe, Ann. *The Memoirs of Ann, Lady Fanshawe.* In *The Memoirs of Anne, Lady Halkett and Ann, Lady Fanshawe*, ed. John Loftis, 100–92. Oxford: Clarendon Press, 1979.

Fanshawe, Richard. *Shorter Poems and Translations.* Ed. N. W. Bawcutt. English Reprint Series. Liverpool: Liverpool University Press, 1964.

Felltham, Owen. *The Poems of Owen Felltham 1604?–1668.* Ed. Ted-Larry

Pebworth and Claude J. Summers. Seventeenth-Century News Editions and Studies. University Park, Pa.: Pennsylvania State University Press, 1973.

Flynn, Dennis. "The *'Annales* School' and Catholicism of Donne's Family." *The John Donne Journal* 2.2 (1983): 1–9.

———. "Donne the Survivor." In *The Eagle and the Dove: Reassessing John Donne*, ed. Claude J. Summers and Ted-Larry Pebworth, 15–24. Columbia, Mo.: University of Missouri Press, 1986.

Foley, Henry. *Records of the English Province of the Society of Jesus.* 7 vols. London: Burns and Oates, 1897.

Gillow, Joseph. *A Literary and Biographical History, or Bibliographical Dictionary of the English Catholics. From the Breach with Rome, in 1534, to the Present Time.* 5 vols. London: Burns & Oates, 1885.

Godolphin, Sidney. *The Poems of Sidney Godolphin.* Ed. William Dighton. Oxford: Clarendon Press, 1931.

Góngora, D. Luis de. *Obras poéticas.* Vol. 1. New York: The Hispanic Society of America, 1921.

Granger's Index to Poetry. Ed. William F. Bernhardt. New York: Columbia University Press, 1986.

Grazebrook, Sidney, ed. *The Heraldic Visitations of Staffordshire Made by Sir Richard St. George, Norroy in 1614, and by Sir William Dugdale, Norroy, in the Years 1663 and 1664.* London: Mitchell-Hughes, 1885.

Greenslade, M. W., ed. *A History of the County of Stafford.* Vols. 3, 14, 17, and 20. Oxford: Oxford University Press, 1970.

———, and J. G. Jenkins, eds. *A History of the County of Stafford.* Vol. 2. Oxford: Oxford University Press, 1967.

———, and D. A. Johnson, eds. *A History of the County of Stafford.* Vol. 6. Oxford: Oxford University Press, 1979.

Greg, W. W. *A Bibliography of the English Drama to the Restoration.* 1951. Repr. London: Bibliographic Society, 1970.

Grimal, Pierre. *The Dictionary of Classical Mythology.* Trans. A. R. Maxwell-Hyslop. Oxford: Basil Blackwell, Inc., 1985.

Guffey, George Robert. *Robert Herrick, 1949–1965; Ben Jonson, 1947–1965; Thomas Randolph, 1949–1965.* Elizabethan Bibliographies Supplements, III. London: The Nether Press, 1968.

Guilday, Peter. *The English Catholic Refugees on the Continent 1558–1795.* Vol. 1, *The English Colleges and Convents in the Catholic Low Countries, 1558–1795.* London: Longmans, Green, and Co., 1914.

Guiney, Louise Imogen. *Recusant Poets, With a Selection from their Work. I.*

Saint Thomas More to Ben Jonson. London: Sheed & Ward, 1938.

Habington, William. *The Poems of William Habington.* Ed. Kenneth Allott. Oxford: Liverpool University Press, 1969.

Hardin, Richard F. *Michael Drayton and the Passing of Elizabethan England.* Lawrence, Kan.: University Press of Kansas, 1973.

Hamilton, Adam, ed. *The Chronicle of the English Augustinian Canonesses Regular of the Lateran, at St. Monica's in Louvain (Now at St. Augustine's Priory, Newton Abbot, Devon),* Parts 1 and 2. Edinburgh: Sands & Co., 1906.

Havran, Martin J. *The Catholics in Caroline England.* Stanford: Stanford University Press, 1962.

Heawood, Edward. *Watermarks Mainly of the 17th and 18th Centuries.* Hilversum, Holland: The Paper Publications Society, 1950.

Heninger, S. K. *A Handbook of Renaissance Meteorology.* Durham, N.C.: Duke University Press, 1960.

Herrick, Robert. *The Poetical Works of Robert Herrick.* Ed. L. C. Martin. Oxford: Clarendon Press, 1956.

———. *The Complete Poetry of Robert Herrick.* Ed. J. Max Patrick. New York: New York University Press, 1963.

Howell, Thomas Bayly. *Cobbett's Complete Collection of State Trials and Proceedings for High Treason and Other Crimes and Misdemeanors from the Earliest Period to the Present Time by John Felton.* Vol. 2. London: R. Bagshaw, 1809.

Jenkins, J. G., ed. *A History of the County of Stafford.* Vol. 8. Oxford: Oxford University Press, 1963.

Jonson, Ben. *Ben Jonson.* Ed. Ian Donaldson. Oxford: Oxford University Press, 1985.

———. *The Complete Poetry of Ben Jonson.* Ed. William B. Hunter, Jr. New York: New York University Press, 1963.

———. *The Complete Poems.* Ed. George Parfitt. New Haven: Yale University Press, 1982.

———. *Ben Jonson.* Ed. C. H. Herford and Percy and Evelyn Simpson. 11 vols. Oxford: Clarendon Press, 1925–51.

Kay, Dennis. "Poems by Sir Walter Aston, and a Date for the Donne/Goodyer Verse Epistle '*Alternis Vicibus*.'" *Review of English Studies* 37 (1986): 198–207.

King, Henry. *The Poems of Bishop Henry King.* Ed. Margaret Crum. Oxford: Clarendon Press, 1965.

La Belle, Jenijoy. "A True Love's Knot: The Letters of Constance Fowler and the Poems of Herbert Aston." *Journal of English and Germanic Philology* 29 (1980): 13–31.

———. "The Huntington Aston Manuscript." *The Book Collector* 29 (1980): 542–56.

Lanyer, Aemilia. *The Poems of Aemilia Lanyer*. Ed. Susanne Woods. N.Y.: Oxford University Press, 1993.

Larson, Deborah Aldrich. "John Donne and the Astons." *The Huntington Library Quarterly* 55 (1992): 635–41.

Latz, Dorothy L. *"Glow-Worm Light": Writings of 17th Century English Recusant Women from Original Manuscripts*. Salzburg Studies in English Literature. Salzburg: Institut für Anglistik und Amerikanistik, Universität Salzburg, 1989.

Le Comte, Edward. *The Notorious Lady Essex*. New York: Dial Press, 1969.

Lewalski, Barbara K. "Writing Women and Reading the Renaissance." *Renaissance Quarterly* 44 (1991): 792–821.

Lockyer, Roger. *Buckingham: The Life and Political Career of George Villiers, First Duke of Buckingham, 1592–1628*. London: Longman, 1981.

McKay, F. M. "A Seventeenth-Century Collection of Religious Poetry: Bodleian Manuscript Eng. poet. b. 5." *The Bodleian Library Record* 8 (1970): 185–91.

Marotti, Arthur F. *Manuscript, Print, and the English Renaissance Lyric*. Ithaca: Cornell University Press, 1995.

Martz, Louis L. *The Poetry of Meditation: A Study in English Religious Literature of the Seventeenth Century*. New Haven: Yale University Press, 1954.

Midgley, L. Margaret, ed. *A History of the County of Stafford*. Vols. 4 and 5. Oxford: Oxford University Press, 1958.

Milton, John. *Commonplace Book*. Ed. Ruth Mohl. Vol. 1, 344–513. New Haven: Yale University Press, 1953.

Mousley, Andrew. "Renaissance Selves and Life Writing: *The Autobiography of Thomas Whythorne*." *Forum for Modern Language Studies* 26 (1990): 222–30.

Nason, Arthur Huntington. *James Shirley, Dramatist: A Biographical and Critical Study*. New York: Benjamin Blom, 1915.

Newdigate, B. H. "The Constant Lovers—I." *Times Literary Supplement* 18 April 1942: 204.

———. "The Constant Lovers—II." *Times Literary Supplement* 25 April 1942: 216.

———. *Michael Drayton and His Circle*. Oxford: Shakespeare Head Press, 1961.

North, Sir Thomas, trans. *Plutarch's Lives of the Noble Grecians and Romans.* Vol. 4. New York: AMS Press, 1967.

Page, William, ed. *A History of the County of Stafford.* Vol. 1. London: Archibald & Co., Ltd., 1908.

Parker, Michael P. "Annotating Aurelian." *John Donne Journal* 6.1 (1987): 159–61.

Paul, Sir James Balfour, ed. *The Scots Peerage: Founded on Wood's Edition of Sir Robert Douglas's "Peerage of Scotland."* Vol. 1. Edinburgh: David Douglas, 1904.

Pearson, David. *Provenance Research in Book History: A Handbook.* London: The British Library, 1994.

Randolph, Thomas. *Poetical and Dramatic Works of Thomas Randolph.* Ed. W. Carew Hazlitt. 2 vols. London: Reeves and Turner, 1875.

———. *The Poems and Amyntas of Thomas Randolph.* Ed. John Jay Perry. New Haven: Yale University Press, 1917.

Rollins, Hyder, ed. *Old English Ballads, 1553–1625, Chiefly from Manuscripts.* Cambridge: The University Press, 1920.

Saintsbury, George, ed. *Minor Poets of the Caroline Period.* 3 vols. Oxford: Clarendon Press, 1906.

Shawcross, John T. *The Complete Poetry of John Donne.* Garden City, N.Y.: Anchor Books, 1967.

Shaw, Stebbing. *The History and Antiquities of Staffordshire.* 2 vols. London: J. Nichols, 1798–1801.

Smith, A. J. *John Donne: The Critical Heritage.* London and Boston: Routledge and Kegan Paul, 1975.

Smith, G. C. Moore. *Thomas Randolph.* Warton Lecture on English Poetry British Academy. London: Oxford University Press, 1927.

Snow, Vernon F. *Essex the Rebel: The Life of Robert Devereux, the Third Earl of Essex, 1591–1646.* Lincoln: University of Nebraska Press, 1970.

Some Canonesses Regular of St. Augustine: St. Monica's Priory, Hoddesdon, Herts. London: Catholic Truth Society, 1939.

Some Account of Colton and of the De Wasteney's Family. Birmingham: Houghton and Hammonds, 1879.

Southwell, Robert. *The Poems of Robert Southwell, S. J.* Ed. James H. McDonald and Nancy Pollard Brown. Oxford: Clarendon Press, 1967.

Spenser, Edmund. *Poetical Works.* Ed. J. C. Smith and E. de Selincourt. 1912. Repr. London: Oxford University Press, 1970.

Staffordshire Pedigrees, Based on the Visitation of that County Made by William Dugdale, Esq. . . . in the Years 1663–1664 from the Original MS Written by

Gregory King. Sir George J. Armytage and W. Harry Rylands, eds. Vol. 63. London: The Harleian Society, 1912.

Stone, Lawrence. *The Family, Sex and Marriage in England 1500– 1800*. Abridged edition. New York: Harper, 1979.

Suckling, John. *The Works of Sir John Suckling: The Non-Dramatic Works*. Vol. 1. Ed. Thomas Clayton. Oxford: Clarendon Press, 1971.

———. *The Works of Sir John Suckling in Prose and Verse*. Ed. A. Hamilton Thompson. New York: Russell & Russell, Inc., 1964.

Sullivan, Ernest W., II, ed. *First and Second Dalhousie Manuscripts: Poems and Prose by John Donne and Others, A Facsimile Edition*. Columbia, Mo.: University of Missouri Press, 1988.

Thomas, Max W. "Reading and Writing the Renaissance Commonplace Book: A Question of Authorship?" *Cardozo Arts and Entertainment Law Journal* 10.2 (1992): 665–79.

Tilley, Morris Palmer. *A Dictionary of The Proverbs in England in the Sixteenth and Seventeenth Centuries*. Ann Arbor: University of Michigan Press, 1950.

Tixall Library, Catalogue of Valuable Books & Manuscripts, Late the Property of Sir F. A. T. C. Constable, Bart. Sotheby, Wilkinson & Hodge, London, 6–7 November 1899.

Townshend, Aurelian. *The Poems and Masques of Aurelian Townshend with Music by Henry Lawes and William Webb*. Ed. Cedric C. Brown. Reading: Whiteknights Press, 1983.

———. *Aurelian Townshend's Poems and Masks*. Ed. E. K. Chambers. Oxford: Clarendon Press, 1912.

Underdown, David. "Kings, Courtiers, and Countrymen." Unpublished paper given at the Newberry Consortium. Newberry Library, Chicago. 18 March 1993.

Wit and Drolery, joviall poems corrected and much amended, with additions by Sir J. M., J. S., Sir W. D., J. D. and the most refined wits of the Age. Ed. E. M. London, 1661.

Wolf, Edwin. *The Textual Importance of Manuscript Commonplace Books of 1620–1660*. An address before the Bibliographical Society of the University of Virginia. 14 January 1949. Charlottesville, Va.: Bibliographical Society of the University of Virginia, 1949.

Wotton, Sir Henry. *"Reliquiæ Wottonianæ": or, A Collection of Lives, Letters, Poems; with Characters of Sundry Personages*. 3rd ed. London: T. Roycroft, 1672.

Woodward, Marcus. *Leaves from Gerard's Herball.* New York: Dover Publications, Inc., 1969.

Woudhuysen, H. R. *Sir Philip Sidney and the Circulation of Manuscripts, 1558–1640.* Oxford: Clarendon Press, 1996.

Young, Michael B. *Servility and Service: The Life and Work of Sir John Coke.* Royal Historical Society Studies in History Series 45. London: Boydell Press, 1986.

Indices

NAMES AND PLACES

Verse

Renaissance English Text Society

Officers and Council

International Advisory Council

Peter Beal, Sotheby's, London
K. J. Höltgen, University of Erlangen-Nürenberg
M. T. Jones-Davies, University of Paris-Sorbonne
Sergio Rossi, University of Milan
Helen Wilcox, University of Gronigen

Editorial Committee for *The Verse Miscellany of Constance Aston Fowler*
 Dennis Kay, *Chair*
 Arthur Marotti
 David Scott Kastan

The Renaissance English Text Society was established to publish literary texts, chiefly nondramatic, of the period 1475–1660. Dues are $35.00 per annum ($25.00, graduate students; life membership is available at $500.00). Members receive the text published for each year of membership. The Society sponsors panels at such annual meetings as those of the Modern Language Association, the Renaissance Society of America, and the Medieval Congress at Kalamazoo.

General inquiries and proposals for editions should be addressed to the president, Arthur Kinney, Massachusetts Center for Renaissance Studies, PO Box 2300, Amherst, Mass., 01004, USA. Inquiries about membership should be addressed to William Gentrup, Director of Memberships, Arizona Center for Medieval and Renaissance Studies, Arizona State University, PO Box 872301, Tempe, AZ 85287-2301.

Copies of volumes X–XII may be purchased from Associated University Presses, 440 Forsgate Drive, Cranbury, NJ 08512. Members may order copies of earlier volumes still in print or of later volumes from XIII, at special member prices, from the Treasurer.

FIRST SERIES

VOL. I. *Merie Tales of the Mad Men of Gotam* by A. B., edited by Stanley J. Kahrl, and *The History of Tom Thumbe,* by R. I., edited by Curt F. Buhler, 1965. (o.p.)

VOL. II. Thomas Watson's Latin *Amyntas,* edited by Walter F. Staton, Jr., and Abraham Fraunce's translation *The Lamentations of Amyntas,* edited by Franklin M. Dickey, 1967.

SECOND SERIES

VOL. III. *The dyaloge called Funus,* A Translation of Erasmus's Colloquy (1534), and *A very pleasaunt & fruitful Diologe called The Epicure,* Gerrard's Translation of Erasmus's Colloquy (1545), edited by Robert R. Allen, 1969.

VOL. IV. *Leicester's Ghost* by Thomas Rogers, edited by Franklin B. Williams, Jr., 1972.

THIRD SERIES

VOLS. V–VI. *A Collection of Emblemes, Ancient and Moderne,* by George Wither, with an introduction by Rosemary Freeman and bibliographical notes by Charles S. Hensley, 1975. (o.p.)

FOURTH SERIES

VOLS. VII–VIII. *Tom a' Lincolne* by R. I., edited by Richard S. M. Hirsch, 1978.

FIFTH SERIES

VOL. IX. *Metrical Visions* by George Cavendish, edited by A. S. G. Edwards, 1980.

SIXTH SERIES

VOL. X. *Two Early Renaissance Bird Poems,* edited by Malcolm Andrew, 1984.

VOL. XI. *Argalus and Parthenia* by Francis Quarles, edited by David Freeman, 1986.

VOL. XII. Cicero's *De Officiis,* trans. Nicholas Grimald, edited by Gerald O'Gorman, 1987.

VOL. XIII. *The Silkewormes and their Flies* by Thomas Moffet (1599), edited with introduction and commentary by Victor Houliston, 1988.

SEVENTH SERIES

VOL. XIV. John Bale, *The Vocacyon of Johan Bale,* edited by Peter Happé and John N. King, 1989.

VOL. XV. *The Nondramatic Works of John Ford,* edited by L. E. Stock, Gilles D. Monsarrat, Judith M. Kennedy, and Dennis Danielson, with the assistance of Marta Straznicky, 1990.

Special Publication. *New Ways of Looking at Old Texts: Papers of the Renaissance English Text Society, 1985–1991,* edited by W. Speed Hill, 1993. (Sent *gratis* to all 1991 members.)

VOL. XVI. George Herbert, *The Temple: A Diplomatic Edition of the Bodleian Manuscript (Tanner 307),* edited by Mario A. Di Cesare, 1991.

VOL. XVII. Lady Mary Wroth, *The First Part of the Countess of Montgomery's Urania,* edited by Josephine Roberts. 1992.

VOL. XVIII. Richard Beacon, *Solon His Follie,* edited by Clare Carroll and Vincent Carey. 1993.

VOL. XIX. An Collins, *Divine Songs and Meditacions,* edited by Sidney Gottlieb. 1994.

VOL. XX. *The Southwell-Sibthorpe Commonplace Book: Folger MS V.b.198*, edited by Sr. Jean Klene. 1995.

Special Publication. *New Ways of Looking at Old Texts II: Papers of the Renaissance English Text Society, 1992–1996*, edited by W. Speed Hill, 1998. (Sent *gratis* to all 1996 members.)

VOL. XXI. *The Collected Works of Anne Vaughan Lock*, edited by Susan M. Felch. 1996.

VOL. XXII. Thomas May, *The Reigne of King Henry the Second Written in Seauen Books*, edited by Götz Schmitz. 1997.

VOL. XXIII. *The Poems of Sir Walter Ralegh: A Historical Edition*, edited by Michael Rudick. 1998.

VOL. XXIV. Lady Mary Wroth, *The Second Part of the Countess of Montgomery's Urania*, edited by Josephine Roberts; completed by Suzanne Gossett and Janel Mueller. 1999.

VOL. XXV. *The Verse Miscellany of Constance Aston Fowler: A Diplomatic Edition*, by Deborah Aldrich-Watson. 2000.